SIR HARRY OAKES

1874-1943

AN ACCUMULATION OF NOTES

Bob Cowan

BOB COWAN

Published by
Highway Book Shop
Cobalt, Ontario
P0J 1C0

ISBN 0-88954-416-6

Every effort has been made to trace ownership of all copyright material and to secure permission from copyright holders. In the event of any question arising as to the use of any material, photographs or illustrations, we will be pleased to make necessary corrections in future printings.

Canadian Cataloguing in Publication Data

Cowan, Bob, 1935-
    Sir Harry Oakes, 1874-1943: an accumulation of notes

Includes bibliographical references and index.
ISBN 0-88954-416-6

1. Oakes, Harry, Sir, 1874-1943. 2. Murder—Bahamas. I. Title.

HV6535.B33N37 2000   364.15'23'092   C00-931538-1

Front cover photos:

Top left:	Courtesy of Special Collections & Archives, Bowdoin College Library, Brunswick, Maine.
Top right:	Courtesy of Museum of Northern History, Kirkland Lake, Ontario.
Bottom:	Courtesy of National Archives of Canada, Ottawa, Ontario.

Back cover photos:

Miners' Memorial:	Author's collection.
Author:	Courtesy of Parken Photo Centre, Cobourg, Ontario.

Printed and bound in Canada

TABLE OF CONTENTS

AN INTRODUCTION

WHO WAS HARRY OAKES?

A great deal has been written over the years about a gentleman by the name of Harry Oakes in books, magazine and newspaper articles, not to mention some movies made for television. However, the following manuscript that you are about to read was not originally intended as the basis for a book, but more as just an accumulation of notes on Harry Oakes, the events, the places and the individuals associated with him. Interspersed within the text are some stories relating to certain individuals and events which add to the general atmosphere that surrounded Harry Oakes and the many places he called home.

We must remember that in addition to Harry Oakes' early life, the basic period that is covered in this text is from the mid thirties and on into the early forties.

In order to provide some background into my initial interest in Harry Oakes, I should mention that back in the early 1980's my employer offered

One of the more relaxed photos of the great Sir Harry Oakes. *Museum of Northern History*

me the opportunity to go to the Bahamas for a three to four year period.

As a result of this relocation, I developed an interest in knowing more about the colourful history of the Bahamas and its people. It was almost a daily routine during lunchtime, under bright blue skies, to stroll along West Bay Street down to the waterfront to view the cruise ships that were in port and to walk back at one's leisure past the Island Shop in the heart of downtown Nassau. The Island Shop was considered one of the better stores on Bay Street and always had the latest publications on its shelves.

On one particular occasion a book entitled *Who Killed Sir Harry Oakes?* by James Leasor caught my attention.

It related to a local tragedy which had taken place right there in Nassau, some forty years earlier and which involved a former Canadian citizen of great wealth, who had discovered the world's second largest gold mine in North America in a place called Kirkland

Lake, in the Northern Ontario region of Canada. In actuality Harry Oakes was a U.S. citizen born in the small town of Sangerville, Maine.

I purchased the book and as I read through it one weekend, it was only natural that I would find it interesting to try to locate some of the old landmark estates belonging to the millionaire Sir Harry Oakes in Nassau and in particular his *Westbourne* estate, where he would meet his tragic and untimely death during the night of July 7th and 8th, 1943.

A touristy police station on West Bay Street in the Cable Beach area of Nassau. *Author's collection*

A subsequent inquiry at a little wooden green shack located on West Bay Street in the heart of the Cable Beach tourist area, which served as what I would call a touristy police station, is probably what developed my sudden interest in the air of mystery surrounding Sir Harry Oakes, his lifestyle, his many friends and, no doubt, some enemies.

As a matter of fact, the senior constable to whom I addressed the question regarding the location of Sir Harry's *Westbourne* estate, rather hinted that it would be best to drop the matter and never did provide me with the location of the Oakes estate. This negative response only made the name of Sir Harry Oakes all the more intriguing.

Following this initial attempt to locate Sir Harry's estate, I inquired from our receptionist at the office the following Monday morning and received a rather concerned look from her. However, she did mention that *Westbourne* was now the site of the present day *Ambassador Beach Hotel* located on West Bay Street, which incorporated a gambling casino — better known as the *Playboy Club and Casino*, with bunnies and all.

As my interest in the matter was now aroused, I was made aware of some of the tragic events that have happened to certain individuals, who over the years have investigated the circumstances surrounding the murder of Sir Harry Oakes. Take, for instance, the much publicized case of Betty Renner, who supposedly made it known while in Nassau in 1950 on holidays, that she intended to research the murder of Sir Harry Oakes. As a result of her curiosity, she was subsequently found murdered herself a few days later and to this day her murder has never been solved. Her death as reported by the authorities was apparently noted as *due to causes unknown*.

Over the years since the death of Sir Harry Oakes, there has been and always will be, this air of mystery, and discussions on the matter still evoke a mark of secrecy with certain individuals in Nassau, even to this day.

While all this happened some fifty-seven years ago, there are certainly some individuals still alive and well in Nassau and elsewhere, who could no doubt shed some further light on the mystery; but they are not all that easy to locate nor in some cases would they speak out on the matter, as I have experienced over the years.

Time is now running out and many of the individuals originally around, who may have been considered as prime candidates as assailants or simply witnesses to this tragic death, are slowly leaving us. The only last possible solution to the whole matter could be a death bed confession.

The murder of Sir Harry Oakes was once classified as *the murder of the century* and has never been solved. *It is not my intention* by writing this material to try to solve the murder, but some of the sources of reference, both individuals and material alike, may give the reader some further food for thought on the matter.

You will note from the list of books which I have referenced, that there has been a great deal written about Sir Harry Oakes and also on the immediate cast of characters, which makes it all the more interesting — from the once second richest man in the British Empire and a Baronet, Sir Harry Oakes; to a Bahamian real estate agent turned millionaire Harold Christie, later to be knighted as Sir Harold Christie; to Count Alfred de Marigny from the Island of Mauritius and his romantic adventures leading up to his marriage to Nancy Oakes; to a Swedish industrialist Dr. Axel Wenner-Gren of questionable political leanings; and finally to an ex-King of England, the Duke of Windsor who married an American lady and who would become the Royal Governor General of the Bahamas during the Second World War.

As you peruse the following material, you must keep in mind that, with the exception of interviews with the late Alfred de Marigny, the late Ernest Callender, the late Reverend Robert Hall, and others in Nassau who wish to remain anonymous, some of the research that went into producing this text was the result of reading many books by a variety of authors — with their own interpretation of what happened; reviewing numerous newspaper and magazine articles, as well as viewing certain film footage.

As a result, it became more and more obvious that there were many disparities among the authors relative to the facts surrounding the individuals, events and places. In some cases the text would appear to have been written in such a style as to merely evoke interest in the book or magazine articles being published at the time, with complete disregard for the actual facts.

A great deal of pleasurable research was undertaken by myself to write this material. It has necessitated my visiting numerous museums and libraries in Canada, the United States, and also in Nassau, including in the latter case the Archives of the Bahamas; the National Library and Archives in Ottawa; personal correspondence with newspapers, magazines, historical societies and university libraries, here and abroad. Visits were made to the filing rooms of newspapers to peruse their *dead files*, as well as visits to cemeteries, colleges, universities, a coroner's office, police detachments and, last but not least, many second hand bookstores in search of old books and periodicals.

Discussions with a fingerprint expert were also undertaken, as were consultations with a fire marshal, homicide detectives, various police officers, and even an attempt to surf the Internet without any great success.

It should also be noted that part of Harry Oakes' own interesting life was spent in Northern Ontario, where he discovered the gold mine leading to his subsequent lifestyle. Oakes was not the only colourful individual in the north as you will see, as many of the early pioneers of the mining industry were characters in themselves and part of the exciting history and legends of the north.

And now as they say, "without any further ado", the following is a summary of the players, places, books, movies, events, stories and whatever else has been researched, which I trust will be of interest to you, with regard to Harry Oakes.

Bob Cowan
Cobourg, Ontario
June 24, 2000

Harry Oakes 1874-1911: His Early Days and Search for Gold

Sangerville and Dover-Foxcroft, Maine ..... Foxcroft Academy ..... Brunswick, Maine — Bowdoin College ..... Syracuse University Medical School, Syracuse, New York ..... Harry's Travels to Australia ..... Harry's Biographical Record — The Whole Truth ..... Death Valley and Finally to the Swastika District of Northern Ontario

Sir Harry Oakes was born plain Harry Oakes on December 23rd, 1874, in the small town of Sangerville, Maine, total population 1,200 people at the time, situated in the northeastern New England states. In 1888 Harry's father moved his family to the nearby town of Foxcroft some seven miles north, which was more populated and offered better schooling facilities. It would eventually become the town of Dover-Foxcroft.

Harry had an older brother, Louis, and three sisters, Gertrude, Jessie and Myrtice.

In July 1992, I made a trip to the towns of Sangerville and Dover-Foxcroft in an attempt to trace some of the early background on Sir Harry Oakes, from his birth place to his final resting place.

I entered the town of Dover-Foxcroft late one afternoon on a beautiful summer day and slowly drove through the town, basically trying to locate the cemetery, where I had hoped to find the mausoleum that was built in memory of Sir Harry Oakes.

Original home of Harry Oakes' family in Sangerville, Maine — circa 1889. *Original source unknown*

As I approached the first cemetery, I immediately turned in and proceeded up and down the rows of tombstones, but did not find any evidence of a mausoleum. Supper time was fast approaching and I headed for the first hotel in town.

The next morning I was up bright and early, drove through Dover-Foxcroft and headed out to the smaller town of Sangerville, where Harry Oakes was born. As I parked my car in front of the local post office, located on the main road, I saw that two elderly gentlemen appeared to have noticed my out-of-town license plates. I got out and walked across the road and greeted them accordingly, following which I introduced myself and

Sir Harry Oakes' mausoleum in Dover-Foxcroft cemetery. *Author's collection*

Grace Bible Church and Christian School in Sangerville on land donated by Lady Eunice Oakes located at Sir Harry's birthplace. *Author's collection*

explained the reason for my visit to Sangerville.

They very kindly guided me in the direction of the original property where Harry Oakes' family home once was and where he spent his early years. As I approached the location I noticed that it was now the site of the Grace Bible Church and Christian School as described on the dedication plaque, which indicated that the land had been donated in memory of Sir Harry Oakes.

I should also mention that right across the road from the Church is a retirement home known as Oakes Manor, which is described as an equal housing

Oakes Manor in Sangerville located across the road from the Grace Bible Church on land donated in memory of Sir Harry and Lady Eunice Oakes. *Author's collection*

opportunity location. There is an inscribed memorial plaque at its entrance, confirming that the property was donated in memory of Sir Harry and Lady Oakes following their deaths.

One of the town's main claims to fame, though not tourism, is that it was the birth place of one Harry Oakes, who later in life would become a gold prospector and eventually a self-made millionaire, who would be knighted by King George VI of England in 1939.

It is interesting to note that in addition to Sir Harry's Baronetcy, another gentleman by the name of Hiram Maxim from Sangerville would also be knighted as Sir Hiram Maxim, the inventor of the machine gun many years earlier.

I then returned to the town of Dover-Foxcroft, home of Foxcroft Academy, where Harry Oakes, his brother Louis and two of his sisters, Jessie and Myrtice, also attended school. The Academy is well known in the New England states and has benefited immensely from some of its former students, who have made donations to the Academy and who have also willed funds to it. As a matter of fact the land, the sports field and some of the extensions to the original Academy, were the result of financial contributions and land donations by Harry and his brother Louis.

A year or so before his untimely death, Harry Oakes had hired an architect to prepare new plans for the restructuring of Foxcroft Academy, however, fate would intervene and the plans were cancelled. In due course his brother Louis would assist with much of the needed financing requirements for the changes to the Academy.

Foxcroft Academy in Dover-Foxcroft. *Author's collection*

In 1961, many years after her husband's death, Lady Eunice Oakes made a substantial donation to Foxcroft Academy in support of the gymnasium fund.

That same day I visited Foxcroft Academy, located along the main road. It was at the Academy that I was referred to the Dover-Foxcroft Library where I was to later meet retired Judge Matthew Williams, who had been a trustee for some twenty-five years at the Academy. Judge Williams provided me with some interesting history of the Academy, as well as of the town of Dover-Foxcroft. A subsequent introduction to Eric Annis at the Lary Funeral Home proved most rewarding relative to my final search for Sir Harry Oakes' mausoleum.

Harry Oakes first attended Foxcroft Academy and following graduation his father decided to send him to Bowdoin College in Brunswick, Maine, in the hope that Harry would obtain a more formal education. Harry graduated from Bowdoin College in 1896.

At some point during his studies, Harry realized that a doctor's annual income was approximately $3,000 and was not considered sufficient for him. As a result he announced to his classmates, that, "I'm going to find a gold mine and make my fortune" — and off he went on his world travels in search of his gold mine, eventually finding his *el dorado* (or the golden one) at Kirkland Lake in the Northern Ontario region of Canada.

Bowdoin College produced many well known influential individuals including Franklin Pierce who would be the fourteenth President of the United States; famous writers Nathaniel Hawthorne and Henry Wadsworth Longfellow; and a multitude of doctors, lawyers and judges.

According to a letter maintained in the Special Collection files at Bowdoin College there is a comment to the effect that Harry Oakes *"was a quiet unassuming boy of average scholastic ability. In athletics he did not make any of the varsity teams, but was a member of his class gymnasium team in his freshman and sophomore years. He was a member of the Zeta Psi fraternity. Although he did not have outstanding personal qualities, he was well liked by his classmates for his quiet way and friendly disposition."* (Bass, W.S. [letter to Miss Lord] quoted with permission of Bowdoin College)

Following his graduation from Bowdoin College in 1896, Harry marked time briefly as a Carter Ink Company agent — a job which he hated. He then headed north during the Klondike Gold Rush where he worked as a prospector in Skagway, Alaska. He continued to work in various places, at one point as a purser on his way to the Philippines, and then did some prospecting in Australia, followed by survey work for the New Zealand government.

Railway station at Swastika, Ontario. *Author's collection*

Oakes' vivid interest in gold mining continued throughout the world and led him finally to Northern Ontario where he arrived by rail in the small town of Swastika, approximately four miles west of Kirkland Lake, in June of 1911. The rest would shortly be history.

In 1938, in view of his new found wealth, Harry Oakes had reached a point when he decided to become an art collector of sorts and proceeded with the purchase of some well known masterpieces. However, not knowing what to do with them, he lent them to his alma mater, the Bowdoin College Museum of Arts in Brunswick, Maine. The collection comprised the following masterpieces:

- Frans Hal's 'Portrait of Pieter Tjarck' (on loan 1938-1947)
- William Hogarth's 'Southwark Fair' (on loan 1938-1956)
- Albert Cuyp's 'River Scene' (on loan 1938-1961)
- Thomas Gainsborough's 'Woodcutter's Return/Cottage Door' (on loan 1938-1963)
- Rembrandt van Rijn's 'Portrait of a Man, also referred to as Young Man with a Sword' (on loan 1938-1973)

A young Harry Oakes of the Class of 1896 at Bowdoin College. *Bowdoin College Archives, Bowdoin College Library*

In correspondence with the Bowdoin College Museum of Arts in November 1992, I was informed that all of the paintings held by the museum were subsequently withdrawn by Lady Eunice Oakes in the last year shown in brackets above, following the death of Sir Harry, and it was the museum's feeling that the paintings were most probably sold by Lady Oakes.

Upon researching the one Rembrandt painting in particular owned by Oakes, the *Portrait of a Man*, it was noted that the next owner of that classic masterpiece following the Oakes family was the Los Angeles Museum of Art, where it is still probably on display.

A number of years following his graduation and the discovery of his Lake Shore Mines, Oakes served on the college's Board of Trustees and received an honorary degree of Doctor of Laws from Bowdoin in 1941 no doubt due in part to his financial assistance to the college.

In a 1965 write-up for the Bowdoin College records the following brief comments were also made about Oakes: *"few graduates of Bowdoin have led such a colourful life as his, reached such peaks of wealth and fame, or died so violently; a lover of the out of doors, he expressed early an interest in mining, and took the Bowdoin courses which were related to work in mineralogy. A self-reliant optimist, he let it be known that he looked forward to making his fortune as a miner"*. (Coles, J.S. [Overview of Oakes Life, 1965] quoted with permission of Bowdoin College)

As part of his continued education following graduation from Bowdoin College, it has often been said that Harry Oakes subsequently attended the Syracuse Medical School in Syracuse, New York, where he was to obtain a medical degree.

Some time in the spring of 1996 I was approached by a medical writer to discuss Oakes' attendance at the Syracuse Medical School; however, at that point I did not have any concrete evidence or background information on Oakes' medical school studies, except what I had heard and read about.

As a result I wrote to Syracuse University in the hope of receiving some information concerning Oakes' attendance at the medical school during the years 1897 and 1898. Some sources claim that he did not complete his medical schooling.

In due course I received a response from the University Archives, which disappointed me a little to say the least, and in this regard I quote the following from their reply:

"Looking through our materials I have been unable to find any reference to Harry Oakes for the two years, 1897 and 1898, that he supposedly attended the Syracuse University Medical School. He is not listed in any of the Medical School bulletins at that time with the other students. He is not listed in the Alumni Index of the University that was printed in 1910 and has pages devoted to non-graduates of the University. He does not have any newspaper clippings on file or any alumni questionnaires returned. I also checked the City of Syracuse Directories for that time and no Harry Oakes is listed as residing in the city."

There have been many stories written on the subject of Harry Oakes and his quest for gold through the years, ranging from his travels to Australia, the Klondike and eventually on to Kirkland Lake in Ontario.

In an attempt to clarify the many different places in which Oakes set about prospecting, I visited his alma mater Bowdoin College in 1995 and came across a Biographical Record of Harry Oakes — Class of 1896, as prepared by Lady Eunice Oakes in February 1949, while she still resided in Nassau. The information was requested by the College in order to prepare their latest General Catalogue of students, who had graduated from the college over the years.

The following would appear to be the most accurate record possible documenting Harry Oakes' early days, following his graduation from Bowdoin College in 1896. (Reprinted with the permission of the Bowdoin College Archives):

1896-1897	Agent Carter Ink Co., Boston, Mass.
1897-1899	In employ of North American Trans. Co.
1899	Ohio Steamship Co., San Francisco, California
1899-1900	Winter — Manila & other ports of the Philippines

8

1900	April — Nome, Alaska
1900-1901	Honolulu, Manila & various ports of the East
1901	Summer — Nome, Alaska; San Francisco, California; San Diego & Los Angeles, California
1901-1902	Different parts of the Far East: China, Japan, Samoan Islands, etc.
1902	November — Australia & later to Rotorua, New Zealand. Also prospected in Mexico and South Africa.
1903-1905	
1906-1911	Mined and prospected in Death Valley district in Nevada.
1911	Staked the Tough-Oakes Mine and the Lake Shore Mines in the Swastika District of Northern Ontario and spent the next years in developing these mines.

It is obvious that most of these travels were for the purpose of prospecting for gold.

There appears to be a lapse for the years 1903 to 1905 in the details. At this point in time, there is no way to elaborate on the data for those years, though based on other sources there is mention of the Belgian Congo, as well as the Yukon.

In an interview in October 1925 with the author Arnold Hoffman, Harry Oakes had made a statement to the effect — *you will see, I know gold mines. I've been in the Philippines, Australia, the Yukon, Alaska and the American West. There's nothing, nothing to compare with Lake Shore and Kirkland Lake.*

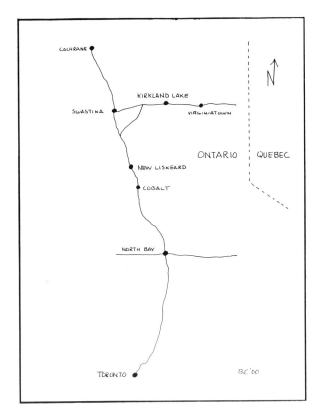

Ontario Road Map

Harry Oakes 1912-1923: Kirkland Lake and the Lake Shore Mines

Kirkland Lake, Ontario ..... Winnie Lake, Ontario ..... Lake Shore Mines Limited — Harry Oakes' El Dorado ..... Harry Oakes — Early Kirkland Lake Days Remembered ..... Harry Oakes' Chateau — His First Residence ..... Dr. Eugene A. Whittredge — Harry's Friend Back Home ..... New Ontario — Better Known As Northern Ontario ..... Northern Ontario Day Dreaming — Going Back In Time ..... Gold Mine Tours — How They Did It ..... Staking A Claim ..... Boston Creek, Ontario — An Unusual Mining Town ..... Roza Brown — Did She Put Kirkland Lake On The Map? ..... Krugerdorf, Ontario — The Hebrew Cemetery ..... Charlie Chow — The Man Who Accepted Paper Shares ..... Jimmy Doig — The Storekeeper ..... Mary Martin — A Friend To Many ..... Northern Ontario Pioneers and Characters — What Would The North Be Without Them ..... Alfred J.Casson — The Group of Seven's Contribution to Sir Harry Oakes ..... Eddie Duke — Photographer par Excellence ..... Highway Book Shop — The North's Best Book Store ..... The National Hockey League — Kirkland Lake's Contribution to Hockey

---

In the early 1900s certain mining ventures were undertaken to explore the mineral possibilities in and around New Liskeard, followed by explorations into Boston Township located just south of Kirkland Lake.

Welcome to Kirkland Lake, Ontario. *Author's collection*

Finally in 1911, more and more development of mining interest and activity led to the staking of a number of claims in and around the present day site of Kirkland Lake.

It was in this year that the first stakings would be recorded, resulting in the discovery of gold in the area and heralding the arrival of a Yankee gentleman by the name of Harry Oakes into Swastika. Oakes would now set about in search of his own mine having previously travelled the world in pursuit of gold, but without any great success.

10

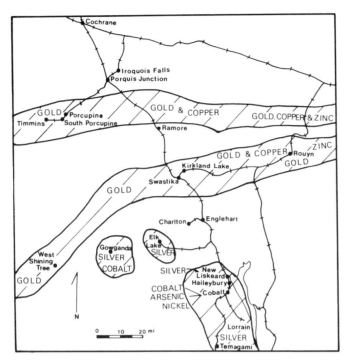

Map 9. *Mineral areas: Cobalt, Porcupine, Gowganda, and Rouyn*

Map indicating mineral areas around Cobalt, Porcupine, Kirkland Lake and others. *Courtesy of Prof. Robert Surtees*

Over the years, Oakes had made it clear to anyone with whom he seriously discussed gold mining or for that matter anyone who was willing to listen to him, that he was determined to establish a one-man mining operation — that is, stake his own claim, develop the mine, finance it and eventually bring it into full production, something that most people thought would never be possible. But Harry did it.

And so it would be that a claim just east of Swastika, would soon be reverting to the Crown for the non-performance of work and Harry Oakes would stake this claim and be on his way to eventual fame and fortune. His source of information was the Bureau of Mines in Toronto.

In 1919 the Township of Teck was incorporated to include Kirkland Lake and the immediate surrounding area. It was not until 1972 that the municipal status of Teck was changed to that of the Town of Kirkland Lake. Government Road was and still is the name of the main street in Kirkland Lake, that runs from east to west, or should I say winds its way from east to west, as the story was once related that the reason for the winding of Government Road was the fact that many years ago the horses pulling wagons through Kirkland Lake, made their own path in order to avoid obstacles and no one seems to have ever bothered to straighten out that path.

Kirkland Lake received its name from one Miss Winnie Kirkland, who was the secretary of L.V. Rorke, Assistant Director at the Department of Mines for the Government of Ontario located in Toronto.

In addition to having had Kirkland Lake named after her, Winnie Kirkland also had the added honour of having Winnie Lake attributed to her, and it has been said that she never did visit these lakes which bear her names. Her descendants have, however, visited Kirkland Lake to see their namesake's place in history.

Miss Winnie Kirkland, after whom Kirkland Lake & Winnie Lake were named. *Original source unknown, Museum of Northern History*

In an effort to locate Winnie Lake on one of my many visits to Kirkland Lake, I called on the Ontario Provincial Police detachment late one evening and inquired about its location.

After some internal office research and a few telephone calls by two of the officers on duty, we were successful with the help of a topographical map in finally locating Winnie Lake. It is located north of the Macassa mine area. The condition of that small bush road precluded my visiting the site with my car, but I went as far as I could.

The joke amongst us that evening while discussing the matter was the fact that possibly someone could call in with a report of a murder at Winnie Lake and the answer was that we would wait till the next morning and call the Ministry of Northern Development & Mines for proper guidance as to its location.

On the night of January 8, 1912, in 36 F degrees below zero weather and heavy snow conditions, Harry Oakes together with two of the Tough brothers, Tom and George, staked a claim which would lead to the establishment of the Tough-Oakes gold mine. It would appear that Harry was short of funds to pay the required recording fee for the claim and as a result entered into a partnership with the Tough brothers.

Later that same year Oakes acquired certain claims covering possible mining sites on the very shores and under Kirkland Lake which subsequently led to the formation of the Lake Shore Mines which was to be his *el dorado* or '*the golden one*'. Lake Shore was incorporated in 1914 with two million shares, half of which remained with members of the Oakes family.

During its lifespan Lake Shore Mines produced in excess of 8.5 million ounces of gold, from its inception in 1918 to its closure in 1968.

Two of the youngest recorded shareholders in Lake Shore Mines were to be the children of R. C. Coffey, who was at one time Harry Oakes' manager of the mine and who had designed the mill and supervised its operations.

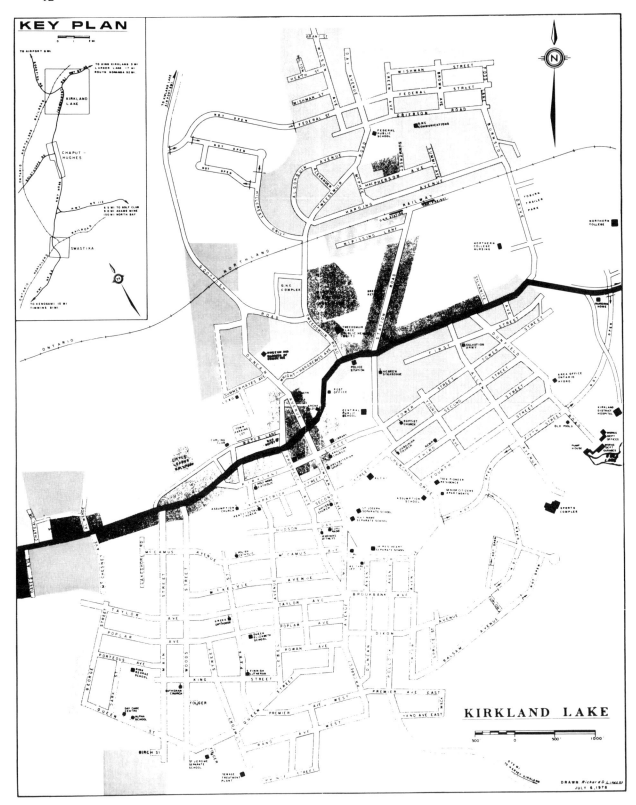

A more recent map of Kirkland Lake. *Courtesy of the Corporation of the Town of Kirkland Lake*

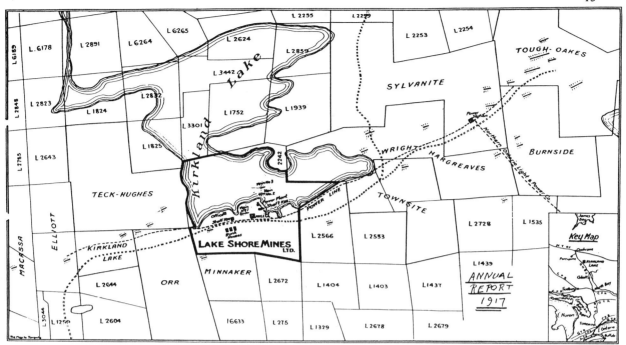

A map of the staking of gold mines in Kirkland Lake in 1917. *1917 Annual Report of Lake Shore Mines, Museum of Northern History*

In the initial stages of trying to raise funds for his mine, Harry tried to advertise in various newspapers and magazines. Apparently one of the leading Toronto newspapers and a leading Canadian magazine refused to accept Oakes' advertising. Their feeling was that Lake Shore Mines was just a *wildcat*. Only the *Northern Miner* newspaper would run the advertisements for Oakes. An interesting sidelight to the matter was that Bill Wright, one of Oakes' mining associates, eventually became owner of *The Globe and Mail* and in addition was at one time considered to be one the richest privates in the Canadian Army. He was to later establish the Wright-Hargreaves Mine.

In 1912, Harry was in dire need of further financial backing to continue the exploration and development of his gold discoveries in Kirkland Lake and as a result returned to his hometown of Sangerville, Maine.

While there he visited with an old school friend Eugene Whittredge, now Doctor Whittredge, whom he approached as a good friend, and spent the better part of an evening in his office lecturing him on his gold discoveries. The real reason for Harry's visit with Whittredge was to ask him if he would care to invest some money in the gold mine that he was developing in Kirkland Lake.

Harry guaranteed Whittredge, who had a dental practice at the time, a very good return on his investment and even promised that he would return to him in dividends after the first year, the amount of his investment; but Whittredge honestly did not have the necessary funds available (a mere $1000) to invest and made it very clear to Harry that if he had it, he would have assisted him. No doubt following Oakes' successful development of the mine and his good fortunes, Whittredge probably regretted the fact that he did not have or could not gather the money needed to invest at the time.

14

Original residences for Lake Shore Mines personnel, which still stand today. *National Archives of Canada PA17716*

It was considered by some that Whittredge was a childhood friend of Harry with whom he hunted rabbits and most likely the last true friend he had back home.

In the June 15th, 1939, edition of the *Northern Miner* on the occasion of Harry Oakes' receipt of a Baronetcy, the following extract of an article written by Oakes himself in the *Miner* of June 28th, 1928, was reprinted giving an outline of Harry's effort in searching for his gold mines. It also provides a very interesting outline of the gold camp in those early days in Kirkland Lake and is reprinted with permission of the *Northern Miner*:

First Finds Were Duds

The rush into Northern Ontario, which was at its height in the spring of 1911, brought many prospectors north of Cobalt and the extended staking in the Porcupine camp led many to look over sections where there was more open ground, which could perhaps be more thoroughly prospected before staking and recording. At that time very good ore was found and worked at Swastika Mine and in June, good ore was developed at the Lucky Cross. The lack of profitable operations on these properties later appeared to be due to the limited extent of their oreshoots. The quality was very fair. However, their showing furnished good reasons to prospect the district in Teck, an unsurveyed township, east and north of these operations. The section east of Swastika was largely favoured in the summer of 1911 and from a prospector's first examination, it was hopeful ground with many quartz veins, iron gouges and well-mineralized fractures, but it was impossible to get any colours of consequence in panning and to date this belt has not produced any ore of consequence.

In midsummer the Wright-Hargreaves was staked on the property belt running through Kirkland Lake, the first strike being made on what is now the south vein of the property and a large interest changed hands at a very modest figure. Most of the ground on this belt of porphyry had been staked several times, perhaps some years previously and an assay running $2.80 is known to have been taken in a previous year near the rich veins, but on the same strip the prospector got an assay near Goodfish Lake running $4.80, staked there instead and still holds the claim.

Tough-Oakes Discovery

The next strike of importance was made late in February 1912, on the Tough-Oakes, which had been re-staked in January. The discovery trench in shallow diggings showed the glaciated top of an oreshoot in a very striking manner, the quartz filling around the enclosed porphyry sections resembling a sort of mosaic work with dark spots of mineral plentifully filled with fine gold. This oreshoot for several feet in width would always give an assay in three figures, but its length was only about 20 feet. When the snow left, late in April, the rich oreshoot on No. 2 vein was found and the high grade value of the camp established. Some of the best of this vein was exposed not far from our cook tent and the weathered, cracked surface was not identified as a vein until a piece of rock was broken off quite casually, showing a piece of free gold the size of a pea. Other showings were found in various parts of the claims in quick succession, but none as rich as the No. 2 oreshoot, which for a width of several inches assayed in four figures and for a width of several feet assayed in three figures. Mill-run tests from which visible coarse gold was excluded, returned $1,200 or more and it was calculated that a section of the rich vein five feet deep and about 80 feet long would produce fifty tons of thousand dollar ore; later about eight carloads shipped to Perth Amboy netted over $650 per ton. This relatively short ore occurrence tapered to the richest small concentration of gold so far found in the camp, and was a hopeful golden stepping stone to further search.

Rich Surface Showings

In midsummer 1912, the south vein of the Lake Shore Mines was found on a point on the south side of the lake, and at about the same time the rich north vein of the Wright-Hargreaves was uncovered on the northeast side of the lake. Rich surface showings were also disclosed on the west side of the lake, the location and strike of these being a very good indication of the rich north veins traversing under the lake a little northeast and southwest. A very rich showing of gold in the south break was found during this summer. In all these discoveries, on the surface samples inches in width would assay in four figures, and feet in width in three figures, while by the first snowfall in the autumn of 1912, there were *indications of quite a tonnage of $50 ore on the surface showings available for about two miles. Of course, the opportunity to see the surface was limited on account of the lake and swamps, and many of the richest showings were soon filled in, after being exposed, by quicksand; other more accessible showings of rich ore were pop-shotted by over-zealous samplers and the high grade scattered through the bush — a very useless proceeding, as the clean cut surface of the hard porphyry, shaved by the glacier, was the best sampling surface which could be presented, even though many return trips for assaying or panning were necessary to obtain a fair idea of the importance of the ore occurrences. Much of the early samplings by visitors was perhaps ten percent efficient. The early prospector-operators were rather a hard-bitten crowd, difficult, perhaps, to the well groomed visitor, to vision as associated with much wealth.*

Abundant Facilities

The situation of the camp was extremely favourable for quick development — every assistance being rendered by the Ontario government by telephone and roads — and very good, though somewhat limited, water power only a few miles away, and it seems strange that a combination of events should cause the lapse of so much time before the camp hit its stride. However, the war and other things intervened and the history of mining camps with similar ore occurrences has shown the difficulty of keeping on the ore. It will be interesting to see whether

The head frame of the Tough-Oakes Mine in Kirkland Lake. *Ontario Archives — OA15380-65*

the apparent additional occurrence of ore found on the lower levels is due to more ore being there, or whether, as is more likely, that a very considerable part of the high grade ore has been missed on the upper levels which the stopes may show later to be as good as below.

It remains to be seen whether a cross section of the whole camp at the 200 foot level is inferior on gold content to a cross section at the 1,200 foot level. So many doctrinaire statements about mining are proved otherwise in two or three seasons that printed statements should be hedged with alibis.

During the mining era there were seven contiguous producing mines along a stretch of three and one half miles — Lake Shore Mines, Wright-Hargreaves, Teck Hughes, Kirkland Lake Gold, Macassa, Sylvanite and Toburn (formerly Tough-Oakes).

It has been said that Lake Shore Mines was the second richest gold mine in the Western Hemisphere after the Homestake Mine in the Black Hills of Dakota in 1887.

Harry Oakes' original home at Kirkland Lake. Harry is the second gentleman from the right. *Museum of Northern History*

The Chateau

The original log structure which was the family home of Harry Oakes in Kirkland Lake, was built around 1919. In 1929 it was partially destroyed by fire, following which Oakes rebuilt it on a grander scale and added a third story to the building. It is now known as the Sir Harry Oakes Chateau and Museum of Northern History.

Harry Oakes' Chateau before his departure from Kirkland Lake — circa 1936. *National Archives of Canada PA17717*

Interior view of Sir Harry's Chateau on occasion of 75th Anniversary celebrations of Kirkland Lake.
Author's collection

The expansion cost of $50,000 was remarkable when you consider that this was the year of the great stock market crash.

The house is located immediately on the shores of Kirkland Lake and facing the site of the former Lake Shore Mines. When I visited the Chateau in the fall of 1998, you could look out any of the northerly windows facing the lake and see the improvements being made to process all the sludge that was dumped from the original mines either into the lake or onto the shorelines. It is the hope of the town and the provincial government alike, to bring Kirkland Lake back to its original state prior to its mining production discovery, for the enjoyment of the people of the town once again, as well as visitors.

Harry Oakes also built a bunkhouse for his employees on the south side of Government Road, which included a hot house where vegetables were grown for the benefit of the workers. The bunkhouse later became the location of the Don Lou Motel.

Following Harry Oakes' departure from Niagara Falls for the Bahamas in 1935, the Chateau continued to be used for meetings and also as a means of providing accommodation for the directors of Lake Shore Mines, whenever they visited Kirkland Lake on business.

In 1965 the Chateau, as it was known, was purchased by the Cochrane Nursing Home and then in 1976 they changed their location, by which time the Chateau had begun to arouse interest as a possible historical structure.

Lake Shore Mines with staff bunkhouse in foreground — circa 1936. *National Archives of Canada PA17635*

The Chateau became the Museum of Northern History and its interior was basically remodelled to accommodate the artifacts and memorabilia of this great northern region of Ontario. In 1980 the building was officially designated as an historical site.

Lady Oakes donated in excess of $300,000 towards the restoration of the Chateau to the same state as when Harry Oakes and his family lived there in the late twenties and early thirties.

Throughout the years 1981 and 1982, the exterior of the building was restored, while in the interior the plaster work was retained and the lighting fixtures reinstalled. The four fireplaces are also original. Changes made included the removal of some walls and the opening up of the second floor to create a striking mezzanine for the display of mining and historical documents, as well as memorabilia of the area.

As you proceed through the house there are many points of interest. One in particular concerns Nancy Oakes' room, where the unique plaster work depicts nursery rhymes, fairy tales, toys and wildlife painstakingly fashioned within the plaster walls by craftsmen of the time.

Close-up of the staff bunkhouse and hot house. *Ontario Archives AO734*

It is worth a visit to the Museum if you happen to be passing through Kirkland Lake or for that matter, why not just make a point of visiting the Museum while travelling in the North. You will be pleasantly surprised and will have a chance to really get a better feeling for the life of Harry Oakes in his days of prospecting. Also you will increase your knowledge of what the North was all about back then.

One of the latest and most interesting displays to have been erected in Kirkland Lake is the Miners' Memorial Sculpture, which was dedicated in July 1994, on the occasion of the 75th Anniversary of Kirkland Lake. It is indeed an outstanding memorial to the more than 1,600 miners who have lost their lives in Ontario mining since the 1930s. It is located at the corner of Government Road and Chateau Drive, just as you drive down to the Sir Harry Oakes Chateau and Museum of Northern History.

The design of this monument includes five individual steel statues representing a stoper, a jacket driller, a scaler, a mucking machine operator and a climbing miner. The entire work of art was the responsibility of artists Rob Moir and Sally Lawrence, who have been its principal creators.

The personnel of the Museum would be only too happy to give you a personally guided tour of the Museum and answer any questions you may have on Harry Oakes and the history of Northern Ontario.

New Ontario

During the early development stages of Northern Ontario and the mining bonanza years from the early 1900s to the mid-thirties, that part of Northern Ontario was often referred to as *New Ontario*.

The reason given by the Provincial government offices for the name *New Ontario*, was apparently to give the public a feeling that something *new* was happening in the northern part of the Province of Ontario and make it sound more attractive and challenging for those wishing to settle in that area.

An interesting reference to the term *New Ontario* was shown in a reproduction of an advertisement in the *Agricultural Temiskaming* newspaper in 1910, advertising cast iron wood cook stoves on sale at The Geo. Taylor Hardware Co. in New Liskeard, with the note *we carry the largest stock of hardware in New Ontario*. As a matter of interest the Farmer's Wood Cook Stove could take 24" pieces of wood and was priced at all of $25, a far cry from today's prices.

Miners Memorial sculpture dedicated in July 1994 during the 75th Anniversary celebrations of Kirkland Lake. *Author's collection*

Adventures in Research

In July of 1994, I made a point of spending a week in Kirkland Lake on the occasion of its 75th Anniversary.

While there I took the opportunity one day of jumping into my car and driving off to visit old abandoned mine sites and photograph some of the once proud head frames and other deteriorating mine buildings. There is a certain feeling to being able to stand there amongst these tall impressive structures and imagine the hustle and bustle of the miners going about their day to day chores during the gold rush period in Kirkland Lake and surrounding area.

On one particular day I headed off in search of the Adams Mine property and as a result travelled on some old dirt roads. On one of these as I drove along I noticed a few red so-called *flagging* tape ribbons on the branches of trees. As I slowed down, I observed something very unusual in the form of metal markers on some posts.

I pulled over to the side of the road, took out my camera and headed down the ditch and up the other side, to note upon closer examination that these were official metal markers, actually indicating that the site had been staked, and interestingly enough they were only dated from November 1993 — some eight months earlier.

I set about photographing in close-up the posts and markers and discovered what I had been looking for — an actual post with appropriate inscriptions recording the staking

Recent staking claim post found on a Kirkland Lake sideroad. *Author's collection*

World's largest staking claim post dated 1965 located in Cobalt, Ontario. *Author's collection*

of a claim — whether it would be an *el dorado*, who knows.

On another occasion as I drove along, I stopped by the roadside and went for a walk into the woods, and as I approached an opening I noticed some rock formations with some green moss growing on them. Remembering some of the stories I had read about where mine discoveries were made by merely removing some of the moss and finding surface gold, I looked around almost as if to make sure that no one was watching me and proceeded with a branch that I had picked up to remove some of the moss. Naturally I did not discover any surface gold, but the thought crossed my mind as I sat down on a stone and reminisced about what it must have been like to really discover gold in this manner.

The day was beautiful and there was not a sound around, with the exception of the wind whistling through the trees. The dirt road was some five hundred feet away, but the lack of the sound of a car was as if I had gone back in time, some seventy or eighty years earlier, when prospectors would set out in the quiet of the north in quest of their dreams.

One of the interesting aspects of my research occurred back in 1992 when I was visiting the Museum in Timmins, Ontario (The Timmins Museum: National Exhibition Centre), and was informed that there were gold mine tours. The guide pointed me in the direction of one of the tours at the old Hollinger Gold Mine, discovered in 1909 by Benny Hollinger, and told me that it was the richest gold producer in the Western Hemisphere.

The tour was my first experience in the art of underground mining and was certainly worth the price of admission. I should mention that when I arrived at the tour site late that afternoon I had just missed the last tour of the day. In conversation with the tour director I mentioned that it would not be possible for me to return the next day, as I was off to Iroquois Falls early in the morning, then directly on to Montreal. As a result, he kindly offered to take me down himself. And off we went in a golf cart down into the mine for a personally guided tour, wearing all the appropriate mining gear.

While the depth we descended was only a hundred or so feet, the display of mining equipment and the simulation of drilling and dynamiting was certainly very impressive and gave one the feeling of being actually down some three thousand feet or more and in a working mine.

A memento in the form of a certificate to the effect that I went on a tour of the mine was given to me, together with a cancelled souvenir cheque from the old Paymaster Consolidated Mines Limited, dated January 5th, 1940. This particular cheque was payable to one Andrew H. Conn of South Bend, Indiana, representing payment of a dividend, however, this particular cheque was for only $33.25, no doubt one of the smaller dividend cheques issued at the time.

On another occasion I visited Virginiatown just east of Kirkland Lake and signed up for another underground tour. This time I was at the site of the Kerr Addison Mine and the tour brought you down almost four thousand feet into a real live mine operation.

As you walked around you could see the miners going back and forth about their work and I should mention that the original descent in one of the old cages was quite the experience. Following the tour there was a draw for a 1988 commemorative gold coin issued by Kerr Addison Gold Mine on the occasion of its fiftieth anniversary, and luckily I was the winner of the coin.

If you are ever up in the mining area and time permits, I strongly recommend that you sign up for one of the guided tours at a local mine, however, as they say, please check with the local Chambers of Commerce or Museums first. And remember, if you go down dress accordingly, as it gets very cool down there.

The following is an article quoted from a publication entitled *What Metals and Minerals Mean to Canadians* and produced by *The Mining Association of Canada, The Northern Miner* and *Industry Canada*. It is hoped that it will give the reader a better understanding of what is involved in staking claims and is reproduced with permission from *The Northern Miner*:

Here's How To Stake Your Claim —

Say you want to stake a mineral claim in Ontario. Under the Mining Act of Ontario, you must first obtain a prospector's license. This is available for a small fee, to all persons 18 years of age and over and to companies.

A mineral exploration claim in Ontario is a square plot of land, measuring about 400 metres on a side and encompassing an area of about 16 hectares. Its boundaries must be oriented in a north-south and east-west direction. The boundaries of the claim must be marked with posts at each corner. The first, No.1 post, is placed at the northeastern corner. Moving clockwise around the claim, the No.4 post is situated in the northwestern corner. Claim boundaries are indicated by blazing trees at intervals or, if the area is treeless, by setting suitable pickets. On the No.1 post must be marked your name, your prospector's license number, the date and the time staked. You must also mark the other three posts with your name and license number.

Within 31 days of staking a claim, you must record the claim, or claims, at the Mining Recorder's Office in the appropriate mining division. (There are nine such divisions in Ontario). You must provide certain information which will identify the location of the claim(s), as well as pay a modest fee per claim staked. You are then issued a set of metal tags which must be affixed to the corner posts within six months. Only then is the claim considered to be properly staked.

At this point, you possess the exclusive right to proceed with exploration and development of the claim. This security of tenure is important for any prospector, geologist or exploration company, for it allows claims to be sold or optioned to other individuals or companies, presumably at a profit.

To hold on to this right, you are required to perform work on the claims or to pay a fee in lieu of work. In Ontario that means performing 200 worker-days of work per claim over five years, beginning with 20 worker-days in the first year. Such work is known as 'assessment work' and it must be reported to, and approved by, the Mining Recorder. Failure to perform the work means you forfeit the right to the claim and the ground opens up for staking by someone else.

Please note that there are differences in the mining laws by region and sometimes a law will be changed. Therefore you should consult with the local mine recording office before staking your claim(s).

An old mining book indicated that the cost of a prospector's license back in the gold rush days was $5.

Certificate confirming underground mine tour. *Author's collection*

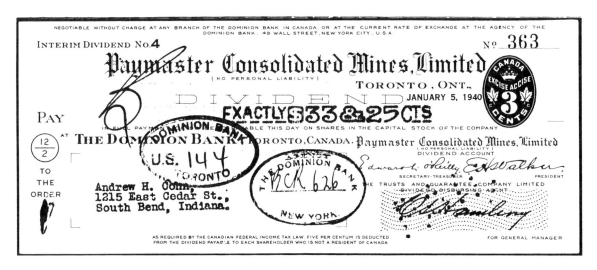

Souvenir cancelled dividend cheque. *Author's collection*

Boston Creek

During some of the interviews that I had with certain individuals in and around Kirkland Lake, I was asked whether I was aware that some of the underworld characters from Chicago travelled on occasion to the town of Boston Creek for some R & R (rest and rehabilitation as we call it). I had in fact not been aware of it. One of the more popular names mentioned was that of one Al Capone.

27

Sample Sketches

Scale: 1:20,000

Complete the group sketch on Part D using this as a guide. Where applicable, the items indicated below must be shown in the sketch.

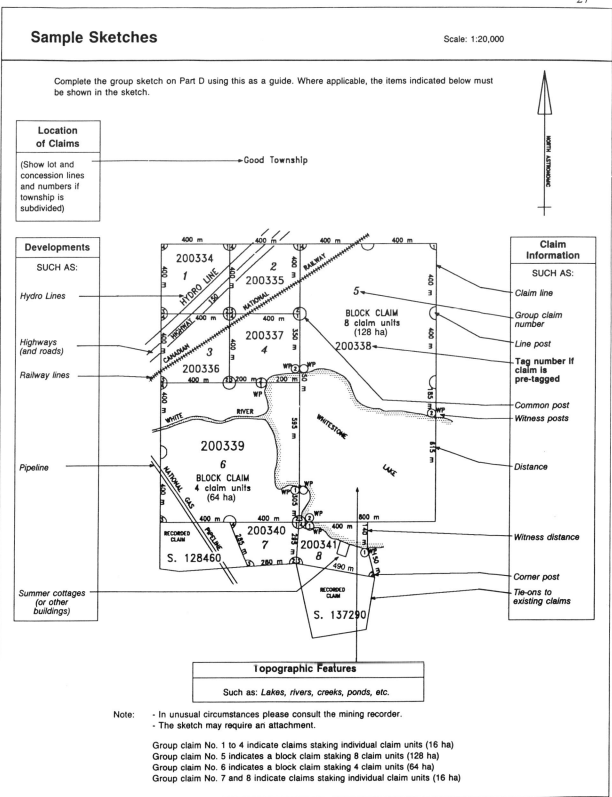

Location of Claims

(Show lot and concession lines and numbers if township is subdivided)

→ Good Township

NORTH ASTRONOMIC

Developments

SUCH AS:

Hydro Lines

Highways (and roads)

Railway lines

Pipeline

Summer cottages (or other buildings)

Claim Information

SUCH AS:

Claim line

Group claim number

Line post

Tag number if claim is pre-tagged

Common post

Witness posts

Distance

Witness distance

Corner post

Tie-ons to existing claims

Topographic Features

Such as: *Lakes, rivers, creeks, ponds, etc.*

Note: - In unusual circumstances please consult the mining recorder.
  - The sketch may require an attachment.

Group claim No. 1 to 4 indicate claims staking individual claim units (16 ha)
Group claim No. 5 indicates a block claim staking 8 claim units (128 ha)
Group claim No. 6 indicates a block claim staking 4 claim units (64 ha)
Group claim No. 7 and 8 indicate claims staking individual claim units (16 ha)

Sample form for the staking of claims. *Courtesy Ministry of Northern Development and Mines*

27

Approach to the hamlet of Boston Creek. *Author's collection*

I made it a point therefore to drive over to Boston Creek where I met a gentleman who provided some background information on the small hamlet, and confirmed the stories that I heard about members of the Chicago mob.

The population of Boston Creek is said to have reached a high point of 750 people during its early days. Keeping track of the population was a problem then because people moved in and out so fast. The following is a brief summary of Boston Creek:

During the twenties several prospects were employing men and Boston Creek soon acquired all the characteristics of a bustling frontier gold camp: a healthy disrespect for the law; two poolrooms providing centres for entertainment and gossip; boarding houses to accommodate passers-through looking for jobs or whatever; a hotel to pass the time between trains; a half-dozen bootleggers, available after hours; and at one time during those wild and woolly days, a policeman was posted in town to provide some law and order. The town even boasted a Chinese laundry and a barbershop. Robert Percy opened the first general store and post office in 1917, choosing the name Boston Creek for the American city he liked and the creek which ran near the camp.

A one-room schoolhouse was erected, probably in 1920-21, following the establishment of a school section in 1920. A small church was serviced weekly by a priest or minister who took turns travelling from Swastika by rail. Before the Hollinger Mine got a

Alfio Bargnesi (third from the left) who at one time had a one-man mining operation in Boston Creek. Third person from right is Albert Anastasia. *Courtesy of Desmond Woods*

camp doctor in 1928, the sick waited for Dr. Edis to pumpcar his way down the tracks from Swastika.

In September 1997, I made a return visit to Boston Creek one evening, to interview a lady who had lived there for some fifty plus years. The main purpose of my visit was to again confirm that what I heard was correct regarding the visit of certain gentlemen from Chicago. The answer was yes and actually Alfio Bargnesi did indeed visit Boston Creek with Albert Anastasia and Al Capone, and she was asked once to take a picture of them, but no copies of the picture were handed about. Wonder why?

While perusing the book *Kirkland Lake — On the Mile of Gold,* written by local author Michael Barnes, I noted that there is indeed mention that one Alfio Bargnesi had a one-man mine operation in Boston Creek. In addition there is a photograph of Bargnesi, together with Albert Anastasia, his wife and family. Anastasia was at one time head of the Brooklyn crime family and referred to as the *Lord Executioner*. On October 25th, 1957, Anastasia was driven to the barber shop at the Park Sheraton Hotel in New York City by his chauffeur, who dropped him off and then parked the car in the underground garage, following which he went for a leisurely stroll. During this time two supposedly unknown gunmen entered the barber shop and shot Anastasia. Word was that a contract had been given to one Joe Profaci, who in turn passed it on to the Gallo brothers from Brooklyn, New York.

Roza Brown

The most outstanding female character around Kirkland Lake during the gold rush days was in all probability a little old lady by the name of Roza Brown. It was said that she was born around 1856 in Budapest, Hungary, but two points that are often questioned are her real nationality and birth date.

Rosie first came to Canada in 1905 with her then husband Lieutenant Louis Brown and headed for Cobalt, Ontario, where they established a bakery and laundry shop on First Street.

It was while they were in Cobalt that a story surfaced to the effect that one night after she had prepared the dough for the next day's bakery products, her husband had come home slightly inebriated and while doing some preparatory work fell into the vat of dough. It was only early the next morning while getting ready to use the dough that Rosie found him. The

Roza Brown's house in Kirkland Lake. *Museum of Northern History*

outcome of the incident was that Rosie cursed her husband in every possible language that she knew and out he went never to be heard of again.

Needless to say, Rosie proceeded to use whatever dough was usable and began filling the bread pans and continued her normal chores. The news of Louis in the dough episode quickly got around and it was not long before Rosie left Cobalt heading in the direction of Swastika and eventually on to Kirkland Lake.

When Rosie first arrived in Kirkland Lake she proceeded to buy property on Government Road which eventually became the site of the Kresge department store. It is said that she paid a mere $100 for it and managed to sell it some fifteen years later for thirty thousand.

In due course she befriended a gentleman by the name of Harry Oakes and a very close friendship developed. As some may recall there is a studio photograph of Rosie standing dressed in her Sunday best, holding a flag pole in her right hand bearing the Union Jack and strung across her is a banner exclaiming *Long Live Harry Oakes*.

Rosie was also notorious in Kirkland Lake for her love of animals. She kept anywhere from five to seven dogs in her house and at times almost as many cats. The sight of her walking down Government Road surrounded by some of her dogs was apparently a common occurrence.

It is known that Rosie always had a loving attachment for the British Royal Family and never missed an opportunity to express her love for the King and Queen and the little Princesses. On one occasion Rosie shipped a live black lamb as a gift to Princess Elizabeth (later to be Queen Elizabeth II) and her sister Princess Margaret Rose. It would appear that the lamb did not make it to the lush green grounds surrounding Buckingham Palace. It did, however, find its way to a new home in the Children's Corner at the London Zoo.

A number of people in Kirkland Lake have memories of the days when Rosie would be ordered by the city fathers to demolish one of her properties, because of building violations, to which she would respond by raising a Union Jack flag on the

Roza Brown showing her admiration for Harry Oakes. *Museum of Northern History*

property in question, declaring that the property now belonged to the King of England or any other member of the Royal Family that she designated, thus preventing its destruction by the Town.

Rosie Brown would also seem to make a point of being one of the first persons to buy a ticket for the opening of any movies on special occasions. In one case a fund raising event was held whereby members of the audience, for a small donation, could go up on stage to kick a picture of Adolf Hitler. Needless to say, Rosie, in one of her more patriotic moods, would again be one of the first to pay her admission and was more than pleased to make a donation to the war fund for the privilege of kicking the picture.

Roza Brown and her love for the Royal Family. *Museum of Northern History*

On March 9th, 1947, at 10.40 p.m., beloved Rosie Brown passed away at the Kirkland and District Hospital after a lengthy illness. Rosie was ninety three years of age and had led a most interesting life among the pioneers of Northern Ontario.

Rosie's body was held at the Symington Funeral Chapel, the final arrangements being delayed pending the arrival of her nephew Dr. Benjamin Salzer from New York. It is said that her funeral procession on a one horse drawn sleigh, was one of the longest ever seen in Kirkland Lake. Rosie was laid to rest in the Hebrew Cemetery in the small hamlet of Krugerdorf some fifteen miles outside Kirkland Lake.

There is a poem entitled *Memories of Roza Brown* which was written by one Olga Neely, who lived on Lebel Avenue in Kirkland Lake at the time and which reads as follows:

Memories of Roza Brown

I have a little tale to tell, about one Roza Brown,
Who made her home in Kirkland Lake, when it was just a town.
She came here many years ago, when she and it were young,
And right until the very end, to Kirkland Lake, she clung.

She came out to this continent, from far off Hungary,
Now this was in the early days, in 1902 or 1903.
From Cobalt Town she landed at Swastika, then the 'Top',
But soon to Kirkland Lake she did advance, and here did stop.

She ran a boarding house at first, and next a laundry place,
And right where Kresge's stands today, her business had its base.
Then for change, she dished out hash, while travelling to and fro,
As on the railroad she was chef, for the old T. N. O.

While she was in the boarding house, she helped out quite a few,
When 'sourdoughs' were looking for the makings of a stew.
Later on she made a living out of real estate, it seems,
But even so, she always looked as if she hadn't any means.

I know that from the early days, this Roza made her mark,
For hers was such a nature as to kindle many a spark.
There were not many folk in town who ever could forget,
This Roza Brown, whose habits were unusual, you bet.

Her home was small and crowded, but besides her, there did dwell,
A pack of dogs, and cats, and other friends of hers, as well.
For she was such a law unto herself, it mattered not,
And even for officialdom, she cared less than a jot.

She had a fascination for parades of any kind,
And managed to attend them all, but not from the behind.
For Mrs Brown would lead them with a flag, and costume too,
All dressed in her long black coat, and with red and white and blue.

For she was patriotic, and she loved the Queen and King,
The Princesses received a little lamb, as offering.
The lamb was black and curly, the finest in the land,
It represented everything that Roza thought was grand.

Now when King George the Sixth, and Queen Elizabeth came here,
To make a tour of Canada, and see both far and near.
They must have been surprised indeed, when they got off the ship,
For there was Roza Brown, to say 'Hello, How was your trip?'

When she set out to pay a call, or just to stroll around,
She'd always be accompanied, this self-same Roza Brown.
For everywhere she went, you see, the dogs went with her there,
No matter who she visited, she didn't give a care.

T'was nothing for the councillors, a visit to receive,
When they transacted business, or were talking with the Reeve.
For Mrs Brown went where she would, and any time at all,
You might perceive her presence, as she went to pay a call.

Now as a pioneer of Kirkland Lake, she'll be preferred,
For no one else like Roza Brown, has ever here occurred.
Her shuffling gait, her costume rare, her temper even free,
But no one ever dared to say a word, to such as she.

I know that she was famous for her kindnesses, at times,
Although she loved a dollar, yet she'd give away some dimes.
And if she ever made a friend, a friend to him she'd be,
But beware of a bawling out, if you did not suit she.

And yet when all is said and done, we really must admit,
That Kirkland Lake was richer for her presence and her grit.
And if she had not come to spend her life up in the 'north',
She wouldn't be remembered, but she will, and for henceforth.

She was laid to rest at Krugerdorf, in nineteen forty seven,
I wonder if we'll see her if we ever get to Heaven.
There'd be a band, it would be grand, with Roza in the lead,
Her flag in hand, she'd take her stand, a sight for all indeed.

And now my story's ended, it has lasted quite a while,
But those who knew this Mrs Brown will all recall her style.
For those of you who missed her, I can say you missed a lot,
But if you had, I promise you, she'd never be forgot!

In January 1998, I finally had the pleasure of meeting Olga Neely who had written the above poem and I acknowledge with thanks her permission to reproduce it. Olga had lived in Kirkland Lake for the greater part of her life.

Krugerdorf is a very small hamlet in Northern Ontario and probably best remembered by many as the site of the Hebrew Cemetery, which comprises the final resting place of Roza Brown.

Easiest access to the cemetery is off Highway 11 just south of the merger with Highway 112 from Kirkland Lake. The road is called the Aidie Creek Gardens Road on the eastern side of Highway 11. You drive all the way down this dirt road past the Aidie Creek Garden Center. As you approach the second intersection you will note a stop sign, beside which is a handmade horizontal sign with the word cemetery on it and the direction to follow.

As you proceed from this intersection you will shortly note on the right hand side a black iron fence, the gates of which are secured with a lock. This is the main entrance to the cemetery.

There does not appear to be any indication of the name of the cemetery and there is no mention of where one can get the key, but access can easily be obtained by lying on your back and slowly sliding under the iron fence, as there is enough horizontal space to do so. I can vouch for this means of entry based on my own experience once in the late fall, when the ground was covered with a light dusting of snow and I was determined to gain access. I trust I will be forgiven for this intrusion.

The direction to the Hebrew Cemetery. *Author's collection*

Once inside you will note that the cemetery is L shaped towards the left, with two small wooden structures on the right — one building is no doubt for gatherings before or after a burial or memorial service and the second one would appear to be the maintenance shed.

On the far left are many tombstones, all of which are inscribed in Hebrew and bear the Star of David emblem. In the very last row and to the right is that of Roza Brown.

As one stands looking at her tombstone, there is a certain feeling of remembering what you have read and heard about Rosie and her many accomplishments, the friends she had, as well as the enemies. Amongst her closest of friends was Harry Oakes. Her enemies were basically any persons who did not like her dogs or animals in general.

Charlie Chow

Another well known individual in Northern Ontario at the time was Charlie Chow, who was born in January 1885. He immigrated from Hong Kong to Canada in the early 1900's and eventually settled in Kirkland Lake in 1916. At first he ran a small restaurant with a few counter stools. As his business and profits increased over the years he eventually built himself a small hotel which opened on April 11th, 1924, a short distance down the street from his original restaurant.

The hotel that he owned and operated was situated on Government Road

Roza Brown's final resting place at the Hebrew Cemetery at Krugerdorf, Ontario. *Author's collection*

and it is just in the past few years that it slowly began to deteriorate to the point where it was finally demolished in November 1993, by the new owners, much to the sorrow of old time residents of Kirkland Lake. A landmark of the area had now disappeared, taking with it a good deal of the history, and the names of many well known guests who stayed there.

During the course of his business ventures in Kirkland Lake, Chow amassed a small fortune because of his willingness to accept paper shares in mining companies as payment for food and lodging.

Charlie's acceptance of shares of such mining companies as Harry Oakes' Lake Shore Mines at a value of fifty cents each as payment, was the start of his financial fortune and some years later when the Lake Shore Mines began to make money, these simple shares began to escalate in value, until at one point they were worth the likes of $64 a share. That, in a way, is how Charlie Chow became so rich. At the time of his death there were many

36

opinions amongst the citizens of Kirkland Lake as to Chow's total worth, some estimates going from $1,000,000 to $8,000,000.

In 1950, Charlie and his business manager, Joe Chung, splurged and bought themselves a Buick automobile for $6,000 including all the available options; however, as the story goes neither one of them knew how to drive. Whenever they wanted to go anywhere they had to ask someone to drive them. When Charlie passed away in 1972 the car was still behind the hotel, with a grand total of forty thousand miles registered on the odometer. Calculations would indicate that over a twenty two year period, the car was driven an average of 1,800 miles a year or 150 miles a month.

One of the true stories about Charlie Chow relates to how one day he was able to assist the manager of the Royal Bank of Canada in Kirkland Lake in meeting a $250,000 mining payroll, as the train carrying the cash from Toronto had been delayed by a snow storm and was unable to arrive on time. Charlie met the payroll in denominations of one, two, five, ten and twenty dollar bills, all from his trusted old safe at the hotel.

Charlie Chow was also to become a legend in the north, together with the likes of Harry Oakes, Rosie Brown and many, many others.

It was interesting to note from one of the old photographs of Kirkland Lake showing Charlie Chow's hotel, that two entrances are shown — one designated *Mens Entrance* and the other *Ladies Entrance*, which no doubt would bring back fond memories for some of the old timers of Ontario relative to the old provincial liquor laws.

Charlie passed away at the Kirkland

Charlie Chow, one of the many individuals in Kirkland Lake. *Courtesy of Eddie Duke, Museum of Northern History*

Charlie Chow's hotel shortly before demolition in 1993. *Courtesy of Les Eaton (Museum of Northern History)*

and District Hospital in Kirkland Lake at the good old age of eighty seven on March 4th, 1972, after a lengthy illness. Funeral services were held at the Symington Funeral

Chapel, followed by interment in the Kirkland Lake cemetery. Chow had donated large sums of money to the Kirkland and District Hospital over the years. He was survived by his wife Leung Chow, son Man Chung Chow and six grandchildren.

Jimmy Doig

Jimmy Doig was the owner of a general merchant type establishment in the town of Swastika, which provided groceries, provisions, flour and feed, dry goods, clothing, hardware and especially mining and prospecting supplies. In some cases he allowed a few of his customers to build up charge accounts.

Among those to whom he offered credit was Harry Oakes. On one occasion Harry went into Jimmy's store, picked up some goods and told Doig to add it to his account. Jimmy refused to add the purchases and told Oakes to replace the merchandise, unless he could pay for it in cash. Oakes told him that he would be receiving as usual some funds from his brother Louis, back home in Maine in a week or so, which would more than cover his balance, however,

Charlie Chow's final resting place in the Kirkland Lake Cemetery. *Author's collection*

Jimmy would still not agree and Harry had to replace the goods.

Apparently Harry left the store enraged and some years later when he was running his Lake Shore Mines, he forbade all of his employees to shop at Jimmy Doig's store, thus slowly forcing him out of business.

As the story continues, Doig was one day down on his luck and decided to take a risk and approached Oakes for possible financial assistance. Harry very kindly gave Jimmy $10,000 and the two of them became good friends once again.

Mary Martin

The name of Mary Martin is associated by most people with the stage play *South Pacific* and eventually with the movie of the same name.

However, according to one of the Toronto newspapers under date of December 27th, 1943, there was a report of the passing of one Mary Martin with the headlines reading *Oakes' Backer Now is Dead*. She was ninety two years of age.

The Canadian Press report referred to Mrs. Mary Martin as the lady who gave financial assistance to the late Sir Harry Oakes, when he first began his exploration of the mining possibilities in and around Kirkland Lake.

Mary Martin was born in Indiana and originally came to Canada as a jewelry demonstrator, who travelled extensively abroad and eventually returned to Canada in 1906. During that year she moved to Northern Ontario as a stenographer for a local lawyer in Haileybury.

She subsequently settled in Swastika where she apparently operated her own secretarial office and social center for prospectors and among those whom she helped with plans and applications was Harry Oakes. She married Ernie Martin, a close associate of Oakes.

It is said that she once controlled the *Violette Claim* which later became part of the original Tough-Oakes mine, and as well had an interest in Lake Shore Mines itself.

Noteworthy Folks of the Early Days

There are a number of individuals, who in some cases can be best described as pioneers and others as characters, who formed the group of dedicated souls who helped develop parts of the rugged and well known townships, which all became part and parcel of Canadian history.

The following are possibly just a few of these individuals — some of whom became famous and others who were just part of the history:

Sandy McIntyre, one of the old time pioneers of Northern Ontario. *Archives of Ontario ACC6805 S11807*

George Bannerman, Joe Boisvert, Roza Brown, Thrift Burnside, Charlie Chow, Ruben D'Aigle, Charlie Dennison, Clary Dixon, Jimmy Doig, Dennis Duffy, Frank Duncan, Bill Dusty, Jim Dusty, Jake Englehart, Charles Cobbold Farr, Ed Hargreaves, Arnold Hoffman, Benny Hollinger, Jim Hughes, Hyman Kaplan, Max Kaplan, Fred LaRose, Walter Little, Bob Martin, Ernie Martin, Mary Martin, Alex Matheson, Sandy McIntyre, Tom Middleton, Jack Miller, George Minaker, Freeman Mitford (later

Lord Redesdale), Gertrude Oakes, Harry Oakes, Father Charles Paradis, Joe Parkin, Fred Schumacher, Henry Timmins, Noah Timmins, Bob Tough, George Tough, Jack Tough, Tom Tough, Al Wende, Bill Wright, Walter Wright and many, many more whose names I may not have mentioned.

Some Special Exhibits, Highlights, And Sources Of Information

Alfred J. Casson is probably best known to many Canadians as having been a member of the famous Group of Seven, a group of Canadian artists, who painted the Canadian scene and recorded the development of Northern Ontario, or as some sources called it at the time, *New Ontario.*

However, it should be noted that Casson was not part of the original Group of Seven, but had replaced Frank Johnston, who had resigned from the Group.

It would appear that Casson's only association with Sir Harry Oakes was that he was commissioned by the Management of Lake Shore Mines in Kirkland Lake to produce an *In Memoriam* book or, as I have been informed, an *illuminated book* in commemoration of Sir Harry Oakes following his death in 1943, relative to his contribution to the mining industry in general. The text of the book reads as follows:

At a recent meeting of the Board of Directors of Lake Shore Mines Limited, it was unanimously resolved to forward to Lady Oakes and family the following expression of sympathy in the sudden bereavement which has plunged them into mourning and brought sorrow to ourselves and many others outside the family circle.

The Board of Directors of Lake Shore Mines Limited extend to Lady Oakes and members of her family their deepest sympathy in the great loss which they have sustained.

The late Sir Harry Oakes, Bart., was not only the President of this Company from its inception down to the year 1935, but he was also the discoverer of Lake Shore Mines and the founder of the Company. He laid the foundation for the development of one of Canada's greatest gold camps, which has produced employment and wealth for thousands of its citizens.

During the long term of years in which he acted as President, his relations with the members of the Board were intimate, and the memory of his great qualities of mind and heart will forever remain with us.

We know that his fine spirit of integrity and high courage will continue to live in our hearts through all the years to come.

As witness the Seal of the Company under the hands of the President and Vice-President, the 20th day of September, A.D. 1943
Lake Shore Mines Limited.

The *illuminated book* can always be found on display at the Museum of Northern History in Kirkland Lake, the former residence of Sir Harry Oakes. The viewing of the book and its masterful art work is definitely a must for art lovers when visiting the Museum.

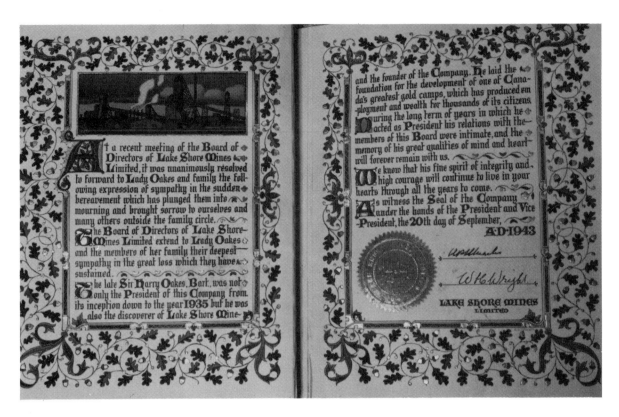

Illuminated Book prepared by Alfred J. Casson of the Group of Seven for the management of Lake Shore Mines as a memorial to Sir Harry. *Author's collection, Museum of Northern History*

It is often said that *a picture is worth a thousand words* and this can truly be said of a gentleman by the name of Eddie Duke, old time resident of Kirkland Lake. Eddie Duke first came to Kirkland Lake in 1929 as a young boy and attended the old Central School.

As time went by Eddie developed an interest in photography and became the major photographer of the northern region around Kirkland Lake, establishing his own shop and studio. There is hardly a mining site around that has not been photographed by Eddie Duke. Annual reports of the mining companies abound with his photos.

A visit to the Museum of Northern History in Kirkland Lake will provide you with samples of his photographic work. I visited with Eddie in December 1998, and was provided with a personal guided tour of his proud photo collection at his home.

While maybe not normally part of an author's manuscript, the name of Highway Book Shop in this case must be included for the simple reason that for anyone interested in the history and the development of the north and in particular the mining towns of Northern Ontario, this book shop is one of the greatest sources of written material. If you are in need of topographical maps — possibly in search of a gold mine — Highway Book Shop has a vast assortment of them.

Highway Book Shop was established in 1957 and is owned and operated by Dr. Douglas Pollard and his wife Lois. Dr. Pollard is a walking encyclopaedia on all kinds of books, recent as well as antiquarian. In addition to being a source of books Highway Book Shop is also a publishing outlet for many local and Canadian authors and their works about the north. It is located on Highway 11 — on the road north some 137 km (85 miles) from North Bay just prior to the cut off to Cobalt, Ontario. As their brochure says, *a book-lover's paradise.*

Highway Book Shop, situated on Highway 11 near Cobalt, Ontario. A book-lover's paradise. *Author's collection*

Kirkland Lake over the years was not just a gold mining boom town, but in the subsequent years it became the stepping stone for many young aspiring hockey players who hoped to enter the National Hockey League and make their own personal mark in the annals of hockey. As a result Kirkland Lake was to be remembered as the town that in part made the National Hockey League famous.

And to back up this statement there are in excess of thirty five known players who started and played part of their careers in Kirkland Lake and eventually graduated to the N.H.L. teams. Amongst these players are the likes of Ralph Backstrom, Roy Conacher, Floyd Curry, Dick Duff, Larry Hillman, Ted Lindsay, Gus Mortson, Bill Plager, Mickey Redmond and goalies Bill Durnan and Daren Puppa.

On December 7th, 1991, in memory of all the hockey players who had passed through Kirkland Lake, an ingot of stainless steel was presented to the people of Kirkland Lake by the Jones Laughlin Steel Co., of Pittsburgh, Pennsylvania. Inscribed on both sides of the ingot are the names of all players involved in this special tribute including the following message from Clarence Campbell, former President of the National Hockey League: *The hockey players of Kirkland Lake have earned recognition for their superior skill and courage with the teams of the National Hockey League.*

Ralph Backstrom, former N.H.L. great. *Courtesy of Ralph Backstrom*

42

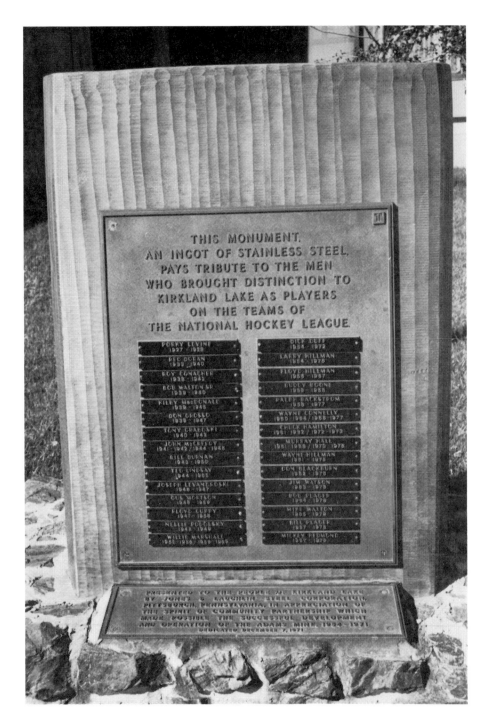

A memorial to the National Hockey League players who lived in, or passed through Kirkland Lake. *Author's collection*

Some of the highlights registered by the players included Ted Lindsay winning the N.H.L. scoring title in the 1949/50 season; Ralph Backstrom winning the rookie of the year in 1959; Bill Durnan winning the Vezina trophy as the best goalie six times during the years 1944-50. It is said that as at 1993, the players who had passed through Kirkland Lake on their way to fame and fortune, had played in 12,563 games, scored 2,330 goals, assisted in 3,601 goals and participated in 35 Stanley Cup victories in the National Hockey League.

3

Harry Oakes 1924-1934: Niagara Falls and Oak Hall

The Discovery of Niagara Falls ..... Harry's Purchase of Oak Hall ..... The Arrival of the Oakes Family to their New Residence ..... A Brief History of Oak Hall ..... The Artistic Aspects of the Residence ..... What Happened to Oak Hall?

In 1608, the explorer Samuel de Champlain recorded in his notes of exploration of Canada, that the Indians along the St. Lawrence River had told him about these falls. Nevertheless, it was not until 1615 that one of Champlain's interpreters and agents, Etienne Brulé, may have visited the falls at Niagara, but nothing definite was recorded to this effect.

The next mention was made by Le Sieur Gendron, a doctor of medicine who lived amongst the native Indians and wrote about the falls in his diary in 1644.

The present day site of the falls has remained a tourist attraction which began as far back as 1783 and has since become a very popular destination especially for honeymooners.

In 1887, the Queen Victoria Niagara Falls Park Commission was established. Years later Harry Oakes, following many of his philanthropic gestures in the area, became a member of the Commission for a two year term in 1933, prior to his eventual departure for the Bahamas.

On July 15th, 1924, Harry Oakes bought an estate from one Paul Schoellkopf, a member of a prominent Niagara Falls, New York family. Oakes undertook to reconstruct, in Tudor style, a good portion of it, which was completed over a period of four years and in 1928 Oakes and his family moved into what was to be known as Oak Hall. In the same year Harry Oakes and his wife Eunice became Canadian citizens.

The building itself had some 37 rooms and dominated an area of 21 acres of rose gardens and grounds overlooking Dufferin Island above Niagara Falls on the Canadian side. Originally the property belonged to one James Skinner and family, a United Empire Loyalist, from 1798 to approximately 1898.

The Oakes family lived in it until 1934, when Harry Oakes decided for financial reasons that it was in his best interest to leave Canada and settle in the Bahamas, where he would not have to pay any income tax and the death duties would be minimal. It was estimated that for every dollar that Lake Shore Mines produced, Oakes handed approximately eighty cents over to the Canadian Government.

During the war years, Oak Hall was handed over to the Royal Canadian Air Force to be used as a convalescent hospital for returning R.C.A.F. personnel from overseas.

In 1952 the property was returned to Lady Oakes. Their son, Sir Sydney Oakes and his wife Lady Greta, lived there for many years before finally returning to reside in the Oakes estates in the Bahamas.

My first visit to Oak Hall was in 1991, on one of Max Haines' *Weekender* excursions, at which time we were given a guided tour of the complete interior of the estate, following which we made a rather strenuous climb up a long staircase to reach a lookout point located at the very top. The view of the surrounding area was worth every effort along the way. Regrettably Oak Hall is no longer open to the public, except for a few rooms on the ground floor. Max Haines is the Crime Columnist for the *Toronto Sun* newspaper.

The interior is a major display of paintings, prints, watercolours and drawings by many noted artists and travellers including the likes of William Henry Bartlett; Thomas Benecke; W. R. Callington; James Pattison Cockburn; Henry Samuel Davis; Washington Friend; Augustus Kollner; Frederick Holloway; Otto Rheinhold Jacobi; Henri Pierre; J.R.Coke Smyth; Isaac Weld and Robert R. Whale. The paintings and other works of art basically depict scenes of the falls and the surrounding area.

Sir Harry Oakes. *Courtesy of Archive Photos*

Sir Harry Oakes' residence, Oak Hall at Niagara Falls. *Author's collection*

A few years ago, my wife and I drove to Niagara Falls and visited the site of Oak Hall, including a visit to the small building on the right hand side as you enter the grounds.

The building itself serves as the headquarters for the golf pro-shop, which is located immediately in front of Oak Hall. In discussion with the gentleman in attendance at the shop, I mentioned my interest in Sir Harry Oakes and he immediately offered to show us the heating and boiler rooms which were located under the pro-shop. As he gave us the underground guided tour, he explained that all of the main furnaces were located in this building approximately one thousand feet away from Oak Hall itself, as it was said that Sir Harry was afraid of fire and wanted the heating system as far away as possible from where he lived — was this true or just another Sir Harry Oakes myth?

Oak Hall is now part of the administrative offices of the Niagara Falls Park Commission. A nine hole golf course was opened on June 17th, 1966, immediately outside the entrance to the hall.

In February 1929, Harry Oakes wrote to the Adjutant of The Lincoln and Welland Regiment in St Catharines, Ontario, concerning his nomination as Honorary Lieutenant Colonel of the Regiment, which he appears to have accepted and which became official on April 4th, 1929.

At this point he was now Honorary Lieutenant Colonel Harry Oakes. Though previous service in the Regiment or the military may be a factor in such an appointment, it is not an absolute prerequisite. This honorary title was most probably conferred upon Oakes as he was a very prominent member of the local community. The honour remained with him till his death in 1943.

4

Harry Oakes 1934-1943: The Bahamas At Last

A Brief History of the Bahamas ..... The Island of New Providence and Nassau ..... Government House — The Royal Residence ..... Harold Christie — Harry's Real Estate Friend ..... The Cable Beach Area ..... The Quaint Village of Gambier ..... Reverend Robert Hall — A Friend of Sir Harry Oakes ..... The Start of Bahamas Air ..... Bahamas General Trust — An Investment Haven ..... The Bahamas Historical Society ..... Land Purchase — A Bahamian Event ..... The Bahamas Police Force ..... Gambling In the Bahamas — To What Extent ..... Prohibition Years — The Rum Runners of the Bahamas ..... Censorship in the Colonies ..... The Royal Bank of Canada ..... The Exchange Control Board — What Not To Do With Your Money ..... The Prince George Hotel — A Meeting Place ..... The Rozelda Hotel — Another Meeting Place ..... Baron Georg and Baroness Marie af Trolle ..... Royal Air Force — The R.A.F. in the Bahamas ..... The Cameron Highlanders ..... Sir Bede Clifford ..... Sir Charles Dundas ..... Dr. Cleveland Eneas ..... Sally Rand — An Exotic Dancer ..... Dr. Axel Wenner-Gren — The Swedish Industrialist ..... The Southern Cross ..... The Athenia — Part of the War ..... The Famous Banco Continental — Mexico ..... Sir Harry's Reasons for Leaving Canada ..... Sir Harry's Sheep Farm ..... Newell Kelly — His Business Manager in Nassau ..... Walter Foskett — His Attorney in the U.S.A. ..... Dover-Foxcroft Cemetery in Maine ..... Hubbard Cottages

---

In 1934 Harry Oakes, resenting the Canadian Government's high tax rate applied to the earnings from his Lake Shore Mines and his possible appointment as a Senator now a thing of the past, decided to move his family and his enormous wealth to the Bahamas, where there was no taxation and the death duty was minimal. A few years earlier in Palm Beach, Florida, Oakes had already met the real estate king of the Bahamas, Harold Christie, who was always seeking people interested in his islands, especially those with money, and Harry Oakes was a perfect candidate.

Harry Oakes had finally arrived in the Bahamas, which has often been described as being *Paradise, the Isle of June*, or the *Jewels of the Caribbeans.*

In reality the Bahamas is geographically described in many sources as comprising some twenty nine islands; six hundred and sixty one cays (pronounced keys) and two thousand three hundred and eighty seven rock formations, all located within an area of approximately one hundred square miles, some 60 miles off the coast of Florida and within fifty miles of Cuba.

The main islands of the Bahamas are New Providence (with its capital Nassau); Grand Bahama (which includes Freeport); Abaco; Andros (actually the largest island in land mass); Eleuthera; Exuma; Cat Island; Bimini (made famous by the writer Ernest

48

A - Westbourne
B - The Caves
C - Gambier Village
D - Lyford Cay
E - Government House
F - Alfred de Marigny's residence
G - Dr. Axel Wenner-Gren's residence
H - Downtown Nassau and the British Colonial Hotel
I - Oakes Field
J - Windsor Field

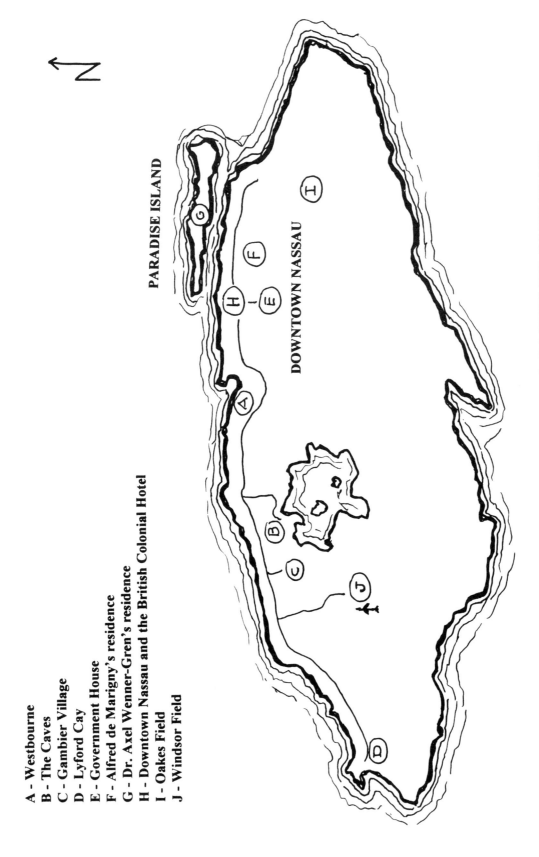

ISLAND OF NEW PROVIDENCE

Map of the Island of New Providence showing the major points covered by this book. *Author's collection*

Hemingway); Long Island; Inagua; San Salvador (discovered by Christopher Columbus) and many more smaller islands. Basically 17 islands are considered inhabited.

Christopher Columbus discovered the Bahamas on October 12th, 1492, when he landed on the Island of San Salvador, also known as Watling's Island (and as Guanahani to the native Indians). There have been subsequent reappraisals of the landing site as proposed by the National Geographic Society in their November 1986 issue, who claim that Columbus landed at Samana Cay, a small island south east of San Salvador. However, as stated by the Minister of Tourism of the Bahamas following the announcement by the Geographic — *he did not really care what island Columbus landed on, as long as he landed in their beloved Bahamas.* Tourism is tourism as you can well imagine.

It is interesting to note that on the Island of San Salvador there are presently three different commemorative sites acknowledging the arrival of Christopher Columbus in the New World. The first monument is just south of Cockburn Town on the sandy beaches in the form of a simple white stone cross erected in 1956. Down the road from this monument is an imposing and monolithic Olympic monument designed to convey the Olympic flame from Athens to Mexico. Around on the other side of the island is a third commemorative Columbus monument, erected in 1891 by the Chicago Herald newspaper and located near Long Bay. The last commemorative monument is the most photographed one on San Salvador.

As the late Bahamian author and historian Dr. Paul Albury once said — *if Columbus could return to San Salvador today he would find the island much as he last saw it. The Admiral would be much pleased to see three monuments commemorating his arrival there in 1492, each marking a different place where he first stepped ashore. He would probably point out the real exact spot of his landing which, of course, would call for a fourth monument.*

The population of the Bahamas is presently estimated at over two hundred and fifty thousand people, a good portion of whom live on the Island of New Providence with Nassau as the capital and where most of the history of the Bahamas evolved and still does.

Being located along the line of the Tropic of Cancer, the Bahamas enjoy a year round tropical climate, though during the period of June to October there is always the possibility of hurricanes passing through the islands. One of the earliest recorded hurricanes which swept up through the islands from the Turks and Caicos Islands to the south, through Harbour Island and on to Nassau causing severe damage along the way, was on September 30th, 1866.

It is said that waves washed over parts of what is now Paradise Island to such a height that some of them almost reached the balcony of the lighthouse situated at the western tip of the island. If you have been to Nassau, you certainly can have an appreciation for the height of the waves as you look out at the lighthouse in Nassau harbour.

Ever since the arrival of the first settlers in 1648, the Bahamas has always been considered a British Colony under the administration of the British Colonial Secretary in London. Independence for the Bahamas came into effect on July 10th, 1973, at Clifford Park in Nassau, with Prince Charles representing the British Government and Queen Elizabeth II. At exactly midnight, to the poignant strains of the Last Post, the Union Jack was lowered for the last time, to be replaced by the new Bahamian flag to the singing of their new national anthem entitled *March on Bahamaland*.

The early motto of the Bahamas was *Expulsis Piratis, Restituta Commercia* and freely translated read as *Pirates Expelled, Trade Restored*. This goes back to the early days of the Bahamas, when Woodes Rogers was appointed Governor General in 1718 with the definite task of ridding the Bahamas of the pirates.

THE BAHAMAS COAT OF ARMS

"EXPULSIS PIRATIS RESTITUTA COMMERCIA"
("Pirates Expelled, Trade Restored")

It is a common misconception that pretty well anyone who ever travels to the Bahamas considers Nassau as an island within itself, rather than just being a town on the Island of New Providence, where Nassau, the capital of the Bahamas, is located.

History would seem to indicate that the Island of New Providence may have been discovered when one Captain William Sayle, leader of the Eleutheran Adventurers went on a voyage to the Carolinas in the southern United States. As they approached land they met with a severe storm, which caused them to drift some distance off course and eventually seek refuge in a harbour in what is now Nassau, and sensing some divine

Original Bahamian Coat of Arms before their independence in July 1973. *Courtesy of the Archives of the Bahamas*

guidance for their rescue, Sayle named the island *New Providence*.

The Island of New Providence is approximately seven miles across from north to south and twenty one miles in length from east to west and one can drive around it, following the shoreline as much as possible, within a two hour time frame and view the beautiful blue and green Atlantic Ocean waters along most of the way.

51

In July 1938, Harry Oakes became one of the twenty nine members of the Bahamian House of Assembly, when he defeated one Milo Butler, a young black Bahamian grocer by 538 votes to 70 in a by-election for the Western District in Nassau. The by-election was necessary when Alfred Adderley was elevated to the Upper House of the Bahamian Government. It was said that Oakes did not conduct a campaign, as his election was a certainty from the start.

In retrospect it is interesting to note that following the Independence of the Bahamas from Great Britain in 1973, the defeated candidate Milo Butler, who had run against Harry Oakes, became the first black Governor General of the Bahamas, as Sir Milo Butler.

In Nassau, Government House — the official residence of the Governor General — is situated on a ten acre estate better known as Mount Fitzwilliam, named after Richard Fitzwilliam who was Governor General from 1733 to 1738. The site was purchased by the Crown in 1801 for the grand sum of £4,000.

The basis of the present structure of Government House was built during the administration of John Kalkett, Governor General from 1802 to 1804.

An Eastern wing was added in 1907 to house the Grand Ballroom and the offices of the Governor General, followed in 1940 by additional quarters erected in the West wing

Government House in Nassau. The official residence of the Duke and Duchess of Windsor during his Governorship. *Author's collection*

The statue of Christopher Columbus in front of Government House. *Author's collection*

(known as the Windsor wing), to accommodate the personal staff of the Duke of Windsor, who was Royal Governor General from 1940 to 1945.

When the Duke and Duchess of Windsor first arrived in Nassau and were about to settle into Government House, the Duchess complained about the interior appearance of the residence, such as the condition of the furniture, the painting of the walls, the wallpapering, as well as the general deteriorating condition of the residence. As a result Sir Harry and Lady Oakes were one of two prominent couples in Nassau, who offered the Windsors appropriate accommodation and in their case it was the use of their *Westbourne* estate, until such time as Government House was properly refurbished.

The statue of Christopher Columbus, which stands below the steps leading up to Government House, was modelled in London by the Aide-de-Camp to Washington Irving and presented to the people of the Bahamas in 1830 by its then Governor General, Sir James Carmichael Smythe.

Harold Christie

One of Sir Harry Oakes' closest friends in Nassau was Harold Christie, who was born of Bahamian parents in May 1896, and was considered one of the major pioneers of land development in the Bahamas. At the time of the death of Sir Harry Oakes, Christie was forty seven years of age.

The members of Christie's family had arrived in the Bahamas in the 1780's with the Empire Loyalists, who left America during the War of Independence from Britain.

In the early thirties, Christie established a real estate firm which still bears his initials H.G. Christie Real Estate Co. He was first elected to the House of Assembly for the riding of Cat Island in 1927.

It was in 1934 that Christie would meet the Canadian multi-millionnaire Harry Oakes during one of Harry's visits to Palm Beach, Florida where he had a residence. Christie outlined to Oakes the benefits of living in the Bahamas, both from a financial point of view and a health one.

In view of Oakes' experiences with the Canadian government concerning the taxation on the earnings from his Lake Shore Mines, the Bahamas seemed like paradise and Harry was not long in making up his mind and moving to Nassau with his family.

A very close relationship developed between Christie and Oakes and as many people would say — *if Christie had property to sell, he knew he would have a deal for Oakes and a commission for himself.* As a result Oakes purchased several homes including *Westbourne*, *The Caves*, followed by the British Colonial Hotel, the Bahamas Country Club and some ten thousand odd acres of property on the Island of New Providence.

In due course, Harold Christie also became a very close friend of the Duke and Duchess of Windsor, following their arrival in Nassau in 1940, and he would also develop a further friendship with Dr. Axel Wenner-Gren, the Swedish industrialist who lived over on what is now Paradise Island.

Christie was one of the founders of Bahamas Airways and the first Chairman of the Development Board (later to be known as the Ministry of Tourism), which was what Christie loved most for his Bahamas.

In 1959, Harold Christie married one Virginia Johnson, who was an old friend who lived in Miami. Sir Harry Oakes had been instrumental in introducing them to each other. Christie at the time was sixty-three years of age.

Harold Christie was knighted in 1964 by Queen Elizabeth II of England, in recognition of the beneficial work that he did in furthering the development of the Bahamas, both as an investment center and as a tourist mecca.

Sir Harold Christie died of a heart attack on September 25th, 1973, in Munich, Germany while travelling on business. The secrets of what really happened that fateful night of July 7th and 8th, 1943, resulting in the brutal murder of his best friend Sir Harry Oakes, surely went with him to his grave. He was 77 years of age at the time of his death and was survived by his wife Lady Virginia Christie.

Cable Beach

There is an area of Nassau called Cable Beach located on West Bay Street, in the hub of the present day hotels including the Nassau Beach Hotel, the Ambassador Beach Hotel (formerly the site of Sir Harry's *Westbourne* estate) and more recently the Crystal Palace Casino and Resort. No doubt at time of writing, the names of these hotels may have changed once again or new ones may have been built.

The remains of the once proud Hobby Horse Racetrack in Nassau. *Author's collection*

The Bahamas had horse racing facilities called the Hobby Horse Race Track which was located across the street from these hotels and interestingly enough during a visit to Nassau in 1992, I came across the remains of the grandstand of the old race track together with the judge's tower. The remains are hidden in the woods, but even now, when you walk up the steps of the grandstand itself, which has survived for more than fifty years, there is a certain feeling that comes over you as you try to picture the Duke and Duchess of Windsor, Sir Harry and Lady Eunice Oakes and other prominent Nassauvians attending some of the races, possibly in the hope of earning some extra pocket money for themselves.

Pari-mutual betting at the race track was operated under the rules of the Canadian Racing Association and all aspects of racing were supervised by the Bahamian Government. Imported thoroughbreds and native horses were raced, but racing was limited to a few days a week.

The Cable Beach area was so named as a result of it being the location where the first telegraphic communication line between Nassau and Miami was established in 1892. The original cable ran from the town of Jupiter in Florida to the Cable Beach area, and Sir Ambrose Shea, then Governor General of the Bahamas, did the honours of sending and receiving the first exchange of messages with the mainland.

The establishment of this communication system provided the Bahamas with its first opportunity to obtain the latest world news, and as well, gave the world access to what was happening in the Bahamas on a more timely basis.

Welcome to Gambier Village in Nassau. *Author's collection*

Gambier Village

A short distance up the road from the Cable Beach area is Gambier Village, one of the quaint native villages around Nassau located in the north western area of the island and claiming to be *the oldest settlement in New Providence*.

From a political point of view, Gambier Village was part of the electoral district which was known as the Western District and under the political responsibility of Harry

Oakes in 1938 as a member of the Bahamian House of Assembly. Oakes ensured that appropriate funds were made available to the village for education and development. It was also a known fact that Oakes himself supported Gambier Village from a personal financial perspective.

During a return visit to Nassau, I made a point one day to drive out to Gambier Village. As I passed Delaporte Point, I turned off the main road and drove up a little dirt road which led me to Gambier and ultimately to the little wooden school house. As I arrived some of the children were playing outside and I approached one of the teachers, who was supervising them and made some enquiries regarding Sir Harry Oakes.

I explained to the lady the purpose of my visit and mentioned that I was aware of a certain memorial photo of Sir Harry, which I understood had been donated to the school as a tribute to him in 1943 following his death. At this point the lady very kindly motioned me to follow her into the school house and look around the classrooms.

Much to my surprise, hanging there on the wall above one of the doors was the famous picture of Sir Harry Oakes, amongst some of the art work of the school children. While it was some fifty years plus later, the picture was still there, though it had faded with the passing of time, but hanging proudly in memory of a great benefactor to the people of Nassau and in particular to the people of this small village of the Bahamas.

The memorial photo of Sir Harry Oakes hanging in Gambier Village School. *Author's collection*

It was interesting to note that all of the school children, boys and girls alike, were dressed in very attractive school uniforms — something you do not see too much of these days, but which is a common occurrence in the Bahamas.

A young Reverend Robert Hall from Gambier Village. *Courtesy of the late Rev. Robert Hall, Nassau*

While I spoke to the lady I inquired if possibly there might still be someone around who had known Sir Harry and it was at this point that she gave me the name of Reverend Robert Hall. I called him and introduced myself expressing my wish to talk to him about his relationship with Sir Harry Oakes, to which he very kindly consented.

Rev. Hall lived in the Yamacraw area of east Nassau, out near Her Majesty's Prison. Though it was my last day in Nassau, I jumped into my rented car and headed out east as fast as I could, because I felt that here again was an opportunity of a lifetime for me to meet someone else who knew Sir Harry in Nassau.

He informed me that he was previously employed by the Bahamian Government as a school teacher and first started his career as Head Teacher at Stafford Creek school over on the Island of Andros, and in due course was appointed as school master at Gambier Village School.

Rev. Hall also told me that his boy played with the Oakes children in their younger days, as Sir Harry's *Caves* estate was located almost face to face with Gambier Village and was within easy walking distance for any of the children.

In late 1938, the then Harry Oakes, as Rev. Hall recalled, purchased five acres of land in Gambier Village from a Mrs. Beatrice Spatakes, an old time resident. The following July, Harry Oakes, now Sir Harry, went about clearing the land with his own tractor and in August he ordered a local contractor to put up a building large enough to be used as a school house and community center.

It is interesting to note that the Duchess of Windsor, through Sir Harry, was also a frequent visitor and a great supporter of the Gambier School in many ways, especially in making donations of books from time to time.

The conversation with Rev. Hall was most interesting and his wife Muriel very kindly provided us with an oscillating fan to help us keep cool in the living room, on what was rather a very warm and humid day. We talked a great deal about Sir Harry, his kindness to the people of Gambier Village and to the native people of the Bahamas in general.

Rev. Hall recalled with great enthusiasm how he and his wife Muriel would occasionally meet Sir Harry and Lady Eunice while walking along Bay Street in downtown

Nassau and how many local people would be amazed, when they would see them talking to such a well known and distinguished couple as the Oakes.

Originally I tried to keep notes of our conversation, however, for no apparent reason, Rev. Hall asked me not to take any. I gladly complied with his request, but needless to say following my departure from his home, I stopped as soon as I was out of sight and proceeded to put down in my note book all that I could remember from our conversation.

There were some interesting remarks made by Rev. Hall about the so-called night watchman (clearly expressed in the singular) at Lyford Cay, the murder of Sir Harry, the possibility of the involvement of a certain prominent Nassau individual and well known business associate of Oakes (and not necessarily Harold Christie, as many would surmise), the use of a blow-torch at the murder scene, the Duke and Duchess of Windsor, as well as his comments relative to the possible involvement of organized crime in the murder of Sir Harry.

Reverend Robert Hall and his wife Muriel, good friends of Sir Harry and Lady Eunice Oakes. *Author's collection*

The question was raised, whether there was any truth in the story that the Duke of Windsor and the Duchess would on occasion stay overnight at a residence in Gambier Village because of the Duke's fear of being kidnapped from Government House by commandos sent ashore from German U-Boats. This question has never been answered, but it has been raised on at least two occasions during my research, including my discussion with Rev. Hall.

Rev. Hall was born near the turn of the century and was approximately thirty-five years of age when he knew Sir Harry and Lady Eunice Oakes in Nassau.

As I prepared to leave, I asked Rev. Hall if I could take a photo of himself and with no hesitancy he obliged. His wife Muriel who happened to come out of the house, asked to join in one of the photos, copies of which I sent to them as a souvenir. As I walked towards my car he called me back and handed me a wallet size black and white picture of himself taken in his younger days. The photo is pinned above my computer as a souvenir of a very kind and obliging Bahamian gentleman with some great memories of Harry Oakes.

Some Comments on Life in the Bahamas in the Early 1940s

It is said that Sir Harry Oakes assisted in the financing and establishment of the Bahamas Airways following his arrival in Nassau. It became one of the Islands' more important transportation means — a kind of predecessor to the present day Bahamas Air, which services the inter island needs of the population of the Bahamas and which is now the country's national air carrier.

It should be remembered that during the late thirties and early forties, the main means of transportation between the islands was by use of the mail boats and at times it would take up to two days to reach some destinations on departure from Nassau proper, provided weather conditions were favourable.

While there are now many air schedules available, including chartered flights, the old mail boat service is still available and provides a cheaper means of transportation for the residents, plus the fact that the national airline and the charter groups are not exactly in favour of carrying live animals and chickens. This service is also an attraction available to the adventurous tourists, who may be interested in a different way of getting out to the Family Islands and at the same time getting to know more about the people of the Bahamas.

In May 1938, Sir Herbert Holt and Lord Beaverbrook (Max Aitken), well known financiers, together with the Montreal Trust Company founded the Bahamas General Trust Company in the Bahamas.

Sir Harry was one of the major shareholders and Alfred de Marigny's good friend John Anderson was a member of the original staff, eventually becoming its General Manager.

The Bahamas General Trust was a corporation whose main business was the provision of trust fund services, which allowed many a wealthy Canadian and others alike, to invest their surplus funds and avoid income tax.

Following Alfred de Marigny's marriage to Nancy Oakes in May 1942, Sir Harry offered de Marigny the position of General Manager to replace John Anderson. He declined the offer as he felt that his personal and property investments, including his newly established chicken farm, were sufficient for his financial requirements. In addition it was de Marigny's intention to avoid any of Sir Harry's offers of financial assistance, as he wished to be self sufficient — to make it on his own — and provide Nancy with the necessary style of life, as would be expected from a good husband.

Also involved in the original plans for the establishment of the trust company were Dr. Axel Wenner-Gren, Harry Oakes and Harold Christie.

As is the case in many places, there is always a Historical Society to maintain a past history and the Bahamas was no exception. As a result the Bahamas Historical Society was established on October 5th, 1959, and was due mainly to the devotion and perseverance of Lady Arthur, wife of the Governor General Sir Raynor Arthur.

The headquarters of the Bahamas Historical Society. *Author's collection*

The Society is a non-profit cultural and educational organization dedicated to stimulating interest in Bahamian history and to the collection and preservation of artifacts relating to its history and its people throughout the many islands.

Following the death of Sir Harold Christie, it was discovered that the Society had on a number of occasions faced financial difficulties and that Christie himself had come to its assistance, unknown to many of the executives and members of the Society, by providing the necessary funds to cover any shortfalls.

The present day headquarters of the Society is located at the corner of Elizabeth Avenue and Shirley Street in downtown Nassau and public lectures by well known Bahamians and invited guest speakers are held on the last Thursday of every month.

In 1946, the British writer Rosita Forbes in her book *Appointment with Destiny* devoted a complete chapter to her experience in establishing herself on the Island of Eleuthera, where she was to build a beautiful home called the *Unicorn* and become a neighbour of Alfred and Ruth de Marigny.

However, the reason for reference to her book is to quote an interesting and rather humorous reflection on the problems that a close friend of hers had faced when he purchased land in Eleuthera and wished to establish proper title to it. The text read as follows:

In the Bahamas most land is owned in common by a whole family. After several generations, it becomes therefore the joint possession of some hundred people. No one of them can sell without permission of all the others, of their heirs wherever they may be — in

Europe or America, in prison or at school — and of their wives, separated, divorced or present (and argumentative!) on the spot.

After seven months of struggle for Lord Monsell, with his house plans ready and clearing already begun, it was discovered by Mr. Toote, our able lawyer — who disentangled controversial statements and a multiplicity of widows, all with highly decorated marriage certificates, much as a spinster deals with her knitting — that one of the supposed owners had never proved his father's will. Inevitably he was in another continent. Two wives claimed right of dower. Two villages were divided as to whether they had ever been married. The oldest inhabitant 'seemed to remember' going to a wedding, but he could not remember whose! Stimulated by a loan of two acres on which to grow mealies and by a four-mile drive in my truck, whose front seat, he said, was just what he wanted for a coffin, 'convenient like and not too hard on the bones', he deposed to our satisfaction and that of the local magistrate.

Subsequently he said he had 'gotten mixed' between two men of the same name. Next week he remembered a third, and thought this would have been the heir if he were alive, but he had gone to 'Australy, where they walk on their heads like flies, being as the earth there is upside down'.

In order to provide police protection to the citizens of the Bahamas, a police organization known as The Royal Bahamas Police Force was established in 1840. A good number of the police officers, both in the force and in the service of His Majesty's prison in Nassau during the period in question, were officers from England and other British colonies, not to mention that a number of them also came from the Royal Canadian Mounted Police in Canada or had obtained a good part of their training with the R.C.M.P.

On learning of the murder of Sir Harry Oakes on the morning of July 8th, 1943, at approximately 7.30 a.m., the Duke of Windsor spent close to three and a half hours debating on whose assistance he should request to investigate the murder. It was his personal opinion that the murder of such a prominent citizen was sure to gain worldwide notoriety and he felt that the murder was too great and serious a case for the local police force to handle.

In retrospect, the Duke could very well have asked for assistance from Scotland Yard, through the British Embassy in Washington or in Ottawa; from the R.C.M.P. in Ottawa or for that matter from the Royal Air Force who were stationed right there in Nassau and who had all the necessary equipment to assist the local police with the initial investigation. Such an investigation by the R.A.F. would no doubt have been very beneficial in organizing and obtaining some much needed information while everything was still untouched. In addition it would have provided an investigative source which would have been considered neutral under the circumstances.

However, the Duke's final decision was to call in Captains Edward Melchen and James Barker from the Miami Police department, which was to go down in history as one of the Duke's greatest mistakes. The only previous contact between the Duke and Melchen, was the fact that when he went to Miami, Melchen would act as his security officer.

The question was always raised as to who was in charge of the investigation, the Miami detectives or the Bahamian Police force? During the trial Judge Oscar Daly asked

Captain Edward Melchen the very same question — Melchen or his associate Captain James Barker. Melchen could not confirm who was the senior person.

A great deal has been said about the history of gambling in the Bahamas and as to whether it was permitted during the Second World War and the Governorship of the Duke of Windsor. Research has shown that it was during Sir Bede Clifford's tenure in office as Governor General of the Bahamas from 1932 to 1936, that he persuaded the Crown to allow a gaming industry to be established, which would only be available to visitors. The Bahamas Country Club in the Cable Beach area was to become the first so-called gambling casino and a very strict dress code was in effect when gambling was allowed. The Club first opened in 1920.

The often talked about Meyer Lansky. *CP Picture Archive*

In reference to a number of sources, as well as in books, magazine and newspaper articles, the finger of guilt for the murder of Sir Harry Oakes has often been pointed at the MAFIA and in particular at Meyer Lansky.

Lansky was born as Maier Suchowljansky on July 4th, 1902, in Grodno, Poland and following his arrival in the United States he had his name changed to Meyer Lansky. He was to be the first Jewish member of the MAFIA following his close relationship with Charles *Lucky* Luciano.

Meyer Lansky was introduced to the Duke of Windsor, then Governor General of the Bahamas in early 1943 in Palm Beach, Florida by who else, but Harold Christie.

It was a known fact that Lansky was responsible for the implementation and operation of the gambling casinos in Havana, Cuba during the Presidency of Fulgencio Batista. In late 1958 Fidel Castro and a group of armed revolutionaries led a revolt overthrowing Batista, who then fled to the Dominican Republic on January 1st, 1959.

As part of the administration under the Castro regime it became obvious that Lansky's gambling empire was at an end and in celebration of Batista's overthrow from power, the Cuban people were led into an orgy of destruction of the gambling machines and any related gaming equipment.

It was, however, known that Lansky being the organizer that he was, already had that necessary back-up plan in mind. The contingency plan in question was the Bahamas and in 1960 his proposition to the Bahamian authorities was put into motion.

We must now remember that Sir Harry Oakes was murdered in 1943, some seventeen years earlier, and a second point to note is that gambling in the Bahamas was allowed to a certain extent in Nassau at the time, although due to the Second World War all gaming licenses were suspended for its duration.

Therefore, how true was the involvement of the MAFIA in the murder of Sir Harry Oakes or was it merely a ruse used by writers to add some intrigue or sensationalism to their stories?

Sir Stafford Sands as head of the Bay Street Boys in Nassau, was eventually instrumental in having a necessary gaming certificate issued in 1963 for a casino in Freeport, Grand Bahama and in 1967 during his appearance before a Commission of Inquiry into gambling, Sands claims to have been offered a substantial sum of money by Meyer Lansky to permit gambling on Grand Bahama, but that he had turned down the offer.

In a book entitled *Crime: An Encyclopedia* the comment is made to the effect that — *solutions abound, but they are no more than scenarios mostly orbiting around the casino issue, whereby Sir Harry refused to have his island paradise spoiled and was hit by the MAFIA.*

On October 28th, 1919, the Volstead Act (named after Representative Andrew J.Volstead of Minnesota) was passed into law by the United States Government and thus started a period known as *Prohibition*, which banned the general manufacturing, sale and transportation of intoxicating liquors and beers.

The importation of liquor into the U. S. was a necessary evil in order to supply the many *speak easies*, which had been set up as a substitute for the former lavish night clubs and drinking establishments.

As the Bahamas was within what was considered a short running distance to the mainland, a great deal of illegal liquor found its way into Nassau and the out islands and then just as quickly to the U. S. Most of the liquor was of good quality and some of the best known scotches available came from Scotland.

Financially it was a most rewarding business and many Bahamians, among them some well known Nassauvians, were involved in the trade. Interestingly enough there does not appear to be any direct reference to any of the so-called Bay Street Boys or any leading members of the well-to-do Nassau society, however, there is mention of Harold Christie — who was also known to Meyer Lansky.

As an indication of the increased revenue to the Bahamian economy that was derived from the importing and exporting of liquor at the time, it is mentioned that prior to Prohibition approximately 38,000 gallons of liquor were imported into the country annually. During Prohibition the quantity increased to 1,340,000 gallons with yearly revenue going up to 852,000 pounds and subsequently dropping to 276,000 pounds following the repeal of Prohibition. The risk of running liquor was great, but so were the financial rewards for the individuals — the captain of a good boat could earn $1,000 a trip and his associate crew member $500, with the possibility of two trips per day scheduled between the Bahamas and the United States.

It is said that the headquarters of the rum-runners was the Lucerne Hotel on Frederick Street in downtown Nassau, which catered to both of the rival underworld gangs operating in Nassau, however, the Commissioner of Police made daily inspections of the hotel to ensure that all was well.

In addition a lady nicknamed *Dog Face Di* was the manageress of the Lucerne Hotel and assisted the local police in keeping everything under control. No problems apparently were ever reported. Amongst the characters were gangsters, extortionists, strong armed thugs, burglars, robbers, confidence men and other assorted types of undesirable individuals.

As described in one source of reference — they paraded about Bay Street and its environs, flashing incredible rolls of thousand dollar bills; they drank and whored and gambled; they carved up the bootlegging and rum-running operations into cartels — just like the good old days in Chicago.

However, as they say — all good things must come to an end and as the Volstead Act was repealed three weeks before Christmas of 1933, business in the Bahamas returned to normal and once again the art of sponging became an important part of Bahamian trade, which would then only last for a short period of time.

Harold Christie's nephew Percy once said that Harold always tended to avoid discussions on his participation in the bootlegging during the Prohibition years, but according to FBI files under the Freedom of Information and Privacy Acts it was indicated that Harold Christie had a criminal record. An Apprehension Order #551 was issued in 1923 relative to his involvement in the illegal sale of a schooner named the *Monarch* to some person who was not a citizen of the United States.

Attempts were made by the FBI to apprehend Christie, whenever he would go to the United States, but without success. Finally the U.S. Government decided that Christie's crime was not an extraditable offence and on October 26th, 1928, J. Edgar Hoover, as Director of the FBI, issued a memorandum to all Special Agents in Charge advising that the Apprehension Order was cancelled.

As the Bahamas was part of the British Colonial Empire at the time of the Duke of Windsor's residency as Governor General and also because the Second World War was in progress, a state of censorship was imposed by the British Government on all incoming and outgoing cables, as well as written communications to and from the islands in the Colonies.

There appears to have been one notable exception which occurred and that was on the very morning that the murder of Sir Harry Oakes was discovered. Etienne Dupuch who was then editor of the *Tribune* had called *Westbourne* estate early to confirm with Sir Harry their appointment for a tour of his sheep farm later that day. Harold Christie answered the telephone and in his excitement informed Dupuch that Sir Harry had been murdered or more precisely according to certain sources — *that he had been shot* (a rather questionable statement, as Christie would later testify that he stayed there that night and had not heard any noise except a few thunder claps and some buzzing mosquitoes).

As soon as the Duke of Windsor received the news of the tragedy, he immediately imposed censorship regulations, but Dupuch had already advised the world and as a result there were many inquiries coming in from foreign newspapers requesting details of the tragedy, as Sir Harry Oakes was indeed a well known world figure.

It took at least one full day before the Duke of Windsor lifted the censorship on outgoing news and it was noted that due to the lack of more informative details of the murder to the foreign press at the time, in particular the *Miami Herald*, news was being gathered from returning tourists out of Nassau as they landed in Miami and there was the concern that the factual reporting of the tragedy was missing.

Reports at first said that Sir Harry had indeed been murdered and were based on rumours circulating in Nassau that morning. None of the travellers would allow themselves to be identified, but the most persistent report was that Oakes had been shot. None of the reports could be confirmed with any official sources in the Bahamas at that time.

Alfred de Marigny himself had sent a cable to his wife Nancy in Bennington, Vermont, informing her of the tragedy and advising her to join her mother Lady Eunice Oakes at the family residence in Bar Harbor, Maine.

The question as to the use of wiretapping of private telephone lines became a matter of curiosity to me, as a number of authors have referred to the events surrounding the investigation by Raymond Schindler and on the occasion of a visit to Nassau in 1992, I asked Ernest Callender, one of the lawyers who had defended Alfred de Marigny. The response was negative, but censoring of overseas calls and mail out of the Bahamas was correct.

In 1944 upon the death of the Duke of Kent in a tragic plane crash, the Duke of Windsor once again imposed censorship on details of the memorial service for his brother, that was going to be held at Christ Church Cathedral in Nassau. The Duke's main concern at that time was the possibly that the Germans would hear details of the location of the service and would send in commandos from one of their U-boats.

In 1908, the Royal Bank of Canada was established in the Bahamas. At the time there was only one other bank in Nassau which was the Bank of Nassau, whose operations were sufficiently precarious that an embezzlement on the part of its manager caused it to suspend payments in 1916.

The following year, the Royal Bank of Canada bought out the assets and liabilities of the Bank of Nassau for some 39,000 pounds.

Royal Bank of Canada on West Bay Street in downtown Nassau. *Courtesy of Dr. Gail Saunders & of Donald Cartwright, Nassau*

One John Gaffney, who worked for the Royal Bank appears to have acted also as head of the Exchange Control Board (ECB) during the war years in Nassau.

As part of the Prohibition era in the United States in 1921, it is recalled that the Royal Bank at one time had over $11 million in cash in its vaults in Nassau and the building itself was guarded by a special group of police officers armed with rifles and bayonets. In those days, the bootleggers were coming back from their liquor runs over to the United States with cold hard cash in their hands, totalling at times up to $50,000 or more on each occasion.

Alfred de Marigny maintained his personal banking needs with the Royal Bank, as did many other residents of Nassau. As a result of this affiliation with the Royal, John Gaffney and one of his associates Lewis Phillips, Manager of the Current and Saving Accounts were called upon to confirm de Marigny's financial worth at the time of the trial. The balances were very much in his favour, contrary to what the Prosecution had hoped for, as they wanted to prove that de Marigny had married Nancy Oakes to obtain financial benefits from her share of the Oakes' fortunes.

As the Bahamas was part of the British Colonial Empire during the Second World War, it was under the strict rules of the Exchange Control Board regulations, which limited the circulation of funds of British subjects, including those residing in the Bahamas. The rules were that permission was required from the ECB in order to move funds outside the limits of the British colonies.

These regulations prevented or prohibited the flow of funds outside of the Bahamas regardless of currency, however, it was a known fact that the likes of Dr. Axel Wenner-Gren, Sir Harry Oakes, Harold Christie and the Duke of Windsor himself, moved funds to Mexico in direct contradiction to the regulations of the Board.

Prince George Hotel on the harbourfront in Nassau. *Toogood's Photography, Nassau*

It would appear that wherever you go in any small town, there is always a central meeting place where drinks and good food can be had and where conversation can be exchanged, and Nassau was no exception. The meeting place was known as the Prince George Hotel, which was considered the local hangout for most of the expatriates living in Nassau at the time. It was centrally located on West Bay Street in the heart of the shopping area and overlooked Nassau harbour.

During the trial, the Prince George was the *meeting place* for the members of the Foreign Press, as well as members of the Prosecution and Defense teams.

On one particular evening during the trial after everyone had a few drinks, someone suggested that Raymond Schindler and a partner enter a dance competition against de Marigny's cousin Georges de Visdelou and his pretty girl friend Betty Roberts. Schindler being a little on the short and chubby side was matched up with a lady who towered over him and the music started.

Schindler had a secret weapon, he had been trained in ballroom dancing in his younger days. Betty and Georges were no match for the competition, but as the story goes when the time came to vote for a winner, the contest ended in a draw and the evening continued on its merry way.

Another location in downtown Nassau was the Rozelda Hotel, where members of the Jury were sequestered for the duration of the trial of Alfred de Marigny from October 18th to November 11th, 1943.

Nancy de Marigny would go there most days for lunch during the trial, whereupon she would meet with Raymond Schindler, one of the investigative members of the Defense team. Schindler would bring her up to date on the proceedings of the trial, remembering that as Nancy was to be called as a witness later, she could not be in the court room prior to having provided her testimony.

As time went by Godfrey Higgs, who was de Marigny's senior defense lawyer, suggested to Nancy that she should consider avoiding being seen at the Rozelda Hotel, as he felt that her presence there could possibly influence the members of the jury who would see her on occasion.

It is also mentioned that Nancy would spend her evenings there with Baron Georg and Baroness Marie af Trolle, who were close friends of Nancy and Alfred and who followed the trial very closely.

In 1942 as part of a lend-lease agreement under the supervision of the U.S. Army Engineering Department, American contractors constructed two large bases on the Island of New Providence — Oakes Field, originally started by Sir Harry Oakes, and Windsor Field named after the Duke of Windsor.

During the Second World War, the British Royal Air Force established an Operational Training School in Nassau. Two of the Units stationed there at the time were the No. 111 Operational Unit (OTU), which provided the final training requirements for the crews that would be manning the long-range Liberator Squadrons of Coastal Command. This unit trained over 600 crews or 5,000 airmen for combat.

The second Unit was the No. 113 South Atlantic Wing, a Transport Command involved in the transport of various aircrafts, together with supplies from Canada and the United States to the combat areas in the Middle and Far East sectors.

During the time that the RAF was stationed on the Island of New Providence, in excess of 2,000 aircrafts were processed through Windsor Field at the western end of the island (where the Nassau International Airport is presently located) on their way to eventual service for the Allies in Africa and other destinations on the war front.

In addition to the air training areas set up in Nassau, the Air Sea Reconnaissance Unit established a frogmen training center along the shores of Salt Cay, which was off the eastern end of the Island of New Providence.

There was also the RAF No.250 Air Sea Rescue Unit which operated from bases located at Fort Montagu in the eastern end of the island and another unit at Lyford Cay at the western end. A further base was located at Harbour Island. The main purpose of the Air Sea Rescue units was to assist in the rescue of the crews of Allied downed aircrafts, as well as survivors of torpedoed naval vessels and merchant marine ships in the waters in and around the Bahamas chain of islands.

The presence of the Armed Forces in Nassau added tremendously to the population and was financially beneficial to the Bahamians and Nassauvians in particular, giving them much needed employment during the construction of the air bases, as well as adding financial revenue as the rate of unemployment was very high and wages were low at the time.

The social life of Nassau also benefited and it was as a result of their presence that Alfred de Marigny would one evening meet two couples whose husbands were in the RAF as Ferry Command Pilots and whose wives were Jean Ainslie and Dorothy Clarke. These two ladies, through no fault of their own, would be thrown into the limelight as a result of their being dinner guests at Alfred de Marigny's home on the very eve of the murder of his father-in-law Sir Harry Oakes.

Both of the ladies were originally called as witnesses by the Prosecution in an attempt to place de Marigny near the scene of the crime, as he had driven the ladies that night to their home which was located next door to Sir Harry's *Westbourne* estate.

They were also cross-examined by the Defense in the form of alibi witnesses, thus ensuring themselves of the mention of their names in the annals of crime whenever the murder of Sir Harry Oakes would be mentioned, as their testimony was very important in establishing de Marigny's whereabouts on that fateful evening.

A further benefit of the RAF's presence would strangely be in de Marigny's favour, as he managed a farm for the raising of chickens and the production of eggs to meet the ever increasing demand of the local people and also the requirements of the RAF. As a sidelight to the whole matter, someone had said that it was ironic that eggs and chickens from de Marigny's own farm were being served at the Rozelda Hotel, where the members of the Jury were sequestered during the trial.

As part of Sir Harry Oakes' charitable donations and assistance in projects, he donated three Spitfires to the war effort (though there is mention that the number may have been as high as five). Two of the Spitfires were supposedly named *The Sir Harry Oakes* and *The Lady Oakes*.

On the day that the murder was discovered Flight Lieutenant Reginald Arthur Gates, Photographic Officer, and Leading Aircraftsman Michael Muir, Photographer of the RAF station in Nassau, at the request of the Bahamian Police Department took four photographs at the scene of the murder and six photographs of Sir Harry's body at the mortuary of the Bahamas General Hospital. They also took photographs of the exterior of the Oakes' *Westbourne* estate. The officers were subsequently summoned to appear at the trial to identify and confirm the authenticity of the negatives and prints used as exhibits during the trial.

Another gentleman, Leading Aircraftsman John Lord, a qualified draughtsman and commercial artist by trade before the war was asked by the Bahamian authorities to make a scale floor plan of the eastern portion of *Westbourne* estate and in particular the rooms, hallways and stairs surrounding the scene of the murder. At the start of the trial he was also called as a witness, to identify the floor plan he had drawn.

As a passing matter of interest, the motto of the RAF is *Per Adura Ad Astra* or *Through Hard Times to the Stars* and that of Sir Harry Oakes, *Per Adura* or *Through Hardship*. An interesting comparison.

During the Governorship of the Duke of Windsor in the Bahamas at the time of the Second World War, there always remained the threat that possibly German U-Boats patrolling the Caribbean waters could infiltrate Nassau harbour and send commandos ashore in an attempt to kidnap the Duke of Windsor and his Duchess.

To overcome this threat, a unit of the Cameron Highlanders, veterans of the Battle of Dunkirk were dispatched to Nassau and as part of their activities they set up defensive posts around Government House and generally made the grounds secure from any potential invaders. They ringed the property with barbed wire to further discourage any attempts at entry.

In order to remain in proper defensive readiness at all times, other members of the Highlanders would make surprise raids on Government House at night from time to time and on occasion when they managed to proceed through the defensive positions, they would slip into Major Gray Phillips room and capture him in his pyjamas, much to his personal embarrassment. Major Phillips was an Aide de Camp to the Duke of Windsor.

On January 10th, 1932, Sir Bede Clifford and Lady Clifford arrived in Nassau and at the age of forty one, he was to be one of the youngest Governor Generals to be posted to the Bahamas.

Sir Bede was responsible for the arrangements made to have Pan American World Airways establish a regular sea plane flight schedule between Miami and Nassau. Pan Am's Nassau terminal was opened by Lady Clifford and the terminal is now the site of the Police Road Traffic station located on East Bay Street, opposite the Eastern Esplanade and not far from the approach of the bridge to Paradise Island. If you live in Nassau and your bicycle has been stolen that is the place to go and look for it.

During his Governorship, Sir Bede Clifford was also responsible for the levelling of the land below present day Fort Charlotte, to make room for a polo and cricket field. This land was subsequently named Clifford Park in his memory and is now used extensively for cricket matches. Polo playing has long since been lost in the history of Nassau following the Second World War.

Sir Charles Dundas was Governor General of the Bahamas prior to the appointment of the Duke of Windsor and it was his intention hopefully to retire from the diplomatic service following his term as Governor of the Islands. However, that was not to be the case.

Dundas is probably best known to Bahamians for the Dundas Center for the Performing Arts located on Mackey Street, which was erected in his memory and is still considered the heart of the local live theatre productions in Nassau, arranged and staged by native Bahamians, as well as expatriates.

There have been many great performances at the Center and during our stay in Nassau in the early eighties, it was always possible to be graced by the presence of the Governor General Sir Gerald and Lady Cash on any given evening.

One of the oldest native Bahamian villages on the Island of New Providence is Bain's Town, better known to many local Nassauvians and expatriates as being *over the hill*, which was considered an exclusively black settlement area in Nassau.

Dr. Cleveland Eneas was a dentist and a distinguished gentleman, who was born in Bain's Town and was closely associated with the Bahamas Historical Society and the Archives of the Bahamas.

Sir Harry Oakes' obelisk memorial monument erected in January 1948 in Nassau. *Author's collection*

His father W. V. Eneas was a well known stone mason and responsible for many of the public work monuments that were erected in and around Nassau. He signed his works with the initials WVE and the date they were finished.

Amongst his works was the Oakes obelisk memorial monument, which was his last and most outstanding. It is the only permanent monument on the Island of New Providence in memory of Sir Harry Oakes. The memorial obelisk was unveiled by the then Governor General of the Bahamas, Sir William Murphy on January 4th, 1948.

It is interesting to note from correspondence in early 1947 between Sir Harry's Nassau lawyer, Kenneth Solomon and Lake Shore Mines in Kirkland Lake that they paid 734 pounds, 18 shillings and 3 pence for four moulds of Vermont white marble for the memorial obelisk. Included in the cost was material, freight and customs, war tax and stamp duty.

Citizens And Visitors

Needless to say, the following story about Sally Rand has no bearing whatsoever on the general content of this text regarding Sir Harry Oakes, but it is mentioned merely as a comment of what went on in the Bahamas at that time.

Sally Rand was a world renowned exotic fan dancer, as well as bubble dancer who was invited to Nassau and did a performance of her famous dances in the presence of the Duke and Duchess of Windsor and invited guests at a Bahamian Red Cross fund raising benefit. Ms. Rand's arrival and show scandalized many of the black politicians and their wives, not to mention the white socialites of Nassau, when they heard of Ms. Rand's performance.

A number of the Nassau socialites attended the fund raiser and it was said that they were amongst the very first the next day to condone the previous evening's performance and in some cases wrote letters to the editors of the two Nassau papers the *Tribune* and the *Guardian* to that effect.

Ms. Rand was born in 1904 in Hickory County, Missouri. During the start of the *Great Depression* it was reported that Ms. Rand was stranded in Chicago, after a show in which she appeared had folded. She took a job dancing in a speakeasy and as a result of trying to save money on the cost of one of her costumes, she began to perform dances with the use of fans, which quickly lowered the cost of her wardrobe and in turn made her a focus of attention in the world of entertainment.

Another prominent citizen of the Bahamas was Dr. Axel Wenner-Gren, a Swedish industrialist and considered one of the world's most successful, with businesses ranging from vacuum cleaners (Electrolux), to refrigerators, to the Beaufort guns used during the Second World War.

His wife was a lady by the name of Marguerite Liggett who was born in Kansas City, Missouri. She had studied opera in Berlin and had long been accused of being a Nazi sympathiser, which only added to the intrigue behind Dr. Axel Wenner-Gren himself.

In April 1939, Wenner-Gren purchased the Edmund C. Lynch (of Merrill, Lynch & Co.) property on Hog Island (later to be known as Paradise Island) off Nassau for $150,000.

Part of the property fronted on what is known to many Nassauvians, as well as expatriates as Cabbage Beach, one of the nicest little stretches of sandy beaches on the north side of Paradise Island. His estate was known at the time as *Shangri-La*.

Later, in early 1961, Wenner-Gren sold his property to Huntington Hartford II, grandson of George Huntington Hartford, founder of the Great Atlantic and Pacific Tea Co. (better known as the A & P food chain), for $9.5 million. Following this sale Wenner-Gren purchased a Nassau home known as *Villa Capucet* and there he spent his remaining days in the Bahamas. He died in November 1961, at the age of eighty.

At one point in time, Wenner-Gren went to Peru with the aim of financing archaeological expeditions to find the lost city of the Incas. While in Peru he presented the country with a million acre park to be known as the Wenner-Gren Archaeological Park and in return the University of Cuzco conferred upon him an honorary doctorate.

Dr. Axel Wenner-Gren. *Toogood's Photography, Nassau*

As a result of this doctorate, he would become known as Doctor Axel Wenner-Gren and it was his wish that everyone call him Doctor to reflect the honour that had been bestowed upon him.

In 1937, Dr. Axel Wenner-Gren purchased a large yacht from Howard Hughes for the sum of $2,000,000. The *Southern Cross* as he christened it, was the fifth largest yacht afloat, was magnificently furnished and even had a private radio station on board. It had a displacement of three thousand tons and had four decks, was 322 feet long, 41 feet wide with a draft of 16 feet and required a crew of forty men.

On a number of occasions when Wenner-Gren was in Nassau, he hosted parties onboard the *Southern Cross* to which he invited the Duke and Duchess of Windsor, as well as Sir Harry and Lady Eunice Oakes.

In addition Wenner-Gren would also take the Windsors on his yacht for journeys to Miami, much to the consternation of Winston Churchill in view of Wenner-Gren's apparent questionable political feelings towards Germany during the war years.

In April 1942, the *Southern Cross* was blacklisted by the British in view of Wenner-Gren's ties with the Axis powers. Three months before, the United States government had also blacklisted Wenner-Gren. At the time he was referred to as the pro-Nazi 'Rockefeller' of Sweden.

The Southern Cross — Dr. Axel Wenner-Gren's luxurious yacht. *Toogood's Photography, Nassau*

As a result of the blacklisting, the Duke of Windsor under his authority as Governor General of the Bahamas, confiscated Wenner-Gren's holdings in the Bahamas which included the Bahamas Dredging Co.; the Grand Bahamas Packing Co.; Sunny Isles Limited; Bank of the Bahamas; Paradise Beach & Transportation Co. and Mababa S. A.

A crew member who served aboard the *Southern Cross* during its entire stay in Nassau was John Dahloff. During an interview he asserted that he never saw any military armament on board the yacht, contrary to what many thought. As Dahloff said, the only weapon was the pistol that the Captain maintained, which was normal procedure on the high seas.

On September 3rd, 1939, the very first day of the start of the Second World War, a British passenger ship the *Athenia* had just left the west coast of Ireland to head out to the Atlantic Ocean, with 1,480 passengers for her Trans-Atlantic voyage to America. Amongst the passengers were more than 500 Canadians, including approximately 375 children.

At around nine o'clock that fateful evening, a German submarine the U-30, commanded by Commander Fritz-Julius Lemp, identified the ship and proceeded to attack, launching torpedoes in her direction, which when striking the ship tore a huge gaping hole in the hull. As a result the *Athenia* began to take on water and sank almost immediately.

Through fate or otherwise, Wenner-Gren's *Southern Cross* was itself on its way across the Atlantic in the direction of Nassau. She was a mere fifty miles away from the *Athenia* at the time of the torpedo attack.

The wireless operator of the *Southern Cross* heard the distress signals and immediately instructions were given by Dr. Axel Wenner-Gren to alter course and head in the direction of the stricken *Athenia*.

The *Southern Cross* arrived on the scene shortly afterwards and proceeded to rescue some 378 passengers who were brought on board. Other ships in the area responded to the SOS signals and headed to the *Athenia* to retrieve as many as possible of the remaining survivors.

In view of Wenner-Gren's pro-German political feelings, the location of the *Southern Cross* in the proximity of the *Athenia* at that particular time, was interpreted by many to be more than just pure coincidence.

The *Southern Cross* continued on her journey towards the Bahamas, transferring the survivors to British destroyers and other cargo ships which headed for Halifax. The yacht then proceeded to her final destination in the warmer enclaves and protection of Nassau's harbour.

The German government denied their part in the sinking and all reference to the event was deleted from the log of the U-30, and furthermore, the crew of the submarine was sworn to secrecy in the matter. It was subsequently mentioned, some time later, that the Commander misidentified the *Athenia* for an Allied troop ship.

On June 3rd, 1941, *Banco Continental* first opened its doors in Mexico City at Avenida Madero No.2, Edificio Guardiola, with an authorized capital of five million pesos.

While stringent foreign exchange controls were in effect during the war years in the Bahamas, somehow funds were finding their way into Mexico supposedly from the likes of Dr. Axel Wenner-Gren, Sir Harry Oakes, Harold Christie, the Duke of Windsor and one John Hastings, then Governor of the State of New York.

It was reported that the Duke of Windsor had deposited the equivalent of nearly $2,000,000 in Mexican Pesos, and it was rumoured that possibly a good portion of this amount represented funds advanced by Sir Harry Oakes himself to the Duke.

In view of the lack of background information on Banco Continental, I undertook to make enquiries with the Library Department at the Banco de Mexico in Mexico City, who subsequently provided me with a copy of the listing of Banco Continental as reported in the Anuario Financiero de Mexico for 1942, which is the equivalent of an annual Bankers Directory.

From the directory the date of the opening of Banco Continental was confirmed as June 3rd, 1941, and the initial authorized capital was $5,000,000 pesos, with $1,275,000 pesos paid in, which comprised 50,000 shares with a nominal value of $100 pesos per share. Banco Continental's objective was to operate as a loans and deposits bank.

The President was John R. O'Connor, together with John A. Hastings as a Director and William O'Connell as Chief of the Commercial Department. All other members of the Board of Directors and officers would appear to be Mexican nationals. Only the name of John Hastings was previously mentioned as a party to the original set up of Banco Continental.

It should be noted that the names of Dr. Axel Wenner-Gren, Sir Harry Oakes, Harold Christie, the Duke of Windsor and John Anderson, were mentioned in an October 23rd, 1943 FBI memorandum as having an interest in investing funds in a financial group in Mexico, however, none of their names appear on record.

In conversation with two retired Canadian officers of the Ferry Command wing of the RAF, who were posted in Nassau during the Second World War, the comment was made to me that a few days following the end of the war some unusual black smoke rose in the western sky and appeared to come from an explosion on Grand Bahama Island. The rumour then was that the smoke was caused by the *explosion* of certain storage tanks belonging to Dr. Axel Wenner-Gren who had a lobster packaging plant on that island.

In order to try to confirm this rather strange statement, I re-read a chapter from the French version of Alfred de Marigny's book entitled *Ai-je Tué?* and compared it to the English version in *More Devil Than Saint* and noted immediately that some text was missing in the translation relating to the incident.

According to a free translation of the French version, the following is based on a conversation between John Anderson, Alfred de Marigny and Georges de Visdelou as recalled by de Marigny:

Anderson confided with de Marigny, that he knew what went on at Paradise Island and the hows and whys of the activities of Wenner-Gren there and in the Bahamas Islands.

De Marigny noted the curious and unusual coincidences between what Anderson said and the rumours that he had heard circulating around Nassau.

A strange thing that happened one day, was that Baron Georg af Trolle, who during that summer had been private secretary to Wenner-Gren, suddenly announced that he was breaking off all relationships with his boss (Wenner-Gren).

Relative to the rumours, Anderson commented — why do you think that the Swede (Wenner-Gren) bought property on Grand Bahama Island and built a lobster packaging plant there?

The packaging plant was known as the Grand Bahama Packing Company Limited. A few years later it was taken over by General Foods of Boston and renamed General Seafoods (Bahamas) Limited.

"Why would I know?" commented de Marigny.

"Use your head" said Anderson—- "do you think that a man who receives income of $25 million a year, is interested in a lobster packaging plant?"

"Well — why did he do it?" asked Georges de Visdelou.

"In the first place, the location chosen was in close proximity to the United States, about fifty miles from Palm Beach, Florida. This place had fresh water and was so deserted that you would not meet anyone around there. He (Wenner-Gren) built enormous storage tanks for oil and petrol. It seemed that he needed it for his packaging plant and his trucks" said Anderson laughingly.

There was a feeling that the petrol was used to fuel the U-Boats of the Axis forces.

Over the years there has been a great deal of speculation, and a number of theories have been put forward, concerning the reasons for Sir Harry's departure from Canada to go and live in the sunny Bahamas. Three of the major theories are described briefly as follows:

1) That he was suffering from asthma and that his doctor wanted him to move to a warmer climate;

2) That he had hoped through large financial contributions to the proper political party in Canada, that he would have been rewarded with an appointment as a Senator, which did not materialize and as a result Oakes moved to the Bahamas. On the other hand as a result of substantial contributions to the St. George's Hospital in London, England, he was eventually rewarded with a Baronetcy and became Sir Harry Oakes. This was better than just being a Senator in the Canadian Government as far as Oakes was concerned;

3) That the Canadian Government was assessing taxes on his earnings from his Lake Shore Mines up to 80% of his gross earned income; whereas in the Bahamas he would be tax free, with the exception of succession duties, which were considered minimal compared to Canada.

Alfred de Marigny recounts that Sir Harry once mentioned to him that his reasons for leaving Canada were both financial and personal due to the Canadian Government's Prime Minister Richard Bennett turning down Oakes' offer of his home in Niagara Falls during a visit by the Duke of York to Canada.

The question of taxation naturally was a serious consideration and is the most likely factor for his decision to relocate to the Bahamas.

A short time before his death, Sir Harry had acquired some farm land in Nassau and purchased a number of sheep with the intention of raising them to help overcome the meat shortage, which was becoming evident in the Bahamas at the time, due no doubt in part to the increased presence of RAF personnel and other immigrants who were now moving to Nassau for a number of reasons besides taxation.

Harold Christie had arranged an appointment for Sir Harry to meet with Etienne Dupuch of the *Tribune* and Raymond Moss of the *Nassau Guardian*, to take them on a tour of the new sheep farm on the morning of July 8th, but fate intervened and Sir Harry would not meet his appointment.

The next day, July 9th, Sir Harry had planned to leave Nassau for Bar Harbor, Maine, where he would rejoin his wife Eunice and the children for the remainder of the summer.

There were two close associates of Sir Harry Oakes in the persons of Newell Kelly and Walter Foskett. Kelly was Oakes' manager for his properties and for all of his investments in the Bahamas, as well as being manager of a company called the Caves Company and also manager of the Bahamas Country Club, which was adjacent to Sir Harry's *Westbourne* estate.

When Alfred de Marigny arrived at *Westbourne* after he had heard of the murder, he learned more details of the tragedy from Harold Christie, who made an interesting remark to the effect — well, at least there's one man who has a good alibi — in reference to Newell Kelly.

According to the transcript of the trial it is indicated that at the time of the murder, Kelly had already left the island on a fishing trip with his friend Dr. D. S. Graham, together with Peter and Marcel Maury. That gave Newell Kelly three potential alibis if needed.

Kelly and his wife Madeleine lived in a cottage on the very grounds of Sir Harry's *Westbourne* estate.

In subsequent conversation with a certain gentleman who knew Sir Harry very well, he suspected that Newell Kelly was not that far away from the island when he was found — on his so-called *fishing trip* the day the murder was discovered. To go a step further it was mentioned that Sir Harry was murdered at Lyford Cay and then taken down by motor launch to Sir Harry's estate, driven by someone who was very knowledgeable of the shore line to the Cable Beach area and the docking facilities at the Oakes' residence.

However, based on Alfred de Marigny's last book, we now know this to be incorrect.

The other gentleman, Walter Foskett, at the time of the death of Sir Harry Oakes, had been an attorney for almost twenty years in Palm Beach, Florida, and had known Oakes for some twelve years.

He was in his fifties at the time and was referred to as *Uncle Walter* by Nancy Oakes and considered a family confidant. During Sir Harry's absences from Nassau, Foskett had full permission to receive and open all correspondence addressed to Sir Harry and Lady Oakes.

Foskett owed his business independence to Sir Harry Oakes, going back to a time when plain Harry Oakes first approached a legal firm in Palm Beach, Florida, in 1931 requesting their assistance in discussing legal matters and seeking guidance relative to his investments in the United States.

On that particular day everyone at the office seemed to be busy and the receptionist informed Oakes that the only person available was one of the younger members of the firm, Walter Foskett.

As you can well imagine it was not a practice to keep Harry Oakes waiting and as a result Oakes took Foskett out to lunch, discussed his requirements and subsequently offered him the responsibilities of being his attorney and legal counsel for himself and his wife Eunice relative to their interests in the United States.

Following the marriage of Nancy Oakes and Alfred de Marigny in May 1942, Walter Foskett was instrumental in assisting Sir Harry in making changes to his will, to ensure that de Marigny would <u>not</u> benefit financially from his marriage to his daughter Nancy.

While Foskett apparently lived in Palm Beach, it was reported in the press at one point, that he was the owner of the Savoy theatre in downtown Nassau, where Georges de Visdelou's girl friend Betty Roberts worked as a cashier.

In 1944, a year following the death of Sir Harry Oakes, the name of Walter Foskett appeared in the annual report of Lake Shore Mines as a member of the Board of Directors, but there does not appear to be any mention of what prompted his appointment in the report.

It would be interesting to know who nominated him to this appointment. Foskett remained a director until 1954.

Walter Foskett passed away in May 1973, at the age of 87. In the Social Directory for Palm Beach, Miami Beach and the Bahamas published in 1952 there is mention that he was then a member of the Bahamas Country Club in Nassau.

In view of Foskett's close rapport with the finances of Sir Harry Oakes before and after his death, would it be fair to say that possibly he had more than a vested interest in Oakes' welfare both financially and otherwise? The name of Walter Foskett did make it to the FBI files and also made for some very interesting reading.

An interesting question to ask either Newell Kelly or Walter Foskett would have been, *when did you last see Sir Harry Oakes alive and where?*

On September 1st, 1943, following the death of Sir Harry Oakes, a report appeared in a local New England newspaper which read as follows:

The body of Sir Harry Oakes who was slain in his Nassau Bahamas mansion July 8th/43 will be interred in an elaborate mausoleum now being built near his boyhood home.

The town vault in Dover-Foxcroft, where Sir Harry's body was temporarily interred pending completion of the mausoleum. Rev. Gordon Reardon is shown following the service. *CP Picture Archive*

Louis Oakes, 71, older brother of the baronet, said no date has been set for transferring Sir Harry's body from the Bassett cemetery vault where it has rested since July 13/43.

Oakes said that construction of the mausoleum in the cemetery here, would take weeks.

The final resting place for Sir Harry Oakes is located in the Dover Cemetery on the easterly outskirts of the town of Dover-Foxcroft, Maine.

The mausoleum is erected in an area measuring approximately one hundred and fifty square feet and stands all by itself, except for the two tall evergreen trees at the entrance and some small well trimmed bushes that lead up to it.

On the front of the mausoleum there is a glass door behind a black grilled gate and as you peer into it, you can see the crypt that contains the earthly remains of Sir Harry Oakes. On the top of the crypt is a bronze bust of Sir Harry, with two urns on either side of it.

When I first looked in I noticed the four urns, but could only see three names inscribed on the marble wall behind the crypt, however, as a result of establishing contact with a local funeral home, I was able to obtain more information on the names of the other members of the family whose urns rest on top of the crypt.

The urns are those of William Pitt Oakes and Sir Sydney Oakes, two of Sir Harry's three sons; Shirley Lewis Oakes Butler, one of his two daughters and finally his beloved and devoted wife Eunice. The missing names are actually engraved on the right hand wall, which is not visible from the entrance.

A certain feeling of wonder passes through your mind as you gaze at the crypt, realizing that Sir Harry rests within its confines and that a great deal of the history of a certain adventurous Yankee, together with his many achievements which were part of his lifetime are there before you.

At the time of my visit to the mausoleum, it had turned out to be a rather dreary, overcast, rainy and miserable type day. As a result some water was dripping through the marble roof down onto the crypt — a rather sombre sight all around.

Following my visit to the mausoleum, I was shown the tombstones and final resting place of Sir Harry Oakes' father and mother, as well as that of his brother and sisters which are located nearby in the same cemetery.

I should also mention that on the day that I visited the mausoleum, there was a small wreath of red roses, six of them to be more precise, resting against the grilled door. I was curious as to who would have placed them there, as the date of my visit was July 8th which coincided with the anniversary date of the death of Sir Harry Oakes in 1943.

Upon inquiry from one of the two florist shops in the town of Dover-Foxcroft, I was informed that on that date, as well as on December 23rd, the anniversary of Sir Harry's birth, instructions are received from a local bank in town to arrange for the necessary floral tributes to be placed at the door to the mausoleum. I subsequently inquired from the bank, however, in the true fashion of banks, the information that I was seeking was considered *privileged information.*

Annually on July 8th and December 23rd, an arrangement of red roses is placed against the door of Sir Harry's mausoleum. *Author's collection*

There seems to be some confusion as to whether the cottages next door to Sir Harry's *Westbourne* estate were called the *Hubbard Cottages* or the *Labouchere Estate*, but for the sake of this writing we will settle for the *Hubbard Cottages*.

It is interesting to note that two of the witnesses, Mrs. Jean Ainslie and Mrs. Dorothy Clarke, wives of RAF pilots stationed in Nassau, lived in *Hubbard Cottage Number Two*, and were driven home on the evening of the murder by none other than Alfred de Marigny. Regrettably this point was being used by the Prosecution to build their case against him, as it was their intention to place de Marigny near the scene of the crime and at the time that it was committed.

In the spring of 1992, I spent two weeks holiday in Nassau visiting with friends we knew when we lived there in the early eighties. I also made a point of visiting certain estates and properties owned by Sir Harry and members of the Oakes family, as well as landmarks consistent with the murder and its investigation which included the *Hubbard Cottages*.

Hubbard Cottage Number Two where Jean Ainslie and Dorothy Clarke resided with their husbands. The residence was located next door to Sir Harry's *Westbourne* estate. *Author's collection*

I believe that it was Raymond Schindler, who while investigating the murder made some so-called dry runs in a car to establish the time that it would have taken Alfred de Marigny to drive the ladies home after the party from his residence on Victoria Avenue and return back home. Taking the time required to travel the distance, adding a reasonable amount of time to possibly commit the crime and return home within the times recorded at the trial, it was noted by Schindler that it was next to impossible for de Marigny to have committed the crime during his drive to and from the *Hubbard Cottages*.

As a matter of interest, I travelled the same distance one Sunday morning when I was there and pretty well came close to Schindler's estimate of thirty five minutes for the return trip. I chose a Sunday morning as there is very little traffic along that stretch of the road from Victoria Avenue to the site of the Ambassador Beach Hotel (formerly *Westbourne* estate).

Sir Harry Oakes and Members of His Family

Harry Goes on a World Cruise ..... Eunice MacIntyre — A Pretty Lady from Australia ..... Nicholas Musgrove — An Extortionist ..... Gertrude Oakes — Harry's Closest Sister ..... His Older Brother Louis Oakes ..... Dr. Paul Ellis — Jessie Oakes ..... Nancy Oakes — Harry's Love and Joy ..... Shirley Lewis Oakes ..... The Green Shutters — One of Shirley's Investments ..... Sir Sydney Oakes ..... William Pitt Oakes ..... Harry Phillip Oakes

---

Following the death of his mother, Harry Oakes went on a world cruise to South Africa, at which time he was to meet Eunice Myrtle MacIntyre from Australia on board a cruise ship. Eunice was on her way to Portuguese East Africa to visit her sister, whose husband was a sugar planter on the Zambesi River. As the cruise progressed Eunice received word that her father had passed away and returned immediately to Australia.

Eunice MacIntyre was at the time a young lady of twenty-four years of age and was described as having *horizon blue eyes, unusually tall and of great beauty*. Harry on the other hand was slightly shorter by three inches and was twice her age — at forty eight.

Eunice was from a reasonably prosperous family, her father Thomas MacIntyre being a government official, who lived in Drummoyne, an agreeable suburb of Sydney, Australia. Eunice worked part-time as a stenographer in a Sydney bank.

At some point following their return to Sydney, Harry proposed to Eunice and they were then married on June 30th, 1923, at the fashionable St Mark's Church at Darling Point in Sydney.

Eunice Oakes in Palm Beach, Florida — circa 1929. *Historical Society of Palm Beach County*

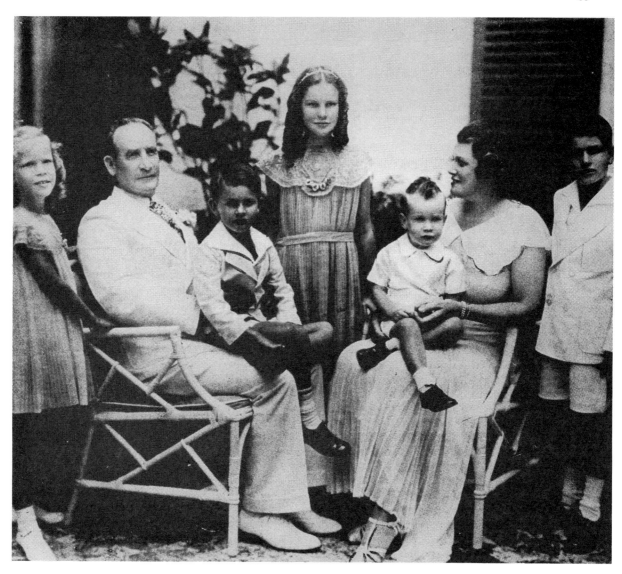

A formal photo of Harry Oakes and his family. *Source unknown*

At the time of the death of Sir Harry Oakes, Lady Oakes was residing at the *Willows* estate in Bar Harbor, Maine, and had not been to Nassau since Easter of the preceding year (1942).

Subsequent to the arrest of Alfred de Marigny, a preliminary hearing was held in the Magistrate's Court and Lady Eunice Oakes attended the hearing accompanied by the Hon. Kenneth Solomon, the Oakes' lawyer for Nassau; Walter Foskett, the Oakes' attorney for the United States and Newell Kelly, the Oakes' business manager for Nassau. This was to be her first visit to Nassau in over a year and was quite a traumatic experience for her. Lady Oakes was dressed in a very sombre black dress, her eyes quite red from crying.

Interestingly enough the three gentlemen Solomon, Foskett and Kelly were all considered close business associates of the late Sir Harry Oakes, as was Harold Christie.

Lady Eunice was already in Miami when the verdict was announced in Nassau on November 11th, 1943, having left by plane earlier that afternoon.

In May of 1969, Lady Oakes decided to visit Kirkland Lake on the occasion of its 50th Anniversary to see what had transpired during her many years of absence. She visited with many of her old acquaintances including Walter Wright who was once the superintendent of Sir Harry's Lake Shore Mines and was later to become a member of the Board of Directors of the company.

Lady Oakes also visited the Museum of Northern History which was formerly Sir Harry's Chateau, where she and Sir Harry lived for many years with the children, before their departure for Niagara Falls and eventually on to the Bahamas.

Don Sampson of Carl's Office Supply on Government Road will always remember Lady Oakes' visit, when a white limousine pulled up in front of his store and an appropriately attired chauffeur stepped out and entered the store. To Don's astonishment, the gentleman picked up and paid for a substantial number of books and returned to the limousine. A number of people had gathered outside the store to see who was in the limousine, however, the windows were all tinted.

At one time Lady Oakes was considered one of the largest Island of New Providence (Nassau) land owners and together with her children inherited a great deal of land previously owned by her late husband.

Included amongst the other rich and famous land owners in the Bahamas at that time were the likes of E. P. Taylor, Huntington Hartford, Sir Victor Sassoon, Dr. Axel Wenner-Gren, Juan Trippe and Arthur Davis to mention only a few.

Lady Oakes passed away on June 9th, 1981, at *Dale House*, one of her residences in Nassau. She was 87 years of age.

At the time of her death she was survived by her two daughters Nancy of London; Shirley Oakes Butler of Nassau; and one son Harry Phillip Oakes also of Nassau. There were four granddaughters and six grandsons.

Some seven years following the death of her husband, Lady Eunice Oakes received a threat in Nassau from a person by the name of Nicholas Musgrove, who claimed that he knew who had killed Sir Harry. *Pay in Tears or Blood — Extortionist Asks Lady Oakes,* read the headline of an article which appeared in the Toronto Star on November 14th, 1950.

The headlines related to the trial of Nicholas Musgrove, a native of the Turks and Caicos Islands (off the southern tip of the Bahamas), charged with one of the attempted extortions of money from Lady Eunice Oakes and her family following the death of Sir Harry.

Apparently, in a move unique in Bahamian law, Chief Justice Bancroft ruled as admissible a *phonograph* record allegedly chronicling a conversation between Nicholas Musgrove and Lady Oakes' secretary Basil Sparrow, former ADC to the Duke of Windsor.

Lady Oakes was told to deposit a large sum of money in a lonely place or *pay in tears, perhaps in blood*. The letter demanding the money was dated May 15th, 1950, and made the note — *who knows but that another attack is planned*. The amount demanded on this occasion was $100,000. The sum of $5,000 at one point seemed to be a popular amount for which the information would be provided as to who killed Sir Harry. Musgrove certainly seemed to be the exception.

Family Members

Gertrude Oakes was one of Harry's three sisters and the closest of the members of his family. She died tragically in January 1935, in a cruise ship collision while aboard the Ward Liner *Mohawk* en route to Mexico, when it was rammed by a Norwegian freighter off the coast at Seigrit, New Jersey.

Gertrude never did marry and in her early days she had moved to Washington, DC, where she was employed by the United States Government as a secretary. From there she would send money to Harry on a regular basis, so that he could pursue his gold mining ambitions. She was rewarded with shares in Lake Shore Mines by Harry and would in due course be financially well off.

Harry tried to persuade her to come up to Kirkland Lake, and become the Secretary-Treasurer, as well as his personal assistant in the operation of Lake Shore Mines. In 1917 Gertrude finally arrived in Kirkland Lake just as Lake Shore Mines began its spectacular gold producing climb.

While residing in the Kirkland Lake area, Gertrude owned a property known as the *Red Pines* at Kenogami Lake situated off the Cochrane highway. When she lived in the area she was known to be a great benefactress and used to send Christmas gifts to the children of the older employees at Lake Shore Mines.

She was also an avid golfer and was involved in the development of the Kirkland Lake Golf Club, eventually becoming a shareholder and executive.

Gertrude was very close to her brother Harry and it was always thought that before her untimely death, she probably knew as much about gold mining and mine management as Harry did himself.

Harry Oakes' brother Louis' estate in Greenville, Maine.
Author's collection

Louis Oakes was Harry's older brother and a civil engineer. He was also known to have sent money to him on a regular basis in the early stages of his quest for his gold mine in Kirkland Lake. As a result of his financial contributions to Harry, Louis like his sister Gertrude, would gain financially from his shareholding in Lake Shore Mines.

In 1924, Louis Oakes was named a Director of Lake Shore Mines, a position which he held until 1932.

Louis' elaborate residence is situated at Greenville, Maine and is a very charming tudor style estate overlooking the neighbouring hills of Maine and on the property itself, almost at the door step, is a golf course.

As was the case with Harry, Louis likewise was a financial benefactor to Foxcroft Academy in the town of Dover-Foxcroft and assisted them in the purchase of additional land, as well as making alterations to the school.

Dr. Paul Ellis was Sir Harry Oakes' brother-in-law, having married his sister Jessie Oakes Babson.

Following the funeral service for Sir Harry held in Bar Harbor, Maine, Dr. Ellis was also present with Lady Oakes and Nancy de Marigny when Captains James Barker and Edward Melchen were called in by Lady Oakes, to brief her on the developments in their investigation of the murder of her husband. It was supposedly at this time that Capt. Melchen gave a very vivid description of the entire murder scene.

Both Barker and Melchen were quite emphatic in assuring Lady Oakes and Nancy that they had proper and positive evidence, including a *certain fingerprint* which would support their claim that de Marigny had been in Sir Harry's room on that night and had murdered him.

Nancy Oakes was born on May 17th, 1924, as the first child of Harry and Eunice Oakes and at the time of her father's death on July 8th, 1943, she was only nineteen years of age and married to Alfred de Marigny.

Nancy spent most of her younger years under the close and watchful eyes of her parents, both at home in Canada and when they travelled through Europe and Latin America.

As she once recalled, for the first few years of her life *the family lived in Kirkland Lake, Ontario where her father had discovered his gold mines. The town she remembered had one main street or road, which was unpaved and there was only one general store.*

When Nancy was nine years of age, she was sent to a private school in the mountains of Switzerland and, as she recalled, some of her classmates came from England, France, Germany, Canada and the United States, including some girls from Palm Beach, whom she knew when she would reside there.

It was at the school in Switzerland where Nancy first met an eleven year old girl from Canada who was to become one of her closest friends, when she would arrive in the Bahamas and in particular during the trial of her husband Alfred de Marigny. The girl's name was Marie Gudewill, who would later become the Baroness Marie af Trolle.

In due course as the family moved to the Bahamas in the mid-thirties, Nancy continued her education over the subsequent years and attended many other private schools. She travelled to South America and to Australia, Bali and Java with her family and in the summer of 1939 when word was that Warsaw, Poland was being invaded and the Second World War was about to start, the Oakes family headed home to the peace, warmth and protection of the Bahamas.

As they were back in Nassau, it would now only be a matter of time before Nancy would discover a handsome and debonair gentleman, who was a great sailor around Nassau and very much a playboy type individual. The gentleman in question naturally was Count Marie Alfred Fouquereaux de Marigny — better known as Alfred de Marigny and Freddie to his close friends.

One day in December 1941, de Marigny walked into the Prince George Hotel in Nassau and a friend of his, John McDermitt, was seated with Nancy Oakes. Introductions followed and it was at this point that Nancy would first meet Alfred de Marigny. At a loss for words, Nancy indicated to him that she knew quite a bit about his sailing accomplishments and all the local and international races that he had won.

Over a period of time Nancy and Alfred began to see each other on a more frequent basis, which would lead to an unusual romantic relationship — here was Nancy seventeen years of age and de Marigny in his early thirties, and a twice divorced man.

On May 19th, 1942, without any forewarning to her parents, Nancy Oakes and Alfred de Marigny were married before a Judge in his Chambers at the Bronx County Court House in New York. She had just turned eighteen two days earlier. At the time de Marigny was 32 years of age — a difference of some fourteen years. Nancy was to be de Marigny's third wife and for Nancy this would be her first venture into the world of matrimony.

Nancy had planned to visit her mother in Canada a few months prior to the wedding with the best of intentions of informing her regarding the plan to marry de Marigny. She felt that she was old enough and did not require her parent's permission and as a result nothing was said to Sir Harry and Lady Eunice till after the wedding.

A few months prior to the death of her father, Nancy had gone up to the Martha Graham School of Dance for some rest as recommended by her doctor. It was while she was at the school that on July 8th she was first advised of his tragic death, following which she immediately went to Bar Harbor, Maine, to be with her mother, her sister Shirley, her brothers William Pitt, Harry and Sydney. Nancy subsequently flew back to Nassau after the funeral services to rejoin her husband Alfred and assist him in the preparation for his defense against the charge of having murdered her father.

Prior to the trial Nancy hired Raymond Schindler, well known private investigator and together with her perseverance in defending her husband, was rewarded with his acquittal of the charges. The Jury however added a rider to the effect that de Marigny be deported from the Bahamas as an *undesirable*.

In order to raise funds for the defense of her husband, Nancy sold her shareholdings in Lake Shore Mines and also cashed in her savings bonds to help pay Godfrey Higgs' fees. De Marigny in turn sold his sailing yacht *Concubine* to Mrs. Higgs for a mere $125; and a white Bahamian, Roland Symonette, who had made and kept the fortune he made during the Prohibition years, bought de Marigny's properties at Governor's Harbour on the Island of Eleuthera on behalf of an investment syndicate.

Following his acquittal Nancy and Alfred left Nassau and headed for Havana, Cuba in December 1943, where they resided for a period of time. Nancy finally left Alfred and headed for Canada where she would take steps to seek an annulment of their marriage.

After the annulment in 1949, Nancy subsequently married a member of the German nobility in the person of Baron Ernst-Lyssandt von Hoyningen-Huene. The marriage took place on December 29th, 1952, at St.Mary the Virgin Anglican Church in Nassau. The Baron was twenty two years of age and Nancy twenty eight. This marriage also ended in divorce.

It is understood that Nancy, then Baroness von Hoyningen-Huene had an adopted daughter Patricia, who would one day marry Franklin Delano Roosevelt Jr., 62 year old son of the President of the United States.

In March 1962, Nancy Oakes was reported to have married Michael Tritton, 30, an Englishman who was in the import/export business. It was Nancy's third marriage at the age of thirty eight. The marriage took place at the residence of the British Ambassador, Sir Peter Garran in Mexico City.

Sydney Oakes was born on June 9th, 1927. He was the eldest son of Harry and Eunice Oakes and was sixteen years of age at the time of his father's death.

Nancy Oakes and her fiancé Baron Ernst-Lyssandt von Hoyningen-Huene at Nancy's residence in Nassau — December 1952. *CP Picture Archive*

As a result of the death of Sir Harry Oakes, Sydney inherited the title of Baronet and became Sir Sydney Oakes.

Sydney was at the family residence in Kirkland Lake at the time of the death of his father, as it is understood that he would go up to Kirkland Lake and work at the mines during the summer months. Subsequently he joined his mother and other members of the family at their residence in Bar Harbor, Maine, following the tragic news.

Sir Sydney married Greta Hartman, a young lady from Denmark, after having served with the British Guards following the end of the Second World War. As a result of the marriage they had four children, two boys William Pitt and Christopher (who being the eldest boy inherited his father's title upon Sir Sydney's death and became known as Sir Christopher Oakes). Sir Sydney and Lady Greta also had two daughters Felicity and Virginia.

In 1952, Sydney moved with his wife and family into Oak Hall at Niagara Falls, Ontario and lived there for several years before returning to the Bahamas. Sir Sydney and Laky Greta were divorced in 1961.

Sir Sydney was killed in a car accident in 1981 in Nassau on West Bay Street just west of Delaporte Village. So hard was the impact of his green Sunbeam Alpine sports car as he hit a light pole that the license plate numerals 976 were imbedded into the pole. It was mentioned that at the time of his death, Sir Sydney was on his way to the airport to meet two important businessmen. He was then fifty four years old.

A press release from one of the Nassau newspapers reported the tragedy of Sir Sydney's death and it is interesting to note that the headlines read *Sir Sydney's Death — Latest in Chain of Family Tragedies,* showing photographs of Sir Harry Oakes and his daughter Nancy, but none of Sir Sydney himself. In addition almost three quarters of the text of the newspaper story related to the past tragedy of Sir Harry's death in Nassau and the marriage of Nancy Oakes to Alfred de Marigny.

The last mortal remains of Sir Sydney Oakes rest in the family mausoleum in the Dover-Foxcroft cemetery in Maine, together with those of his father Sir Harry and his mother Lady Eunice, his brother William Pitt and sister Shirley.

Shirley Oakes was born on April 10th, 1929, and was the second daughter of Harry and Eunice Oakes. She was fourteen years of age at the time of her father's death.

Shirley made her social debut in Philadelphia in 1947 and London in 1950. She was a classmate of Jacqueline Bouvier, who was later to become Mrs. Jackie Kennedy, wife of the thirty fifth President of the United States. Shirley was one of the ten bridal attendants at the wedding of Jacqueline Bouvier and John Kennedy.

Her curriculum vitae as she termed it was as long as her husband's — Institut d'Etudes Politiques, University of Paris 1949-1950; School of Law, Columbia University 1954; Virginia Swinburne Brownell Prize for History at Vassar College, where she was a member of the Phi Beta Kappa. Other well known institutions of learning that she attended included Yale University and Wadhurst College in Kent, England.

She also worked for the New York law firm of Davidson, Dawson and Clark and served as an officer in the Foreign Department of the Empire Trust Company of New York. Shirley also held the position of Vice-President and Director of a Nassau company called British Colonial Hotel (Holdings) Co. Ltd., which administered the British Colonial Hotel that her father had purchased some years earlier.

Shirley Lewis Oakes and Allan Churchill Butler leaving the church following their wedding in Nassau. *CP Picture Archive*

In April 1967, Shirley married one Allan Churchill Butler. Together they established a bank in Nassau known as Butlers Bank Limited and in due course she became one of its directors while her husband served as its Chairman.

Shirley's marriage to Allan Butler broke up in 1981, the very same year that she was seriously hurt in a car crash on her way back to Nassau from a party at Lyford Cay on West Bay Street. Apparently she was at the Club House and as she left, someone driving behind her noticed that she had left her purse on the roof of her car and flashed their high beams in an attempt to get her attention. Regretfully it would appear that Shirley misunderstood the signal as an indication to pick up speed rather than to slow down or stop and as a result she began accelerating her car.

A short while later Shirley lost control and ran into a tree. She was immediately hospitalized and was paralysed. She died in August of 1986.

The Green Shutters pub on Parliament Street in Nassau.
Author's collection

As part of Shirley's investments in Nassau she owned a residence on Parliament Street, which was to become the location of a well known eating and drinking establishment called the *Green Shutters*. A recent advertisement refers to the *Shutters* as an authentic old style English pub offering such delicacies as *bangars and mash; steak and kidney pie; roast beef and Yorkshire pudding* and naturally local seafood platters, as well as the best of imported beers both on draught and bottled. The food is just great. The history of the premises dates back to the 1860's and was formerly a private residence.

The *Green Shutters* is presently one of the Friday night hangouts in Nassau for expatriates, as well as local Nassauvians and a good meeting place for discussions on local politics, politicians themselves and other local and worldly events. In other words a real gossip hangout. Would the *Green Shutters* be a good place to discuss Sir Harry Oakes?

While doing some research at the Museum of Northern History in Kirkland Lake, I came across a slip of paper in one of the files on which someone had written Shirley Oakes name and a comment to the effect that she had attended Vassar College. I looked up the lady's name in the Toronto telephone directory and called her. She confirmed that she was two classes behind Shirley at Vassar College and knew her as a most pleasant and intelligent young lady.

This lady's sister had taught Shirley at Baldwin School and at the start of the fall semester one year, she asked all the girls to write an essay on what they had done during the past summer. As time passed, the teacher noted that one of the girls was leaning against her desk in complete tears, which prompted the teacher to speak to the head mistress to explain what was happening in her class. As it turned out the young lady in question was Shirley Oakes, who had lost her father that past summer of 1943.

William Pitt Oakes was born on September 10th, 1930. He was the second son of Harry and Eunice Oakes and was thirteen years of age at the time of his father's death.

As the story goes, some time following the death of his father, William Pitt stood at a cocktail party at the British Colonial Hotel in Nassau one evening speaking to one Rex North, a leading society columnist.

During his conversation with North, William Pitt spotted the squat features and smallish figure of someone he knew very well across the room. He gestured towards him and said to North, *"There is the man who knows how my father was murdered and why."* The gentleman's name was never revealed, but can we guess to whom William Pitt was referring?

In 1952 William Pitt married Eunice Bailey of London, England.

William Pitt died in New York on April 26th, 1958, at the very young age of twenty eight and at the time of his death, he and his wife Eunice had been in New York while he combined a business trip with a medical check-up.

Harry Phillip Oakes and his bride the former Christiane Botsch leaving the Church following their wedding in Hamburg, Germany. *CP Picture Archive*

While in his suite at the *Westbury Hotel*, William Pitt was stricken with a coronary thrombosis, possibly complicated by a liver ailment which led to his death. His sister Shirley further confirmed that her brother had suffered from a heart murmur for a number of years.

The last mortal remains of William Pitt Oakes also rest in the family mausoleum at the Dover-Foxcroft cemetery in Maine, together with the remains of other members of the Oakes family.

In March 1961, it was announced in the press that William Pitt's widow Eunice married the millionaire Robert David Lion Gardner at St. Thomas Church in New York. Gardner was the sixteenth owner of Gardner's Island which is situated off Long Island, New York, and which had been given to an ancestor by King Charles I in 1639. Eunice was 30 and Gardner 50 years of age.

The youngest of the Oakes children was Harry Phillip Oakes, who was born on August 30th, 1932, to Harry and Eunice Oakes. At the time of his father's tragic death in 1943, he was only eleven years of age.

In late 1957, Harry met Christiane Botsch while they were studying at the University of Toronto. He was taking a business course, while Christiane was studying English and anthropology. After a short four month romance they were married in March 1958.

Based on a Nassau newspaper clipping under date of May 10th, 1983, a celebration was held at the Lyford Cay Club on the occasion of the twenty fifth wedding anniversary of Harry and Christiane Oakes. The invitations indicated that it was a black tie affair. It also mentioned on the card — no gifts please.

Amongst the members of the family in the reception line were their three sons Harry Newell, Philip and Michael, as well as their daughter Bianca who was then attending Tulane University in New Orleans. Also in attendance was Harry's older sister Baroness Nancy von Hoyningen-Huene (Nancy Oakes) and her husband Baron Ernst-Lyssandt von Hoyningen-Huene.

6

The Duke and Duchess of Windsor

His Royal Highness The Duke of Windsor ..... A King's Story ..... Montgomery Hyde — A Man Called Intrepid ..... The Duchess of Windsor — Her Story

---

On December 10th, 1936, King Edward VIII of England had already made his decision to abdicate as King of England in order to marry — *the woman I love* — the American Wallis Simpson. On that particular evening, he read the following address to the people of his beloved England and the members of the British Commonwealth:

At long last I am able to say a few words of my own. I have never wanted to withhold anything, but until now it has not been constitutionally possible for me to speak. A few hours ago I discharged my last duty as King and Emperor. And now that I have been succeeded by my brother, the Duke of York, my first words must be to declare allegiance to him. This I do with all my heart. You know the reasons which have impelled me to renounce the throne, but I want you to understand that in making up my mind I did not forget the country or the empire which, as Prince of Wales and lately as King, I have for twenty five years tried to serve. But you must believe me when I tell you that I have found it impossible to carry the heavy burden of responsibility and to discharge my duties as King as I would wish to do without the help and support of the woman I love. And I want you to know that the decision I have made has been mine, and mine alone. The other person most nearly concerned has tried up to the last to persuade me to take a different course. I have made this, the most serious decision of my life, only upon the single thought of what would, in the end, be best for all.

This decision has been made less difficult for me by the sure knowledge that my brother, with his long training in the public affairs of this country and with his fine qualities, will be able to take my place forthwith without interruption or injury to the life and progress of the Empire, and he has one matchless blessing, enjoyed by so many of you and not bestowed upon me, a happy home with his wife and children. During these hard days, I have been comforted by Her Majesty, my mother, and by my family. The ministers of the Crown and, in particular, Mr. Baldwin, the Prime Minister, have always treated me with full consideration. There has never been any constitutional tradition between me and them and between me and Parliament. Bred in the constitutional tradition by my father, I should never have allowed any such issue to arise. Ever since I was Prince of Wales and later on when I occupied the throne, I have been treated with the greatest kindness by all classes of the people wherever I have lived or journeyed throughout the Empire. For that I am grateful. I now quit altogether public affairs and I lay down my burden. It may be some time before I return to my native land, but I shall always follow the fortunes of the British race and

Empire with profound interest, and if, at any time in the future, I can be found of service to His Majesty in a private station, I shall not fail.

And now we all have a new King.

I wish him and you, his people, happiness and prosperity with all my heart.

God bless you all! God save the King!

Following this address, King Edward VIII became the Duke of Windsor and from that moment on, his life and relationship with the Royal Family would take a different turn. A whole new life began for him and in due course he would be directed to the Bahamas by Winston Churchill to assume the position of Royal Governor General, accompanied by Wallis Simpson — then to be the Duchess of Windsor. Their meeting with Sir Harry and Lady Eunice Oakes would then only be a matter of time, as well as their introduction to Harold Christie and Count Alfred de Marigny.

A matter of time also before the Duke of Windsor's involvement in one of the most publicized murders in the history of the Bahamas.

Arrival of the Duke and Duchess of Windsor in Nassau in August 1940. *Toogood's Photography, Nassau*

The Duke of Windsor was born on June 23rd, 1894, to the then reigning King George V and Queen Mary.

The Duke and Duchess of Windsor were married on June 3rd, 1937, at the Chateau de Cande in France, which had been lent to the Duke for the occasion by his friend Charles Bedeaux, who would later commit suicide following his having been charged with treason and conspiracy with the Nazis in occupied France during the early part of the Second World War.

The Duke of Windsor took up residence in Nassau as the Royal Governor General of the Bahamas on August 17th, 1940. He was to be the 54th Governor General and arrived with his Duchess aboard the Canadian merchant ship the *Lady Sommers* which had picked them up in Bermuda a few days earlier.

The Duke and Duchess of Windsor visiting the RAF station in Nassau. *Author's collection*

He succeeded Sir Charles Dundas, the previous Governor General who had been requested by Winston Churchill to relinquish his post in order to allow for the appointment of the Duke of Windsor. It was Churchill's desire that the Duke of Windsor be kept as far away as possible from England, due to his political feelings which he had expressed on many occasions over the past few years.

The Windsors left the Bahamas on May 3rd, 1945, a short time before the normal term of a Governor General's appointment of five years.

The Duke was informed of the murder of Sir Harry Oakes at 7.30 a.m. on the morning of July 8, 1943, by his Aide-de-Camp, Major Gray Phillips, but he did not take any decisive action, it is said, for some three hours and fifteen minutes, at which time he finally placed a call to the Miami Police Department and spoke with Captain Edward Melchen.

On July 23rd, 1943, the Duke of Windsor was in Miami on private business and was faced by the local press, whose main interest was to question him regarding his request for two Miami detectives to investigate the murder of Sir Harry Oakes in Nassau, a British colony.

The Duke commented that the murder was a great shock to everyone and was *no reflection on the Nassau police*. He further confirmed that *he was prompted by the fact that the Miami officers had the equipment and experience, not available in the Bahamas, for fingerprint work, photographing and other methods needed for the probe*.

In 1951 the Duke of Windsor published an autobiography of himself under the title *A King's Story*, which was considered to be the official memoirs up to that point in time of His Royal Highness the Duke of Windsor, formerly King Edward VIII of England.

In August 1996, the Public Broadcasting Service aired a television special entitled *Edward on Edward* written and directed by Prince Edward, nephew of the Duke of Windsor. The story basically was on the life and times of the Duke of Windsor including his abdication as King, to marry Wallis Simpson.

During the program, a brief comment is made of the Duke's Royal Governorship of the Bahamas during the Second World War and a remark in particular to the *unfortunate incident* when the Duke called for the assistance of the Miami police in the investigation into the murder of Nassau's most prominent citizen and millionaire Sir Harry Oakes.

The Duke died of cancer in a Paris hospital in May 1972. Nine days before his death he was visited by his niece Queen Elizabeth II, which was the first token recognition by the Royal Family since his departure from England following his abdication in 1936, some thirty six years earlier.

A similar autobiography written by the Duchess of Windsor as her memoirs was subsequently published in 1956 under the title *The Heart Has Its Reasons* and was also considered her memoirs up to that point.

The interesting aspect of these two books is that in the case of the Duke of Windsor's book, there is no mention of his residency as Governor General of the Bahamas, which was considered by many historians to have been a major point in his life, as it was to be his last royal function on behalf of the British Government. The Duchess on the other hand devoted a complete chapter to their residency in Nassau with mention of the murder of — *their closest friend, Sir Harry Oakes.*

Upon the Windsors arrival in Nassau in August 1940, Sir Harry and Lady Oakes lent them their *Westbourne* estate as living accommodation, while Government House was being refurbished. An interesting note is that the Windsors apparently slept in the very same room in which Sir Harry Oakes was to meet his tragic death some three years later.

The British secret agent Montgomery Hyde on the staff of Sir William Stephenson (from A *Man Called Intrepid* fame) had been assigned the responsibility of reporting on the activities in Nassau of the Duke, Sir Harry Oakes, Harold Christie and naturally Dr. Axel Wenner-Gren in particular, concerning their involvement with the money transfers to Mexico.

In March 1941, Montgomery Hyde visited with the Duke of Windsor in Nassau and while he was having a discussion with the Duke on the question of security, Sir Harry Oakes arrived at Government House with a sixteen man delegation from Mexico, which included

General Maximino Camacho, Governor of the Province of Puebla and brother of the Mexican President Avila Camacho.

At the time it was a known fact that Britain had broken off diplomatic ties with Mexico, after they had expropriated all British oil companies in the country, without making any offers of compensation. The Duke of Windsor as Governor General of the Bahamas, was no doubt aware of the diplomatic problems and should have ensured that no Mexican nationals be allowed into the Bahamas. I guess being a friend of the Duke of Windsor had its privileges and this incident was one of them.

After Hyde left the Duke of Windsor's office, he immediately went over to the office of Leslie Heape, the Colonial Secretary and convinced him to send an Immigration Officer to Sir Harry's British Colonial Hotel, where the Mexicans were residing and verify the status of their passports. As a result of the spot check, it was uncovered that one of Sir Harry's guests was actually on the FBI's black-list and wanted for un-American activities.

General Maximino Camacho, Governor of the Province of Puebla in Mexico, being welcomed to Nassau by Harold Christie and Sir Harry Oakes. *CP Picture Archive*

The apparent objective of the meeting of the Duke of Windsor and Sir Harry Oakes with the group of Mexican businessmen, was relative to the eventual formation of a Mexican financing group in Mexico City, through the transfer of funds from the Bahamas contrary to the stringent foreign exchange control which applied to all Bahamian residents, including the Duke of Windsor.

Hyde was born in Belfast, Northern Ireland in 1907 and was the author of more than forty books, mostly biographies and studies in criminology and sociology. Hyde was a practised barrister and worked in the British secret intelligence during the Second World War.

In his book entitled *Crime Has Its Heroes*, Hyde describes the background of a number of murders and in his remarks on the Oakes case, he comments to the effect that he felt Harold Christie's claim that he did not hear any commotion the night of the murder was indeed correct — *as Christie was not in his room at the time,* having left *Westbourne* to visit his mistress and returning at dawn in time to discover the charred body of his best friend Sir Harry Oakes.

The fact that he was *supposedly* seen by Captain Edward Sears in the downtown area of Nassau shortly after midnight, would substantiate the feeling that Christie had left *Westbourne* to go and visit *with someone* and if he had testified to that effect, he would have compromised the lady. For understandably chivalrous motives he was unwilling to do so, thus the reason for testifying as he did, to the effect that he had spent the entire night at *Westbourne*.

The Duchess of Windsor was born Bessie Wallis Warfield on June 19th, 1896, in a summer holiday cottage at Blue Ridge Summit, a slightly run down health centre in Pennsylvania.

Her father died when she was only a few months old. In due course she dropped the name Bessie, which was the name of her mother's older sister Mrs. Bessie Merryman. Wallis also felt that there were more than enough cows called Bessie to her liking. Her second name Wallis, though the name of a man, was given to her in memory of her father — Wallis Warfield.

Wallis was twenty years of age when she first married U.S. Navy Lieutenant Earl Winfield Spencer Jr., on November 8th, 1916, at the Christ Episcopal Church in Baltimore, Maryland. Following their marriage they lived on various naval bases across the United States. Spencer's wish at the time was to be posted overseas and participate in combat, however, this wish never materialized and the Spencers remained in the United States for the duration of the war.

As time went by the marriage began to deteriorate, partly due to Winfield's drinking problems and Wallis eventually left him. At first both families would not see divorce as the solution to the problem, as divorce was not considered appropriate in those days. In due course she finally did obtain the divorce on December 10th, 1927.

In the interim she did have occasion to travel to China, where she eventually met her second husband, Ernest Simpson, who was in the process of obtaining a divorce from his wife. Wallis and Ernest were married on July 21st, 1928, within a year of her first divorce.

It was during her trip to China that Wallis Simpson purchased *the Chinese screen*, which eventually found its way into the home of Sir Harry and Lady Eunice Oakes, as a gift for having made their *Westbourne* estate available to her and the Duke of Windsor following their arrival in Nassau. The screen comprised six cream coloured pasteboard panels with a *Chinese* motif which when completely extended covered an area of approximately ten feet in length.

With the Duke's appointment as Governor General of the Bahamas, the Duchess served as Chairperson of the Bahamas Red Cross Society for the duration of their stay and was also appointed Honorary President of the Daughters of the British Empire. Both of these social functions were part and parcel of the fate of being the wife of a Bahamian Governor General.

She always considered her stay in the Bahamas as their *Elba* or *St. Helena* in reference to Napoleon's exile to those islands and on many occasions when writing to close friends, she crossed out the official title on the letterhead relative to Government House and replaced it with either one of the above references.

The Duchess outlived the Duke and died on April 24th, 1986, at the age of 90.

7

Count Marie Alfred Fouquereaux de Marigny

Alfred Freddie de Marigny ..... His Concubine ..... Marquis Georges de Visdelou Guimbeau — The Playboy ..... Grissou — The Cat ..... Elizabeth Mary Roberts — A Pretty Nassau Lady ..... Charles Rolle — The Butler and Friend ..... Curtis George Thompson — A Close Friend ..... Baron Georg and Baroness Marie af Trolle — Close Friends of Nancy Oakes ..... Alfred Ceretta — de Marigny's Friend ..... Brenda Frazier — The Debutante ..... Howard Robard Hughes ..... Captain Robert Millar — His Majesty's Prison ..... Ms. Rosita Forbes — The British Writer ..... Rollie Symonette — A Nassau Businessman ..... Ernest Hemingway ..... More Devil Than Saint — The First Book ..... Alfred de Marigny — Houston, Texas January 1993 ..... Alfred de Marigny and Harold Christie ..... Alfred de Marigny and the Duke of Windsor ..... Alfred de Marigny and His Deportation from the Bahamas ..... The Marriage Annulment ..... De Marigny's Attempt to Immigrate to Canada ..... Back to Montreal ..... The Islands of Mauritius — The Starting Point ..... John Herbert Anderson — A Nassau Friend

---

Alfred de Marigny was born on March 29th, 1910, in the Mauritius Islands.

In his early days he lived with a grandmother and two spinster aunts and was told at the time that his real mother had passed away when he was three years of age.

As the years went by Alfred developed a very inquisitive mind and learned as much as he could about life in general. In the long run this curiosity would benefit him in facing many of the problems and challenges that he would encounter later in life.

In due course he left Mauritius to attend a Jesuit school in Normandy, where for the next six years he would be at the top of his class and when he reached the age of eighteen, he had finished his secondary education and had passed the entrance exam for Cambridge University.

Following his education abroad Alfred returned to Mauritius for a visit with his relatives and one day while playing tennis, who should be playing against him in a set of doubles but his real life mother, who was indeed still alive and well. She had divorced his father and had remarried in Port Louis.

At that point he decided to remain on the island and see what life would bring him, following which Alfred saw his cousin Georges de Visdelou, who had also come back from studies abroad. Little did Georges know at this point that he would play a very important part in the future life of Alfred de Marigny. Georges was from a wealthy family and spent most of his youth in France.

Within six months, de Marigny would again see his real father for the last time and leave Mauritius forever heading off to London with his cousin Georges.

In London the two of them established themselves in the appropriate social circles where they would meet a number of influential people using their titles of Count and

Marquis to their best advantage. At one point following his arrival in Paris, de Marigny met a young lady by the name of Lucett Alice Cohen, a real charmer apparently and the daughter of Sir George Cohen, a well-to-do Alsacian financier who included amongst his distinguished neighbours Barbara Hutton, the Woolworth heiress.

As Alfred de Marigny continued to escort Lucett to various social functions, a romantic relationship developed and they were eventually married on June 3rd, 1937, the same date as the wedding of the Duke and Duchess of Windsor. The marriage took place in Paris and was performed by a local Magistrate.

This was to be Alfred de Marigny's first venture into matrimony and it would end in divorce in Florida some thirteen weeks after their arrival in America.

It is interesting to note from the two books authored by Alfred de Marigny, that not one of them contains any photos of Lucett Cohen, which would prompt the question — who was this mysterious lady?

The crossing to America was on board the *Normandie*, one of the luxury French liners of the time and de Marigny would meet the well known writer Ernest Hemingway, with whom he would renew his friendship again in Havana, Cuba following his deportation from the Bahamas in 1943.

As part of one of his weekends of socializing, de Marigny was subsequently a house guest of Coster Schermerhorn and his wife Ruth. Schermerhorn was the senior partner of the firm Fahnestock and Company which was formed by Ruth's family.

A romance developed between Ruth and Alfred, which led her to seek a divorce from her husband in Nevada following a ninety days residency requirement. Ruth and Alfred were married on November 28th, 1937, in Reno, Nevada.

In the interim waiting period, de Marigny would board the steamer *Mungaro* and begin his journey towards the Bahamas. Upon his arrival in Nassau he would make the acquaintance of the Prince George Hotel, which would act as his home away from home. The Prince George was located down by the harbour front, and acted as the meeting place for native Bahamians, expatriates and visitors alike.

While establishing himself in Nassau, he would also meet Harold Christie, real estate agent extra-ordinaire, member of the Bahamian government and member of the Bay Street Boys — that exclusive Nassau clan of white businessmen.

Christie arranged for de Marigny to go on a tour of the out islands and more specifically to the Island of Eleuthera, where he would buy land and eventually build himself a home at Governor's Harbour.

However, it became obvious that the new lifestyle in the Bahamas would not suit Ruth and she could not adapt to the new surroundings. In due course a further divorce was on the horizon for de Marigny which became final in April 1940. However, Ruth and de Marigny made an agreement that she could continue to live in his house on Eleuthera for a period of time.

In early 1939, the possibility of a second world conflict rose again and as Britain and other countries prepared for war, many wealthy families would now begin their influx into the Bahamas, which certainly was far enough away from the battlefields and hostilities of war, that no harm could come to the so-called refugees.

A young and debonair Alfred de Marigny and Nancy Oakes in Nassau. *CP Picture Archive*

De Marigny's full name and title was Count Marie Alfred Fouquereaux de Marigny, a very impressive one, however, it was de Marigny's wish when he first arrived in Nassau to be referred to as Alfred de Marigny and in this regard he informed the two leading newspapers accordingly. The title of Count was a hereditary French title in his family and one that he did not want to use, though when living in London, the title was of great benefit to him in his social pursuits. His cousin the Marquis Georges de Visdelou Guimbeau, on the other hand never hesitated to use his title as a Marquis to his best advantage wherever he went.

Alfred de Marigny had lived the greater part of his life near the ocean in Mauritius and it was a natural for him when he arrived in Nassau to further his interest in sailing and as a result he helped establish the Nassau Yacht Club.

Little did he know at this point that his love for sailing would be part of the decision by four members of the jury to ask for his deportation from the Bahamas as an *undesirable*, following his acquittal on the charges of having murdered his father-in-law, Sir Harry Oakes.

De Marigny became part of the social circuit in Nassau and saw Nancy Oakes at a family reception, hosted by Sir Harry and Lady Eunice at their *Caves* estate and it would not be long before he would see her again at the engagement party of one of Nancy's best friends Marie Gudewill.

Along came New Year's Eve 1942 when de Marigny, having now developed a closer social and romantic relationship with Nancy, was invited to Baron Georg and Baroness Marie af Trolle's home, to participate in the celebrations to welcome in the New Year.

And as we now know Nancy Oakes and Alfred de Marigny were married on May 19th, 1942, at which point Nancy called her parents in Bar Harbor, Maine, to inform them of the marriage. During a conversation with her father, he very bluntly asked Nancy, *"How much money do you want?"* However, as time went by everything would work out well between Nancy, Alfred and her parents. Or so everyone thought.

On May 27th, 1943, Nancy was to leave the island and head north to the Martha Graham School of Dance in Bennington, Vermont for some rest following certain medical attention. Alfred remained in Nassau and tended to the ever growing needs of his newly purchased and developing chicken farm.

On the evening of July 6th, 1943, de Marigny was down at the Prince George Hotel with his usual circle of friends, when he was introduced to the wives of two Royal Air Force pilots in the persons of Jean Ainslie and Dorothy Clarke, whom he invited to the party at his home the following evening.

At the start of the dinner party, the guests were all seated outside enjoying themselves when suddenly a tropical storm began to develop and it was necessary for everyone to rush indoors. During the dinner the lights began to flicker, at which point de Marigny proceeded to light up a few hurricane lamps and as he inserted his hand inside the globe of one of the lamps with a burning match, he burnt the surface of his hand. Two of the guests, Jean Ainslie and Dorothy Clarke both noted this incident.

As the day dawned on Thursday July 8th, 1943, little did Alfred de Marigny realize that his life would now change forever on the discovery of the murder of his father-in-law, Sir Harry Oakes, at his *Westbourne* estate.

Victoria Avenue in Nassau where Nancy and Alfred de Marigny resided. *Courtesy of Dr. Gail Saunders and of Donald Cartwright, Nassau*

Nancy Oakes de Marigny on one of her visits to see her husband during the trial. The title of the book is *My Country and My People* by Lin Yutang, 1938. *CP Picture Archive*

At approximately 6.30 p.m. on the evening of Friday July 9th, 1943, Alfred de Marigny was charged with the murder.

De Marigny's trial would commence in the Supreme Court of the Bahamas on October 18th, 1943, and end on November 11th, 1943, a total of twenty two court days, ending with his acquittal on the charges of having murdered Sir Harry Oakes.

On the morning of November 15th, 1943, de Marigny was informed by his lawyer Godfrey Higgs that a rider had been added to the verdict by the Jury, unbeknownst to the people in the court room due to the excitement, to the effect that he be deported from the Bahamas as soon as possible as an *undesirable*.

On Monday December 6th, 1943, Alfred de Marigny and Nancy left Nassau for Havana, Cuba arriving there two days later, thus ending his ties with the Bahamas until his return in June 1990, some forty seven years later at the invitation of the Bahamian Government.

They travelled to Havana on a small, uncomfortable, cabinless motorized freight boat which had been chartered for the occasion. On arrival they stayed temporarily at the Hotel Nacional and were later to rent a house in Varadero, a suburb of Havana.

De Marigny was often referred to as *Frenchie* by Sir Harry Oakes, no doubt because of his heavy French accent which apparently touched on the Charles Boyer style.

The last time that Alfred de Marigny saw Nancy was in Montreal in 1946 and there is a last photograph taken of them socialising together one evening in the Normandie Room at the Ritz Carlton Hotel.

On April 18th, 1946, de Marigny called for a new investigation into the murder of his father-in-law, claiming (as he did in 1990) that Sir Harry died of bullet wounds. At that point in time the Duke of Windsor had left the Bahamas and de Marigny's request remained unanswered.

In March, 1975, de Marigny, together with his wife, a very attractive American lady, settled in Florida. It was de Marigny's wish that details of his family be left out of any stories or publications, as he felt that privacy was necessary.

The de Marignys lived in a very pleasant neighbourhood of Houston called oddly enough *River Oakes*.

In 1990 he published his last book entitled *A Conspiracy of Crowns: The True Story of the Duke of Windsor and the Murder of Sir Harry Oakes* and as part of his publisher's promotion, he came to Toronto in July of that year, but no public appearances were made though he was interviewed by a number of leading Toronto newspaper columnists.

It has been noticed during the course of his appearance in the Magistrate's Court immediately following his arrest and subsequently during his trial in the Supreme Court, that Alfred de Marigny always appeared to have a smile on his face and would speak to those whom he recognized in the crowds milling about, when he would walk to the Court House. Whenever Nancy was in the crowd he always had a smile for her.

After having read a great deal about Alfred de Marigny and also having had the pleasure of meeting him personally, it is hard to believe that he did not take the whole matter of his trial more seriously. As an indication of his conviction that he would not be found guilty, de Marigny had arranged for his butler to bring his car to the side of the Court House.

It was obvious that de Marigny had no intention of going anywhere but home with Nancy following the trial.

De Marigny had many friends in Nassau in all walks of life, from plain native workers, to businessmen, lawyers, police officers and the social elite and yes, even the Duke and Duchess of Windsor.

Following his acquittal on the murder charges, Alfred de Marigny and his cousin Georges de Visdelou were subsequently charged with the illegal possession of four drums of gasoline and fined 100 pounds each. It was a known fact that there was strict rationing of gasoline during the war years and these four drums in particular bore RAF markings to add to their problems. Magistrate Frank Fields, who had heard the preliminary hearing in the Magistrate's Court in Alfred de Marigny's trial, was the presiding magistrate in this case.

De Visdelou pleaded guilty, but de Marigny pleaded not guilty and was convicted by the Magistrate on the following charges:

1)   That they at Nassau, New Providence, on the 8th and the 13th of July, 1943, did have in their possession or convey, four metal drums valued at approximately 10 pounds and 180 gallons of High Octane gasoline also valued at approximately 10 pounds, together valued at 20 pounds, the property of the Royal Air Force, Nassau, reasonably suspected of having been stolen or unlawfully obtained.

2)   Further that they at Nassau, New Providence, between the 8th and 13th of July, 1943, did without the authority of a license acquire 180 gallons of High Octane gasoline otherwise than from a supplier of gasoline.

Col. Frederick Lancaster said the drums in question were not brought into court as evidence because this type of fuel was highly explosive and there was an element of danger in having High Octane gasoline drums in the court room.

As part of a follow-up on some material that I had written, I decided to call Alfred de Marigny on January 28th, 1998, to obtain his comments and clarifications, however, it was with deep regret that I learned in talking to one of his sons, that Alfred had passed away earlier that very same day.

One of Alfred de Marigny's main interests in life was sailing and as he was surrounded by the sea from his birth in the Islands of Mauritius to his life in the Bahamas, he became a very adept sailor. When I visited with him in 1993, he happened to step out of the room for a brief moment and his wife suggested that I ask him when he came back — if he knew how to swim?

Taking her advice I did ask Alfred the question, to which he responded that — *if you are a good sailor, there is no reason to fall out of your boat and therefore no need to swim.*

As a result of his interest in sailing competitions, he became a champion Star Class yachtsman and assisted many young local Bahamians, including Capt. Durward Knowles, in acquiring the knowledge and expertise needed for the sport. He bought sailing yachts, which he gave to some of his close friends and was influential in organizing the Nassau Yacht Club, which ran in direct conflict with the Royal Nassau Yacht Club.

While he was married to Ruth Fahnestock and had settled in the Bahamas in 1937, de Marigny was the proud owner of a Star Class yacht which he had re-christened *Concubine*.

The definition of the word concubine according to Webster's dictionary is — *a woman with whom a man cohabits without being married*. Under that definition of his marital status at the time, de Marigny felt that his sailing yacht was indeed a *Concubine*.

Following the trial, de Marigny thought that he should rename his yacht the *Exhibit J* as a reminder of the famous fingerprint exhibit that was used by the Prosecution against him at his trial and almost cost him his life, but in actuality he had sold the yacht to the wife of his lawyer Godfrey Higgs.

Georges de Visdelou

Georges de Visdelou, Alfred de Marigny's cousin, was depicted as a *bon vivant*, an intellectual and a cartographer who had been accepted by the Royal Geographical Society in London after publishing a paper about the discovery of Mauritius by the Portuguese.

Georges de Visdelou and his girlfriend Betty Roberts, together with the cat *Grissou*. *Corbis Images*

Georges was also described as — *an impenitent, irresponsible hedonist, amusing, with a devil-may-care attitude*, who together with Alfred de Marigny, succeeded in scandalizing some of the more important members of Nassau's society circle.

Following the acquittal of Alfred de Marigny, Georges left the Bahamas on December 10th, 1943, and headed for Haiti. His girl friend Betty Roberts turned down an apparent last minute marriage proposal from him and remained in Nassau.

During a telephone conversation with Sir Durward Knowles in early 1998, he informed me that it was he who took de Visdelou over to Haiti by motor launch leaving Nassau at three o'clock in the morning. The crossing was done in twenty four hours in German submarine patrolled waters.

There was a subsequent rumour that Betty Roberts went to New York and married a Russian Count. Nothing further was ever mentioned about de Visdelou, although in a discussion with Ernest Callender in 1992 he did mention that he had heard that Georges passed away a few years earlier in London, England.

De Visdelou had a cat called *Grissou*, which some people say played a very important part in the defense of Alfred de Marigny, for on the night of the murder of Sir Harry Oakes, *Grissou* was in de Marigny's bedroom at the time that Georges returned from having driven Betty Roberts home.

It would appear that the cat was caught up in the blinds and drapes around the window and was preventing de Marigny from falling asleep. As a result when Georges returned, de Marigny called to him to come and remove his cat, thus accounting for de Marigny's whereabouts at that particular time.

Pictures of the cat being held by Georges de Visdelou and Betty Roberts graced the pages of many magazines and newspapers during the course of the trial.

The name *Grissou* apparently came from a French word meaning firedamp which was known as an explosive gas.

Elizabeth Mary Roberts

Elizabeth Mary Roberts was better known to her many friends in Nassau as just plain Betty Roberts. She worked as a cashier at the Savoy Theatre. There is also mention that she worked at the Windsor Hotel in Nassau as a front desk clerk.

Ms. Roberts was described by one person as — blond, fair skinned, blue eyed, buxom, cocky and sexy, and that she insisted her real home was with her mother. She was said to be sixteen or seventeen years of age at the time of the murder.

She appeared at Alfred de Marigny's trial as an alibi witness for the Defense, for on the evening of the murder she was also one of the dinner guests at de Marigny's home and remained with Georges de Visdelou, after the departure of most of the other guests.

Following the trial, Judge Sir Oscar Daly made a point of complementing Ms. Roberts on her deportment during the period of questioning, which he felt must have been most trying for her in view of her young age and suddenly being placed in the limelight, as her face and every word she said would appear in the world press.

Charles Rolle

Charles Rolle was de Marigny's black butler, who also appeared as an alibi witness for him during the trial and who confirmed that the dinner party at de Marigny's on the eve of Sir Harry's murder had broken up around twelve-thirty.

Rolle was questioned by Captains Barker and Melchen during their visit to de Marigny's home in search of the clothing that he had worn on the evening of the dinner party. They seemed quite surprised that all the suits previously worn by de Marigny were indeed pressed and hanging very neatly in the closet, as if someone were trying to hide some evidence from them.

At this point Capt. Melchen immediately challenged de Marigny that quite possibly he was indeed hiding something from them. Rolle interjected and made it very clear to Barker and Melchen that it was always the custom in Nassau for a gentleman's butler to make sure that all clothing was indeed properly cleaned and pressed immediately after use.

Rolle further testified at the trial that he saw de Marigny leave with Jean Ainslie and Dorothy Clarke to drive them home and that Georges de Visdelou and Betty Roberts were still in the house when he returned.

This would make the time of de Marigny's return to his residence to be approximately 1.30 a.m.

George Thompson

When de Marigny first arrived in Nassau, he travelled over to Eleuthera from Nassau one day on a local mail boat, whereupon he met a young Bahamian by the name of George Thompson. De Marigny was impressed with Thompson from the conversation that they had on board the boat and offered him a job of supervising the construction that he was going to undertake at Governor's Harbour.

George informed de Marigny that he was interested, but that he was also indebted to the captain of the mail boat on which he was working in the amount of twenty pounds and would not be able to accept the job offer. De Marigny would not see it and gave him sufficient funds to pay off his debt and provide him with a little extra pocket money.

As a result George accepted the offer and became de Marigny's right hand man. De Marigny re-christened him *Curtis*. A close friendship developed and would be proven during the trial.

According to de Marigny, the police investigating the murder brought Curtis to the police station and advised him to admit that he had taken de Marigny to *Westbourne* the night of the murder. Thompson refused to agree to such a statement and remained loyal to de Marigny.

In 1990, de Marigny, while revisiting Nassau, called on Thompson who was nearly seventy years of age and still active and in demand as a captain of one of the boats in the fishing fleet that sails out of Nassau Harbour.

Baron Georg af Trolle

Baron Georg af Trolle was the private secretary at one time for Dr. Axel Wenner-Gren and married into the upper class society of Nassau. His sole support was irregular contributions from an official committee set up to administer Wenner-Gren's assets.

His wife was formerly Marie Gudewill from Montreal, Canada and a very close friend of Nancy Oakes. It is said that Baroness Marie could not touch or control her assets in Canada due to the British Exchange Control regulations in effect in the British Colonies at the time.

It was at the home of the Trolles that Nancy first danced with Alfred de Marigny before the start of their romantic escapade.

Raymond Schindler, who was hired by Nancy de Marigny, together with Professor Leonard Keeler, resided with the Trolles whenever they were in Nassau to assist with the defense of de Marigny. The reason naturally for staying with the Trolles was that the added expense which would be incurred by staying at a fashionable Nassau hotel was not within de Marigny's trial budget at the time.

Marie and Baron Georg were married on March 29th, 1941, at Christ Church Cathedral in Nassau followed by a reception in the penthouse at Sir Harry's British Colonial Hotel. The bride was given away by Sir Harry Oakes and Nancy Oakes was one of the bridesmaids.

The best man was Capt. Hjalmar Rothman, crew member of Dr. Axel Wenner-Gren's *Southern Cross*.

Alfred Victor Ceretta

A good friend of Alfred de Marigny was Alfred Victor Ceretta, better known as *Freddie*, who was an engineer from the United States, employed by a firm which had obtained the contract over Sir Harry Oakes, to develop and build a new airfield which was to be named *Windsor Field*. The air field would in due course become the site of the present day Nassau International Airport at the west end of the island.

This airport was not to be confused with *Oakes Field*, which Sir Harry had himself built in the eastern part of the island and of which the runways are still visible, though covered over with grass and wild brush. *Oakes Field* was used by the RAF for training during the war.

Following the dinner and as the guests were beginning to leave, de Marigny was preparing to drive the two ladies back to their residence next door to *Westbourne* and invited Freddie Ceretta to come along with him. Ceretta declined and de Marigny drove them home alone. As someone later commented, if you are about to go and murder someone you surely do not invite one of your friends to go along with you.

Brenda Frazier

In 1939 Brenda Frazier, the very attractive niece of Sir Frederick and Lady Jane Williams-Taylor was visiting with them in Nassau. The Williams-Taylors lived at the *Hermitage*, one of the private residences along East Bay Street. The *Hermitage* was constructed by Lord Dunmore and used as a summer retreat by him during the years 1787 to 1796, and is presently the residence of the Roman Catholic Bishop of the Diocese of Nassau.

In later years during a dinner party hosted by Brenda Frazier, one of her guests announced in a rather loud and authoritative voice that she knew who had killed Sir Harry Oakes and proceeded to inform everyone that *it was Harold Christie*, not knowing that Christie himself was sitting at the other end of the table.

So the story goes, Christie rose from his chair demanding, *"How do you know this?"* Before she could answer, he collapsed to the floor. To everyone's relief, Christie recovered. And so ended a further story surrounding the murder of Sir Harry Oakes as nothing else was said by anyone, certainly not Christie.

Howard Hughes

Howard Hughes was born on December 24th, 1905, in a small family frame house on Crawford Street, just east of what is presently downtown Houston, Texas. The exact date of his birth has always been a point of confusion, as there are no records of his birth being registered in the Texas Division of Vital Statistics in Austin or for that matter with the Houston Board of Health.

In January of 1993, I met with Alfred de Marigny and his charming wife at their home in Houston, Texas. During our conversation de Marigny mentioned an event that happened in Nassau when Brenda Frazier, the New York society debutante, had been invited to his home on Victoria Avenue for supper with Nancy, himself, and some friends. Accompanying Brenda Frazier was none other than Howard Hughes, who arrived very shabbily dressed. In those days in Nassau it was normal for men to arrive at parties in somewhat more formal attire.

De Marigny informed Hughes of the matter and very politely asked him to leave, or as de Marigny prefers to recall, *"I threw him out."* The story continued to the effect that a few days later de Marigny bumped into Hughes at the Prince George Hotel bar and the two of them had a few drinks together as if nothing had ever happened.

Captain Robert Millar

Captain Robert Millar acted in the dual capacity of Naval Reporting Officer for His Majesty's Government, with that of Superintendent of His Majesty's prison in Nassau at the time of the murder of Sir Harry Oakes. He was responsible for the safety and well being of Alfred de Marigny during his incarceration in Nassau prison pending and during his trial.

It was with Capt. Millar that Montgomery Hyde, Secret Intelligence Agent for the British Government, resided whenever he came to Nassau to review the security conditions surrounding the Duke and Duchess of Windsor.

Millar was a former Royal Canadian Mounted Police (R.C.M.P.) officer in Canada, the R.C.M.P. being the official government police force of Canada.

Rosita Forbes

Rosita Forbes was a very well known English writer and traveller, who was born in Swindersby, Lincolnshire, England in 1893.

She visited almost every country in the world during her lifetime and travelled extensively in Arabia and North Africa, using the experience of her travels as the basic source of material for the many travel books that she wrote over the years.

In due course Ms. Forbes made the acquaintance of Alfred de Marigny, subsequently writing a book in 1946 entitled *Appointment with Destiny*, which reflected a great deal on her life on the Island of Eleuthera in the Bahamas.

While living at Governor's Harbour on Eleuthera, Rosita Forbes acquired property and invested approximately $60,000/$70,000 at the time in the development of her residence which was called the *Unicorn*. She resided next door to Alfred and Ruth de Marigny.

One of the problems that developed for Ms. Forbes on Eleuthera and eventually caused her to become well known to de Marigny, was the fact that it was her understanding that she was to receive her water rights from de Marigny's property. However, this was not de Marigny's understanding and as a result he was called to Government House, where a face to face meeting between de Marigny and the Duke of Windsor developed. De Marigny finally retained his water rights and Ms. Forbes was obliged to make her own arrangements for her water supply.

It would appear that it was at this meeting with the Duke of Windsor that Alfred de Marigny described the Duke of Windsor to the Duke's Aide de Camp, as *nothing more than a pimple on the ass of the British Empire.*

This run-in with the Duke of Windsor would be one of a number that de Marigny would have over the years. As Alfred de Marigny said to me, "*The Duke of Windsor was not my best friend,*" and he felt that these types of encounters most likely led to his being charged with the murder of his father-in-law Sir Harry Oakes.

Approximately one month following his arrest for the murder of Sir Harry Oakes, Alfred de Marigny was known to have sold his three houses, together with 101 acres of land that he owned at Governor's Harbour, to a development company headed by Rollie Symonette.

Symonette was a member of the Bahamian House of Assembly in Nassau and a fellow sailor with Alfred de Marigny and commodore of the Nassau Yacht Club, which de Marigny helped establish.

A few days following his acquittal, de Marigny happened to pass by Symonette's office down by the harbour and during their conversation, he noticed a roll of beautiful one inch hemp rope on the floor. Upon commenting on it to Symonette, de Marigny was informed that the rope was his. De Marigny asked him what he meant and Symonette said — *it was a special order from Hallinan (the Attorney General). I imagine he had something in mind for it, if you were found guilty.*

De Marigny asked for only a small piece of the rope as a souvenir and for future good luck.

Ernest Miller Hemingway

During his lifetime of travel, Alfred de Marigny met a number of well known individuals and amongst them, was Ernest Hemingway whose friendship he valued both before his arrival in the Bahamas and subsequently following his deportation when he went to Cuba.

Ernest Miller Hemingway was born in July 1899, in Oak Park, a small suburb of Chicago, Illinois, and in 1934, Hemingway heard about the islands of the Bahamas and especially the little Island of Bimini. He subsequently bought himself a boat which he named *Pilar* and set out the next year for the Island of Bimini.

Following the order of deportation from the Bahamas in 1943, Alfred de Marigny and his wife Nancy headed for Cuba where they befriended Ernest Hemingway and his many friends in Havana. De Marigny had originally met Hemingway while crossing from France to America on the French liner Normandie and the two of them became good friends.

During their stay in Havana, the de Marignys visited or were invited on a number of occasions to Hemingway's retreat called Finca and the following are two short quotes relating to their visits with Hemingway.

From Mary Welsh Hemingway's book entitled *How It Was,* written in 1976:

With the appearance of Nancy de Marigny we had new diversions. She was a graceful, dark girl whose father had been mysteriously murdered, and she was on her way to her family home in the Caribbean. She was flirty in a wistful, waiflike way and after dinner showed us ballet steps she had been learning, the Capehart producing accompaniment. We, and especially Bumby, were enchanted, and Ernest and I moved into his room so that she could have my room for the night. A day or so later Bumby, mesmerized by our young guest, announced he was going with her to Miami and on to her Caribbean island. He would return soon, he said.

The reference to *Bumby* is actually to Jack Hemingway, Ernest Hemingway's son, who had a romantic involvement with Nancy Oakes and who considered himself quite the playboy type and became acquainted with Nancy and Alfred de Marigny while they were in Cuba. Jack had many occasions to meet them during their stay.

In a further comment from a book entitled *Ernest Hemingway: A Life Story*, written in 1969, the following passage is quoted in reference to visitors to Hemingway's *Finca*:

On a typical Sunday, besides the ever present jai-alai players and other ex-patriate Basques, one often found visiting a sportman or a writing friend from the north ... and sometimes Nancy Oakes and her husband, Count Freddy Marigny.

On the morning of Sunday July 2nd, 1961, Hemingway ended his life as he tripped the trigger of his double-barrelled shot gun and killed himself, only nineteen days short of his sixty second birthday.

Some Writings and Opinions

Alfred de Marigny thought it best to write a book and did so in 1946 entitled *More Devil Than Saint*, some three years after the murder of his father-in-law Sir Harry Oakes and his subsequent acquital of the charge. De Marigny felt that this was his only means, at that time, of explaining to the world what had happened to him while he was in Nassau and how he was wrongfully charged on July 9th, 1943, with the murder. He had made plans to write the book a few years earlier, but in view of two attempts on his life while living in Havana, he reached agreement with his publisher to postpone publication of the book pending a more opportune time.

In May 1945, while passing through Toronto, Alfred de Marigny said during an interview that he was going to write a book about the case — *I want to put down the facts. The book will be ghost written, but I have already prepared about 200,000 words of notes.* He claimed and confirmed that 11 or 12 witnesses at his trial had changed their statements between the time they signed them before the police and when they testified in court.

They just said they had changed their minds. I want to put down what they swore first and what they testified and ask just why the change was made, said de Marigny.

In the same year a French edition of the book entitled *Ai-je Tué?: Le Monde est Ma Prison* (*Have I Killed?: The World is My Prison*) was published in Montreal and it would appear that de Marigny had written the original text of his book in French and then had it translated into English as *More Devil Than Saint*.

A good part of the book relates to the accusation of murder and the eventual trial, however, the text also provides a very informative background into the life of Alfred de Marigny — from his upbringing on the Islands of Mauritius to his worldwide travels to London, Paris and New York, as well as his romantic adventures.

In 1990, de Marigny wrote the follow-up book entitled *A Conspiracy of Crowns: The True Story of the Duke of Windsor and The Murder of Sir Harry Oakes*, which he felt was needed in order to update and clarify some of the points in his life and as he had said in the closing remarks in his first book — *Perhaps some day before I die, I can write the end of the story. But not now. The story is still unfinished.*

The jacket of the original book made for interesting reading — *the confessions of a modern lothario who lived dangerously, loved not wisely but too well, and faced the gallows for a murder he didn't commit.*

On the back cover there is a short note about de Marigny and refers to him — as *yachtsman, playboy and businessman*, which is indeed a true description of the gentleman.

While on a visit to our Houston office on a project in January 1993, I made a point of telephoning Alfred de Marigny at his home, in the hope that an appointment could be made to meet with him and discuss the contents of my previous letter sent to him in 1991.

In retrospect my original letter to de Marigny was my first attempt at communicating with someone closely associated with the tragic death of Sir Harry Oakes and who else but his own son-in-law, who had been charged with the murder and subsequently acquitted.

If my memory serves me right, I had close to forty questions outlined in my letter, however, as his wife said to me — *Alfred did not like writing and the opportunity of meeting with you, would hopefully make up for it.*

An invitation for me to drop by their temporary residence was gladly accepted on a Saturday evening and a very pleasant time was had, including a wonderful roast beef supper with all the trimmings.

Count Marie Alfred Fouquereaux de Marigny in Houston, Texas.
Courtesy of Mrs. Alfred de Marigny

Alfred de Marigny informed me that he was eighty three years of age and appeared to be in very good health. His facial appearance had not changed from that shown on the back jacket of his book *A Conspiracy of Crowns*.

I thought that he had an outstanding sense of humour and in my estimation he is also a very outspoken individual, when recalling some of the incidents that we discussed, both the humorous ones and at times the more serious ones while he lived in Nassau.

In October 1993, the CBC aired a program entitled *Scales of Justice*, hosted by Edward Greenspan, presenting a further made-for-television presentation on the subject of the life and eventual murder of Sir Harry Oakes and the ensuing trial of his son-in-law Alfred de Marigny. During the closing scenes Alfred de Marigny is interviewed in Rawson Square in Nassau and makes the following statement regarding the murder and the involvement of Harold Christie in Oakes' tragic death:

Sir Harry Oakes had no power to license casinos. It would have been ratified by the Government in Nassau and local politicians.

Christie and the Duke were the persons to deal with. Furthermore it was public knowledge that Sir Harry had already decided to move his family and his wealth to Mexico. Finally the idea of Sir Harry going off in a storm at midnight to a special meeting with a Mafia figure on a boat is ludicrous. Among other things, when the body was found in the

114

morning, his false teeth were in a glass by the side of the bed. No one goes off to a meeting without his teeth.

He did not leave Westbourne that night. This is my opinion.

At this point further comments are made by Edward Greenspan and then de Marigny resumes his commentary as follows:

More than one individual acting on behalf of Harold Christie killed Sir Harry.
Why? Christie was a promoter. Used and misused Oakes' money on many land deals. He was also involved with Oakes and the Duke of Windsor in money laundering deals with Axel Wenner-Gren in Mexico City in violation of wartime British currency restrictions.
When Oakes discovered that Christie had swindled him in several matters, he decided to take steps to collapse Christie's empire. His intention sealed his own death warrant. Christie and his co-conspirators needed a fall guy.
I was an outsider and fit the bill to a T.

In defense of the accusations brought forth by Alfred de Marigny against Harold Christie, his nephew Percy Christie in Nassau made the following statement as part of the presentation:

Alfred de Marigny has accused Sir Harold Christie of murdering Sir Harry Oakes.
In Sir Harold's defense, he was renowned for the fairness of all his dealings and it was accepted by all concerned that he was not capable of such a murder and had no motive for it. Further he would not have enjoyed the many friends and clients that he had all over the world in business and politics if he were in any way the type of man de Marigny described, whereas de Marigny was deported on the unanimous recommendation of the jury as 'undesirable'.

As you may recall the recommendation of the Jury for de Marigny's deportation was based on the fact that they had the position of a hung jury, with four members being Plymouth Brethren who had voted him guilty, not of the murder of Sir Harry Oakes, but of the fact that he did not observe the day of the Lord. It would appear that Percy Christie did not read Alfred de Marigny's last book, otherwise he would not have made such a statement about de Marigny's deportation.

It was always Alfred de Marigny's contention that there was no love lost between himself and the Duke of Windsor and this fact was also mentioned in his second autobiography written in 1990.

De Marigny first met the Duke of Windsor at the Ascot races in England and again when he was invited to a social gathering at Charles Bedeaux's chateau in France, with the third meeting to be in the Bahamas aboard Dr. Axel Wenner-Gren's yacht the *Southern Cross* in Nassau Harbour.

There were a number of occasions when de Marigny would almost go out of his way to upset the Duke of Windsor and one of them occurred when a fire at a Nassau liquor store prompted the owner to have a warehouse sale. De Marigny knew the owner very well and also the fact that there were five cases of Hennessy Five-Star cognac, which came from occupied France and were to be auctioned off. Alfred told his friend to run the ad on one of the last pages of the newspapers, but to just mention the date and time, not the location.

As a result de Marigny came into possession of a good supply of this valuable French cognac, the exact brand that the Duke of Windsor liked and naturally had hoped to purchase at the auction.

A few days later the Duke sent his Aide-de-Camp, George Woods over to visit de Marigny and ask him for a few bottles of the cognac. De Marigny informed Woods that there was no question of giving the Duke any bottles of the cognac, but that he would be more than pleased to sell him some at a reasonable cost. Insulted with the offer, the ADC returned to Government House.

A week or so later, de Marigny sent the Duke two bottles of the Hennessy cognac with his compliments, enclosing his business card. Interestingly enough the Duke of Windsor acknowledged the gift and sent de Marigny a note of thanks.

Another incident happened when the Hollywood movie star Madeleine Carroll visited Nassau on the occasion of the première of the movie that she starred in with Sterling Hayden, entitled *Bahamas Passage*.

The movie was premièred at the Savoy Theater in Nassau on December 11th, 1941, with the Duke and Duchess of Windsor in attendance, as the guests of honour. The proceeds of the evening went in support of the Bahamas War Committee fund raising efforts.

Following her arrival in Nassau, Madeleine Carroll was at the Prince George Hotel one evening when she happened to overhear de Marigny and his friend Georges de Visdelou speaking in French which intrigued her, as she herself had a good knowledge of French and loved the language. Ms. Carroll invited them over to her table where the necessary introductions followed.

As the friendship progressed that evening, she told de Marigny that the Duke of Windsor had planned a reception at Sir Harry's British Colonial Hotel following the premiere of her movie the next evening. Ms. Carroll was not up to another one of those cocktail parties at which point she and de Marigny made plans to return to his residence with Georges and Sterling Hayden following the première.

When I met de Marigny in 1993, he described to me the events that followed to the effect that as Ms. Carroll left the theater and ran across the street, Sir Harry followed by Harold Christie and the Duke of Windsor's Aide-de-Camp, George Woods ran in hot pursuit of Ms. Carroll trying to catch up with her and persuade her to go with them to the planned reception. She turned around and told her followers that she was going with de Marigny and his friend Georges.

Needless to say this little incident further estranged the relationship between de Marigny and the Duke of Windsor.

Alfred de Marigny said to me that following his marriage to Nancy Oakes, Sir Harry informed him that it was not appropriate for him and Nancy to avoid appearing at functions at Government House whenever the Duke of Windsor extended invitations to them. De Marigny's response was that these receptions *were not his cup of tea* and he preferred not to attend. Needless to say this attitude upset Sir Harry and their absences at various functions were no doubt noticed by the Duke himself.

While Alfred de Marigny was acquitted on the charges of having murdered his father-in-law by a verdict of 9-3, the Jury recommended to Sir Oscar Daly, the presiding Judge, that de Marigny be deported from the Bahamas as an *undesirable.*

In the excitement following the announcement of the *not guilty* verdict by James Sands, the Jury foreman, no one heard the Jury's subsequent recommendation of deportation.

Sir Oscar explained to Mr. Sands that it was not within his jurisdiction to act on the Jury's recommendation, but that the matter would be referred to the Attorney General for whatever action would be deemed appropriate by him.

In this regard I quote directly from the closing minutes of Sir Oscar's hand written notes under date of November 11th, 1943, which read as follows: *Foreman states jury consider Colonel Lindop should have been called. Foreman states unanimous recommendation of the jury that the accused be deported immediately.* There is definitely no mention of Georges de Visdelou in the recommendation, though many authors have been misled with this information and have included Georges in the recommendation.

It is possible that Georges de Visdelou's departure from the Bahamas almost at the same time as de Marigny's, may have been a subsequent recommendation of the Attorney General after the fact, as both de Marigny and de Visdelou were considered a challenge to the socialites in Nassau and also to the Duke of Windsor.

At first de Marigny made it very clear that he would challenge and fight the deportation order. He and Nancy subsequently left the Bahamas on December 6th, 1943, for Havana, Cuba, where their exile would begin and de Marigny himself would never return to the Bahamas until 1990, when he and his wife would be invited back by the Bahamian Government.

Prior to his departure many efforts were made by the Duke of Windsor in contacting London to find a means of transportation to fly de Marigny back to the Island of Mauritius. However, as Britain was involved in wartime activities there were certainly no flights available between these two locations and the response from London was a negative one. Under the circumstances, de Marigny made his own arrangement and left for Havana, Cuba, where he would again meet up with his friend Ernest Hemingway.

De Marigny confirmed that he had received a telegram from Commandante Miranda, Under-Secretary of State in Havana, who was also a great Star Class yachtsman, informing him that he could have his passport visaed for Cuba and to bring his yacht, but he had sold the yacht to raise funds for his defense. Nancy was to accompany him to Cuba.

De Marigny and Nancy settled in Havana and some time later she would herself head for Montreal where she would again meet up with Alfred a year or so later.

Meanwhile de Marigny remained in Cuba and at one point joined on as a third mate aboard the *Kelowna Park*, a Canadian merchant ship which was due to head out for Canada.

As the story goes, the ship hit a stray mine during its crossing and as a result of the damage inflicted, headed for repairs in Halifax, Nova Scotia. While the ship was docked in Halifax, de Marigny received a thirty day shore leave and headed immediately for Montreal to meet up with Nancy.

While in Montreal de Marigny made application to the Canadian Immigration authorities in the hope of eventually settling in Canada as an immigrant. However, the Acting Immigration Commissioner who interviewed him commented to the effect that — *under present wartime regulations the only class of immigrants accepted are either British subjects or American citizens who are bonafide agriculturists with sufficient capital to establish themselves in this country.* A rather unusual statement under the circumstances.

He was eventually refused admission to Canada and was to be deported. In the interim he was held in the Immigration jail, but two Montreal Jewish businessmen, Harry Rajinsky and Moses Miller, came forward and posted the necessary cash bond of $50,000 for his release pending the final hearing of his application.

De Marigny wondered why these two gentlemen came to his assistance and it was only after speaking with them one evening at dinner, that he realized that some years before, he was instrumental in assisting them with the escape from Germany of one of their friends Edith Meyer. He had last seen her in Paris some nine years earlier.

Alfred de Marigny made several visits to Montreal and established himself with the Jewish community where he had many friends. This close rapport is further evidenced by the fact that the dedication of his last book *A Conspiracy of Crowns* read in part as follows:

.... and to Montreal's Jewish community of the mid-forties, led by Moses Miller, Philip Joseph and Harry Rajinsky. In the darkest hours of my life, they defined for me the word friend.

In 1990 de Marigny made a return visit to Montreal on the occasion of the launching of his latest book and looked up Moses Miller and Harry Rajinsky, however, their names had disappeared from any telephone directory reference. He took the opportunity, however, to visit the site of the apartment building on Lincoln Street in downtown Montreal, where he had lived for three years before eventually leaving Canada.

The island country of Mauritius comprises the Mauritius and Rodrigues Islands located in the Indian Ocean some five hundred miles east of the Madagascar coast, and covering 788 square miles. Port Louis is the largest city and its capital.

The Island of Mauritius is subject to a subtropical climate very much like that of the Bahamas and it was from Mauritius that Alfred de Marigny first left for Europe, having lived most of his younger days by the ocean.

English is now the official language, but French and Creole were and are still spoken by many of the citizens. Alfred de Marigny learned all his French in Mauritius and as a result inherited from Oakes the nickname of *Frenchie*.

De Marigny's cousin Georges de Visdelou also came from Mauritius, as did Col. Reginald Erskine-Lindop, Commissioner of the Bahamas Police at the time of the murder.

Another friend of Alfred de Marigny was John Anderson, who was said to have worked personally for Dr. Axel Wenner-Gren, the Swedish industrialist and millionaire, who lived in his estate on Paradise Island. Anderson was also the General Manager of the Bahamas General Trust in Nassau.

On the morning that the murder of Sir Harry Oakes was discovered, it was from Anderson that Alfred de Marigny first heard the news of his tragic death, as they passed each other on West Bay Street in Nassau.

As de Marigny and his wife Nancy were about to leave Nassau in December 1943, following the deportation order recommended by the Jury and acted upon by the Attorney General, it is said that Anderson paid de Marigny eight hundred pounds in settlement of an original debt of one thousand pounds. De Marigny gladly accepted, in view of his own financial circumstances at the time as a result of the expenses surrounding the trial.

It is also interesting to note that John Anderson's name made it into the now declassified files of the Federal Bureau of Investigation, as recorded in an FBI agent's memorandum to his director dated October 23rd, 1943. (see last pages of Chapter 13)

8

The Murder of the Century — As It Was Called

The Year Was Nineteen Forty Three ..... Dinner Guests at Alfred de Marigny's Party ..... Dinner Guests at Sir Harry Oakes' Party ..... Harold Christie — Harry's Best Friend or So They Say ..... Dorothy Macksey — Harold's Fateful Secretary ..... Frank Christie ..... Charles Herman Hubbard ..... Mrs. Dulcibel Effie Henneage ..... Sally Sawyer and Veronica McMahon ..... July 8th, 1943 — A Day Like Any Other Day in Nassau? ..... The Murder of Sir Harry Oakes ..... The Murder Scene — Some Comments ..... Sir Harry Oakes — The Head Wounds ..... Hair Singeing — A Clue to the Murderer ..... Some Small Fires ..... Blood: Pool Patterns: Spill Patterns: Impact Spatters ..... Exhibit J — The Famous Little Fingerprint ..... Lividity — Part of the Death Scene Evaluation ..... Rigor Mortis ..... Murderer or Murderers? — Some Theories ..... A Murder Weapon – Again A Few Theories ..... Palo Mayombe — A Voodoo Theory ..... Rawlins — One of Two Night Watchmen ..... Who Knew Sir Harry Was Leaving the Island? ..... Dr. Leonard Huggins ..... Dr. Lawrence Wylie Fitzmaurice ..... Dr. Ulrich Ricky Oberwarth ..... Dr. Hugh Arnley Quackenbush ..... Col. Reginald Alexander Erskine-Lindop ..... Major Herbert Pemberton ..... Col. Frederick Lancaster ..... Lieutenant John Campbell Douglas ..... Elizabeth Betty Renner ..... Cyril St.John Stevenson — A Last Attempt to Investigate the Murder ..... Sir Oswald Raynor Arthur ..... Edward Majava — Another Witness ..... Lord Beaverbrook — Did You Do It Harold? ..... Evalyn Walsh McLean — The Hope Diamond

---

Aside from the fact that the murder of Sir Harry Oakes occured in the Bahamas in 1943 and took up a good portion of the news headlines around the world on July 8th of that year, other events happened that may be of interest to some.

At the movies, *Casablanca* with Humphrey Bogart, Ingrid Bergman, Paul Henreid, Claude Rains, Conrad Veidt, Sydney Greenstreet and Peter Lorre, won the Oscar for best movie with Paul Lukas winning an Oscar as Best Actor for his part in the movie *Watch on the Rhine* and Jennifer Jones as Best Actress for her part in *The Song of Bernadette*.

In the music field some of the top songs or melodies for that year were *Oklahoma; Surrey with the Fringe on Top; Shoo Shoo Baby; Oh What A Beautiful Morning* and *Mairzy Doats*, with the latter song comprising some *unusual lyrics* which went as follows:

> *Mares eat oats and does eat oats,*
> *And little lambs eat ivy,*
> *A kid will eat ivy too,*
> *Wouldn't you ?*

In the sports world, the Detroit Red Wings hockey club won the Stanley cup; the Chicago Bears took the professional football title in the United States; the Kentucky Derby was won by a horse called *Count Fleet* ridden by jockey Johnny Longden and last but not least the World Series was won by New York of the American League.

The U.S. Open golf tournament and the Indianapolis 500 motor car race were not held that year due to the war. In the world of beauty pageants, one Jean Bartel of Los Angeles, California, won the title of Miss America.

During the week of July 4th, the movie *Flight for Freedom* starring Rosalind Russell and Fred MacMurray was playing at the Savoy theatre in Nassau, while *Once Upon a Honeymoon* with Cary Grant and Ginger Rogers was playing at the Nassau theatre.

The Allied armed forces had begun to land in Sicily in preparation for the eventual invasion of Italy which was then underway.

Marshall Vasselevski of Russia appeared on the cover of Time magazine for that week.

The brutal murder of Sir Harry Oakes made headline news in many newspapers around the world and in some cases relegated the news of the Allied invasion to the sideline.

In 1943, prices showed the cost of a new car at $900 and a new house at $3,600. A loaf of bread was going for a mere ten cents, a gallon of gas was only fifteen cents and a gallon of milk was sixty two cents.

Of interest to those in Kirkland Lake, was the fact that gold was traded on average at $35 an ounce during that year, which is interesting when one looks back and remembers that Sir Harry Oakes gave shares in his Lake Shore Mines as payments for food and other needs — the shares were then accepted at various prices going as high as fifty cents.

On the evening of July 7th, 1943, Alfred de Marigny hosted a dinner party at his home on Victoria Avenue in Nassau, though his wife Nancy was away at the Martha Graham School of Dance in Bennington, Vermont for health reasons at the suggestion of her doctor.

Over the years there has always been some confusion concerning the number of guests at the dinner party on that evening and the following are the names of those as testified by de Marigny at the trial:

Alfred de Marigny	Georges de Visdelou
Mrs. Dorothy Clarke (*)	Mrs. Jean Ainslie (*)
Freddie Ceretta	Oswald Moseley
Betty Roberts	Donald McKinney
Mr. & Mrs. Alva Brooks	Mrs. King

(*) Dorothy Clarke and Jean Ainslie lived in *Cottage Number Two* at the *Hubbard Cottages*, which was situated next door to Sir Harry's *Westbourne* estate and de Marigny drove the two ladies home on that particular evening.

De Marigny felt he had room for one more guest that evening and called Harold Christie earlier in the day, but he declined the invitation and supposedly told de Marigny that he would be at Sir Harry's residence for dinner and spending the night there.

Apparently nothing unusual or exciting happened during the course of the evening at de Marigny's home, with the exception of the occasional power failure due to the tropical storm, which led de Marigny to light some hurricane lamps at which point he suffered burns to his hand.

Little did de Marigny and some of his guests realize that evening, that they would soon be involved as witnesses in what would be considered the *murder of the century* and participate in one of the greatest criminal trials ever held in the Bahamas.

It is interesting to note that John Anderson, a close friend of Alfred de Marigny, was not at his party the previous evening, however, the very next morning who should de Marigny come across while driving along West Bay Street, but Anderson himself. Anderson informed him about Sir Harry's death. How did Anderson first hear about it and where was he coming from at mid morning?

On the same afternoon and evening as the party at de Marigny's home on July 7th, Sir Harry Oakes also hosted a gathering of some of his friends at his *Westbourne* estate which comprised the following:

Sir Harry Oakes	Harold Christie
Charles Hubbard	Dulcibel 'Babs' Henneage
Sally Sawyer (*)	Veronica McMahon (*)

(*) Ms. Sawyer and Ms. McMahon played tennis with Sir Harry and Harold Christie in the afternoon. Afterwards they sat on the veranda, enjoyed some refreshments and left before the other guests arrived.

Oakes' dinner party started around 8.30 p.m. and lasted till approximately 11.00 p.m., following which Sir Harry and Harold Christie retired for the night in separate and almost adjoining bedrooms on the second floor at 11.30 p.m., prior to which they had a general discussion in Sir Harry's room as he would be leaving shortly for Bar Harbor, Maine, to rejoin Lady Eunice and the children for the remainder of the summer.

Mrs. Henneage and Charles Hubbard had already departed.

Enid Fernandez, the Oakes' cook, and Mabel Ellis, the Oakes' maid, were in attendance during the evening and following the clean-up of the kitchen, left for their respective homes in east end Nassau.

A gentleman whom I met in Toronto a number of years ago made a comment to the effect that he understood that the Duke and Duchess of Windsor were also present at the dinner party at Sir Harry Oakes' estate. A subsequent newspaper clipping also mentions that possibility, but in all cases the comments would appear to be just hearsay as there is no definite proof that they were present at Sir Harry's home that evening.

Word was that the Duke and Duchess spent the evening at Government House with some friends, and played cards. Around ten o'clock following the departure of their guests, the Duchess told the Duke to finish his cigar and cognac, at which point they retired for the evening.

It would appear that all of the leading players on the island had now been accounted for — or so we hoped.

Harold Christie's father was a member of the Plymouth Brethren religious group and it is interesting to note that four members of the Jury at the trial of Alfred de Marigny were also members of this group. It is said that they were responsible for adding the recommendation to the verdict of acquittal, that Alfred de Marigny be deported from the Bahamas as an *undesirable*.

It was always Christie's claim that the murder of Sir Harry was committed by a voodoo priest out of jealously, but the actual scenario of how the murder was committed has never been discussed by him. Interestingly enough no one has ever asked him for his opinion except Lord Beaverbrook some years later, but without any results.

There has been mention that Harold Christie had a police record and that he had also benefited from the rum-running days of Prohibition, as did many of the other Bay Street Boys.

Harold Christie, Nassau real estate entrepreneur and close friend of Sir Harry Oakes. *CP Picture Archive*

Keeping in mind what has been said above, it would be of interest for the reader to refer to the comments which appear in the *Federal Bureau of Investigation* memorandum dated October 23rd, 1943, as there is definitely some official reference to Christie and a possible criminal record in the United States. (see last pages of Chapter 13)

It was Alfred de Marigny's contention that by the spring of 1943, Christie was well indebted financially to Sir Harry Oakes and that Christie had doubled-crossed him regarding the transaction on the sale of land which would become a new military airfield at the west end of the island.

As a matter of interest, it is noted that Christie also slept at *Westbourne* on Sunday, July 4th and again on Tuesday, July 6th — the previous night.

On the question of Harold Christie having slept in the bed at Sir Harry's estate on the night of the murder, it was reported in the *Miami Herald* on October 23rd, 1943, that

Major Herbert Pemberton during a cross-examination by the Defense remarked that, "*It was not heavily ruffled, but someone had lain there because there was an indentation on the pillow.*"

In addition Sir Oscar Daly, the Presiding Judge, asked the question, "W*ere the sheets rumpled?*" — to which Pemberton replied, "*Very little.*"

We should at this point bring up the question of Harold Christie's part in the trial of Alfred de Marigny, as Christie was one of the first witnesses to be called by the Prosecution. It must also be remembered that quite possibly Christie was the last person to see Oakes alive that evening (except for the murderer or murderers) and the first person to see him dead the following morning. His testimony set the scene of what pretty well happened that fateful night — at least according to Harold Christie.

Christie maintained when he was cross-examined by the Defense, that he had spent the night at Sir Harry's estate regardless of the fact that the only things that disturbed him during that night were the sound of buzzing mosquitoes and a few thunderclaps, which in both cases awakened him, all this while his closest friend was being murdered in a room some sixteen feet away.

It appeared that there was no question of his having left *Westbourne* according to his testimony, contrary to the statement made by Alfred de Marigny in his last book to the effect that Harold Christie was seen leaving the estate on his own by two night watchmen and heading in the direction of downtown Nassau.

Christie's appearance in the witness box was described as that of a very nervous gentleman, who would continuously wipe the prespiration off his forehead and at one point Erle Stanley Gardner, who was representing the Hearst newspapers during the trial, noted that Christie took almost ten to fifteen seconds before answering some questions put to him by Godfrey Higgs. In a quiet Court House such a delay seemed to last an eternity.

H. G. Christie Ltd., Harold Christie's home away from home. *Author's collection*

On May 2nd, 1962, Harold Christie's American born secretary, sixty year old Dorothy Macksey was murdered, adding fuel to the allegations of the keepers of the Oakes' legend that Miss Macksey had come to — *know too much about the Oakes murder and was eliminated.*

On May 18th, 1962, it was reported in the press that Harold Christie had posted a $2,800 reward for any information relative to Miss Macksey's murder. A similar amount had previously been posted by the Bahamian Government.

An interesting note was that Miss Macksey's clothing was sent over to the Metro Crime Laboratory in Dade County, Florida for analysis and forensic testing. It was not until 1980 that a proper Forensic Science Laboratory was set up in the Bahamas.

Officers from Scotland Yard arrived in Nassau in June of 1962, in a further attempt to re-open the investigation into the murder of Sir Harry, as well as the tragic murder of Miss Macksey. As reported in the London Daily Express, the officers received — *a lack of co-operation from local police officials and a polite unwillingness of local residents to help.*

Frank Christie was the brother of Harold Christie and was also involved in the real estate business as manager of H. G. Christie Real Estate in Nassau.

On the morning that Harold Christie discovered Sir Harry's body, he immediately called his brother Frank to tell him what had happened and to come out immediately, however, Harold in the excitement neglected to tell Frank where he was. As Frank drove out along West Bay Street he noted that cars had gathered outside Oakes' *Westbourne* estate and surmised that this was the place. Or did he already know?

Charles Hubbard was a retired Woolworth executive, who moved from London, England, to Nassau, and became a neighbour of Sir Harry Oakes. He owned the *Labouchere Estates*, which were situated two properties over from Sir Harry's *Westbourne* estate on West Bay Street at a distance estimated to be five hundred feet. The estate is better known as the *Hubbard Cottages.*

Hubbard, while living near Sir Harry, was not a frequent visitor and prior to the dinner party on that fateful evening, had only visited with him on two or three occasions.

On the evening in question, he arrived at Oakes' *Westbourne* estate with Mrs. Dulcibel Henneage around 7.00 p.m. and left with her at 11.00 p.m. to drive her home, returning to his residence at 11.45 p.m.

The following morning at 7.30 a.m., Hubbard received a call from an excited Harold Christie over at *Westbourne* asking him to come over immediately. As he arrived at the scene on his bicycle, Dr. Hugh Quackenbush was also arriving. Hubbard remained at *Westbourne* for a few moments, then returned to his residence. There was no apparent need for his presence and there is no indication why Christie called him over in the first place.

During his testimony at the trial, Hubbard remarked that Sir Harry was in a jovial and high spirited mood on the evening of the dinner party, no doubt in preparation for his departure to rejoin his family in Bar Harbor, Maine.

Some years after the murder, Charles Hubbard also met a tragic death when he lost control of his car and crashed into a *casuarina* tree as he drove along West Bay Street outside his home.

A close friend of Harold Christie was Mrs. Dulcibel Henneage who was described as the wife of a British Army officer, assigned to the War Office in London. She was classified as an English evacuee living in Nassau, together with their two children and had rented a cottage near Harold Christie's home in east end Nassau.

She was normally referred to under the nickname *Babs* or *Effie* and was considered as a pretty woman in her late twenties, rather young in comparison to Harold Christie's age at the time.

Prior to her invitation to dinner at Sir Harry's on the evening of July 7th, she had spent the afternoon with Charles Hubbard at his home next door to Oakes, in company of her two children and a nurse, who subsequently went home later that afternoon with the children.

Mrs. Henneage and Charles Hubbard then proceeded to Sir Harry's residence for drinks and eventual supper.

Her name was often linked to being the *mistress* in a relationship she supposedly had with Harold Christie, which led to the question, who was she really romantically involved with — Christie or Charles Hubbard? In order to settle this question I asked Alfred de Marigny during a conversation one day, to which he confirmed that indeed she was Christie's *lady friend*.

She apparently lived at *Porter House* located on East Bay Street and this could quite possibly explain the statement made by Capt. Edward Sears, to the effect that he saw Harold Christie driving in downtown Nassau on the evening of the murder, as it would be necessary to go through Nassau in order to head out to her residence.

There always appeared to be the question that remained unanswered as to whether Harold Christie did indeed leave *Westbourne* the night of the murder to visit with Mrs. Henneage afterwards. The records show that she was called as a witness, however, the cross-examination merely concerned her presence at and departure time from Sir Harry's dinner party.

It would seem that one of the Defense attorneys could have easily asked Mrs. Henneage in a discreet manner, as to her activities that night after being driven home by Charles Hubbard, in an attempt to establish Harold Christie's whereabouts which was most crucial. The question — *did you see anyone else later that night*? could have blown the case wide open depending on the answer.

Sally Sawyer and a friend, Veronica McMahon had played tennis with Sir Harry Oakes and Harold Christie at the Bahamas Country Club on the afternoon before the murder, next door to *Westbourne* estate.

Sally was Harold Christie's niece. Very little is known about her, nor whether she lived in the Bahamas or was merely visiting with her uncle in Nassau at the time. Following the tennis match, Sally and Veronica left the party before the other guests Charles Hubbard and Mrs. Dulcibel Henneage arrived to join Sir Harry and Christie for dinner.

Even though Sally Sawyer was one of the guests at Sir Harry's estate during the afternoon prior to the murder, she was never called upon to testify concerning her presence at *Westbourne* that afternoon or for that matter to possibly provide an opinion on the disposition of Sir Harry and Harold Christie or the other guests on the afternoon leading up to that fateful night.

We must now proceed to the morning of July 8th, 1943, — possibly a day like any other day in Nassau, or so everyone thought.

However, on this particular morning, the number one citizen of the Bahamas and the richest Baronet in the British Empire, Sir Harry Oakes, would be found bludgeoned to death in his bed at his palatial *Westbourne* estate in Nassau at approximately 7.30 a.m. by his very best friend Harold Christie, who had been an overnight guest.

Original plans were for Sir Harry to play a game of golf with the Duke of Windsor in the morning, to be followed later with a tour of Oakes' new sheep farm, together with

Etienne Dupuch of the *Tribune* and Raymond Moss of the *Nassau Guardian*. A tour which had been organized by Harold Christie.

Prior to leaving the office on his way to see Sir Harry, Dupuch called *Westbourne* to confirm the appointment for later that day, but Harold Christie answered the phone and at that point proceeded to inform Dupuch that Oakes was dead. Dupuch asked Christie to confirm what he had just said and then proceeded in his capacity as a newspaperman to advise the outside world of what had happened.

The estimated time of death according to medical consultation was set at between 2.30 a.m. and 5.00 a.m. and Christie had supposedly slept in the second bedroom down from Sir Harry's room, a distance of some sixteen to seventeen feet away. Close enough no doubt for Christie to hear any unusual sounds emanating from Oakes bedroom and smell any smoke from the fires that had been set, which no doubt must have blown around in view of the tropical storm outside.

According to Christie the windows at *Westbourne* were not always kept closed and depending on the direction of the storm, no doubt a number of them would normally have

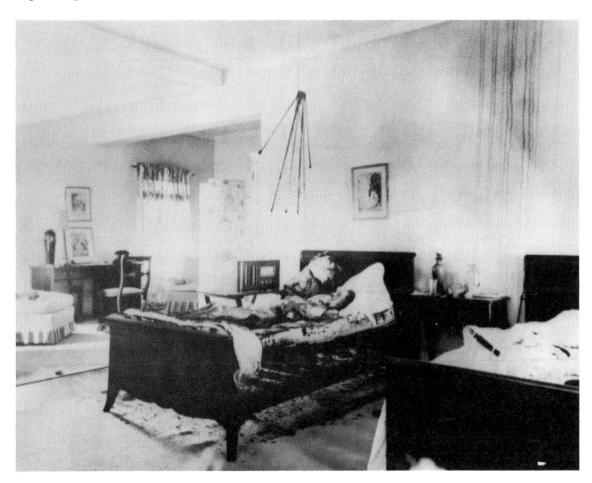

View of the bed from the north side with body. *Corbis Images*

been left open. The rooms in question ran from north to south and as was usually the case, the storm would have most likely come from the northeast side — which was the ocean side. As a result there is every possibility that some of the smoke would have filtered through to Harold Christie's room.

Sir Harry's entire family was off the island at the time, with Lady Oakes at their home, the *Willows* in Bar Harbor, Maine; Shirley with two of her three brothers, William and Harry Jr., were also with their mother, while Nancy (Alfred de Marigny's wife) was at the Martha Graham School of Dance in Bennington, Vermont. Sydney was said to be at the Oakes' residence in Kirkland Lake, Ontario.

When the body was found by Harold Christie it was lying horizontally on its back and diagonally across the bed in a west-to-east position. A close-up photograph of the wounds to Sir Harry's head showed that blood had flowed from the proximity of the left ear,

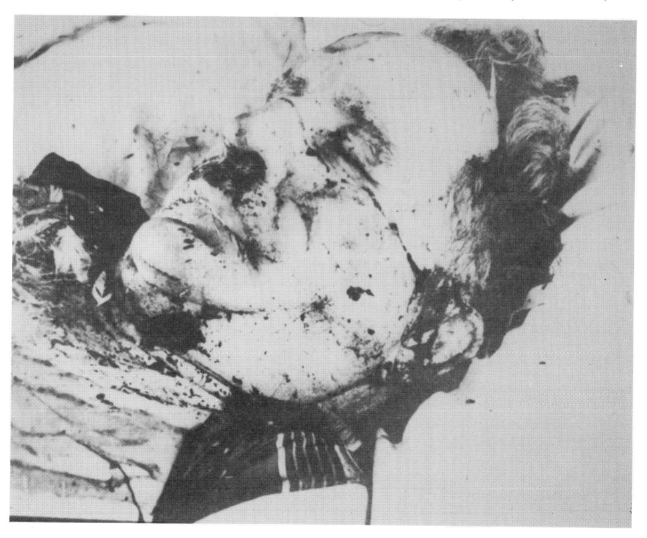

Close-up of the head wounds to Sir Harry Oakes. *Archive Photos*

across the left cheek and over the bridge of the nose. We must remember that the blood was as a result of injuries originally inflicted above the left ear and more precisely as four triangularly shaped wounds. It is therefore obvious from the position that the body was found in, that the flow of blood defied the laws of gravity, which in this case would normally have run down the back of Sir Harry's neck and onto the pillows or sheets.

It is understood from consultation by the author with medical personnel and books, that for the blood to coagulate, a time period of approximately two to three minutes would be required under normal circumstances. In this case it would have meant that quite possibly the murder took place away from the bed, either somewhere in the room itself near the entrance or immediately outside the room and that Sir Harry's body was at one point in a face down position, but in my estimation definitely not away from the site of *Westbourne* as many an author has surmised. Quite possibly the coagulation may have taken a little longer than normal due to the humid climatic conditions prevailing in Nassau and occurring in particular during and after storms, which is common in the Bahamas and the islands.

There are theories that the murder took place outside of *Westbourne* and during an interview with a gentleman in Nassau in April 1992, he seemed to imply that the murder quite possibly took place up at Lyford Cay and that the body was taken back to *Westbourne* by motor launch. The driver of the motor launch was indicated to be a close business associate of Oakes in Nassau and quite familiar with the rugged shoreline from Lyford Cay to the Cable Beach area and to the landing at *Westbourne*. The night watchman who was on duty at Lyford Cay at the time of the incident was well known to this gentleman to whom I spoke. Other stories say there were two night watchmen at Lyford Cay and that both of them were found dead shortly after Sir Harry's murder occurred. By contrast, in the case of the sole watchman theory, he seemed to have led a normal life and died of natural causes.

In contradiction to the above statements is the fact that according to the transcript of the trial there is mention that a pair of Sir Harry's white pants and a shirt were found on the bed next to the one he was sleeping in, all without any indication of blood stains. This is further substantiated by a photo of the room showing a second bed in the background on which you can actually see the pair of white pants, with a black belt and a shirt. This was considered proper attire for playing tennis in those days. Based on this information and evidence, it would appear that Oakes never left *Westbourne* and possibly rose to meet his attacker or attackers, following which he may have been struck on the head and fallen to the floor.

As the body of Sir Harry Oakes was removed from the bed, a copy of the *Miami Herald* was found on the bed where he lay. It would appear that quite possibly under these circumstances Sir Harry rose from his bed to investigate a noise and threw the newspaper back on the bed, which would be a normal reaction. He could have been lying on the bed or sitting in the chair at the time; however, Christie's testimony says that Oakes was on the bed when he left him to go to his own room that evening.

As one may recall there were blood stains on certain areas of the doors and walls which may explain that a possible struggle with the assailant(s) in the hallway may have occurred and that Oakes was then forced back into the bedroom.

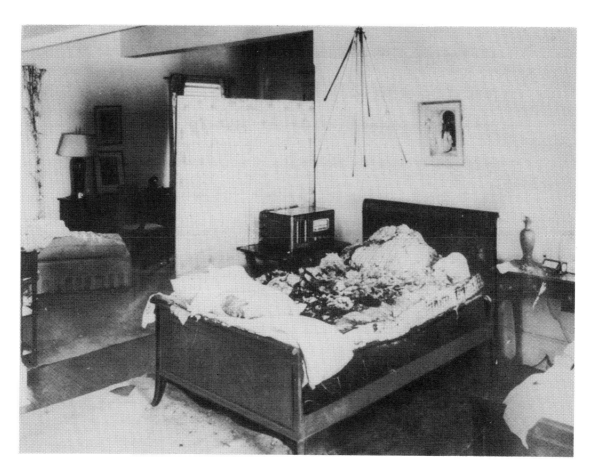

View of the bed from the north side following removal of body. *Archive Photos*

It is understood that the portion of *Westbourne* where the master bedroom was located was of all wood construction and would certainly have carried the sound of someone coming up the stairs and walking along the veranda or hallway, which could have awakened Sir Harry.

The final medical verdict of the death of Sir Harry Oakes was that death was caused by shock, haemorrhage around the brain and fracture of the skull. No one has ever challenged the cause of death.

An attempt was made to obtain a copy of the death certificate, but the only document available was a copy of the *death record* issued by the local funeral home in Dover-Foxcroft, which for personal reasons is not reproduced in this manuscript.

During an interview on the Canadian CTV program W5 in 1990, Alfred de Marigny was asked a question relative to the fact that how could Harold Christie, who was sleeping in a room within sixteen feet of Oakes' room, not hear any of the noise or commotion? As part of his response, de Marigny made a comment to the effect that the walls in the rooms did not reach up to the ceiling level. A rather unusual statement indeed, but such construction is quite possible. There is no photographic evidence of this statement as it pertains to Sir Harry's room.

It would appear almost impossible for Sir Harry to have been murdered outside his estate and the body brought back to *Westbourne*. There is also the question of his false teeth having been found in a glass on the night table between the two beds. In this latter case, no one who wears false teeth would — as the saying goes, *don't leave home without them*.

Following a discussion with Alfred de Marigny in Houston in January 1993, it was still his conviction that Sir Harry Oakes was shot to death. In reading the text of his book and his interview with one of the *surviving* night watchmen it would appear that they should have heard the three or four shots. On the other hand the watchmen were only able to hear the tearing of cloth from their location in a wooden guard shack located a short distance away from the house. The cloth torn could possibly have been the pillow from which the feathers were spread over the body, however, the statement to the effect that they heard such a sound seems rather strange under the circumstances.

If we return to the scene that faced Harold Christie when he opened the door and discovered the limp body, his first reaction was to reach for a pillow from the adjoining bed and place it under the head of Sir Harry in order to prop him up. It was Christie's belief that quite possibly at that time there was still some hope of reviving him and he proceeded to put some water into a glass and pour it into Sir Harry's mouth.

During the trial Godfrey Higgs in his cross examination of Christie, showed him a picture of Sir Harry with the injuries clearly shown on his face. Nevertheless, Christie claimed that he believed that Sir Harry was still alive.

A rather unusual reaction when it would certainly appear that Sir Harry was dead. To add to the melodrama of the scene, Christie then went for a towel in the adjoining room, soaked it in water and then returned to the scene of the murder and went about wiping Sir Harry's face, for what purpose at this point will never be known.

Christie appeared to be in a state of shock (if indeed he was) since he continued to run around in his borrowed pyjamas and finally began to seek help. He first called Charles Hubbard, Sir Harry's neighbour who had been a guest the previous evening at the dinner party. He then proceeded to call Dr. Hugh Quackenbush, Col. Reginald Erskine-Lindop and finally Mrs. Madeleine Kelly, wife of Sir Harry's Nassau manager and neighbour of Oakes, who lived in their residence immediately adjoining *Westbourne* estate.

Harold Christie did not have a watch and was unable to tell at what times he was awakened during the night to first kill mosquitoes and for that matter when he supposedly heard thunder claps. How accurate was his timing with regard to when he went to sleep or when he awoke — provided Harold Christie was at *Westbourne* all the time?

We must also establish the scene of the crime as it first appeared and the following is a good description of the condition of the room in which Sir Harry Oakes was found, as given by Major Herbert Pemberton, Acting Deputy Commissioner of the Bahamas Police, one of the first police officers at the scene:

Sir Harry's bedroom showing burn marks on the carpeting and clothes closet, together with potential blood stains. Lines in photo represent someone's accidental cropping of the photo. *Corbis Images*

I saw burnt marks on a green carpet that covered the floor. The door to the hallway had black smudge marks. There were also smudge marks on a clothes closet just inside the door on the left. The portion of the rug near the closet was badly burnt. There were twin beds in the room and the body was on the southern one. On the northern bed I found a pair of white trousers and a shirt. Around Sir Harry's bed, there was a considerable amount of burnt material and the surface of the bed was badly burnt, especially the wooden head at the northwest. The furniture appeared to be in order. An electric fan was in motion at the foot of the northern bed, blowing in a southerly direction. Above the bed was a burnt frame of a mosquito net. Between the two beds there was a small table with a reading lamp, a thermos, a tumbler and a set of false teeth. At the south of the bed was a table with a radio. Running parallel to the bed, approximately three feet away was a large light grey wooden screen. The screen was open and ran almost the full length of the bed. The western end of the screen was recessed into an angle between the wall and a cupboard and it was necessary to go around the eastern end to get to the bed. On the eastern portion of the screen, on the side away from the bed, there were smudge marks.

Famous Chinese screen beside Sir Harry's bed. De Marigny's fingerprint was supposedly taken from the second panel on the right. *Archive Photos*

To the northwest of the L-shaped bedroom there was a bathroom. There was a considerable amount of burnt material on the bathroom floor and in the wash basin. In the northeast corner there was a door that led into a bedroom, then there was another bathroom and another bedroom. The distance from the far bedroom, occupied by Harold Christie, to Sir Harry's room was 16 feet and 11 inches.

There are two other items that were in the room which were not listed in the above scenario and that would be a pair of Sir Harry's reading glasses and a can of insecticide spray, which his maid Mabel Ellis had left on the floor near the northern door when preparing the room.

Aside from the two missing items from Major Pemberton's testimony, it would appear that there is sufficient detail from which a few conclusions can be drawn.

One of the interesting notes is the distance between Sir Harry's room and that in which Harold Christie was, which makes one wonder how Christie *could not have heard any noise* emanating from Oakes' room or for that matter smell any smoke from all the little fires that appear to have been set throughout the room. That is if Christie was indeed in the next room, as some comment was made to the effect that the bed in which Christie supposedly slept, was not exactly ruffled.

The feathers that were spread over Sir Harry's body are often questioned as to whether they were spread on purpose, to give the scene a type of voodoo aspect, or merely part of the actual murder scenario, whereby someone tried to suffocate Sir Harry with the pillow and in the ensuing struggle the pillow was torn.

Some of the main wounds to Sir Harry Oakes' head were those inflicted on the left side and when Dr. Lawrence Fitzmaurice, Acting Chief Medical Officer of the Bahamas was called upon under questioning during the trial, to describe the mortal wounds to Sir Harry's head he provided the following description:

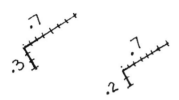

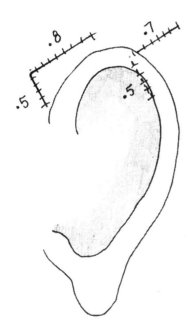

Drawing of head wounds.   *Author's collection*

There was a wound in front of the upper part of the left ear approximately .8 by .5 inches in size. A probe could be inserted in an inner, forward and slightly downward direction approximately a distance of one inch. There was a second wound approximately two inches above the first about .7 by .3 inches in size. A probe could be inserted less than a quarter of an inch (through the scalp only). There was a wound immediately behind the upper lobe of the left ear, approximately .7 by .5 inches in size. A probe inserted in a forward and slightly downward direction went in a considerable distance and seemed to go inside the skull. There was another wound approximately 1.5 inches above the third wound, about .7 by .2 inches in size. A probe could be inserted less than a quarter of an inch. The four wounds were all on the left side. A peculiar feature of the wounds was that they were all somewhat triangular in shape with their apices pointing towards the front of the head. There was evidence that there had been bleeding from all four wounds as well as from the nose and possibly the left ear. There was a slight abrasion on the back edge of the upper lobe of the left ear.

The following comment would be of interest regarding the wounds to Sir Harry's head as described in a book on criminal history relative to gun shot wounds:

At close range, from one to three feet, a more or less triangular wound about 1.5 to 2 inches in diameter could result. There is evidence of scorching and tattooing, also singeing of hair by flame unless the weapon was fired through clothing. Beyond a range of three feet the shot begins to spread out and at four feet the wound appears as a central hole with small perforations around it.

Following the discovery of the body of Sir Harry Oakes, an investigation of the scene of the tragedy revealed that there were numerous signs that fires had been set around the room on the walls, on the floor carpeting, on some pieces of furniture, the guard rails leading up the stairs, plus the fact that the mosquito netting that hung over Sir Harry's bed had also been burned — for some reason the wooden frame survived the fire. Attempts to burn Sir Harry's body were also evident as there were areas of the bed that were burned.

There are two photographs of the crime scene showing the body of Sir Harry on the bed, one is taken from the south side and one from the north side. Upon perusal of the photographs it is obvious that the sheets and covers were completely burned on both sides of the bed and burned in such a way as would seem to indicate that quite possibly a blow torch was used, as the burn marks appear to have been in a back and forth motion.

As a result of these attempts to set the various fires it was the conclusion of Capt. James Barker, that the murderer would have had burn marks on his clothing and on his body, especially on the hands and it was his intention to question anyone who may have been in or near the room.

Barker first examined the hands and hair of Harold Christie, the most likely suspect as he had supposedly spent the night at *Westbourne*, but he did not find any tell tale signs of any burns on him.

Sketch of a blow torch possibly used to set fires in the room and to the victim. *Author's collection*

He next examined Oakes' son-in-law Alfred de Marigny, who was not a suspect at that early stage of the investigation, however, the detectives felt that there may have been some questionable relationship between himself and Oakes, that would have prompted him to want to murder his father-in-law.

According to Capt. Barker's expertise there were four degrees of burns possible under the circumstances: (1) hair subjected to heat sufficient to cause extreme brilliance; (2) tight curling; (3) singeing and (4) burns destroying the hair near the surface of a tissue (this latter stage being easily recognizable by the ash residue adhering to the burnt stump or shaft). Although very technical, this was Barker's professional opinion which he expressed at the trial.

As Barker proceeded with a microscopic examination of de Marigny, he noted some *hair singeing and burns* to his hands, his eyebrows and arms, some singeing to the hair on his head and possibly to his beard. As a result of these possible burn marks, de Marigny was asked to explain how they might have occurred.

At first de Marigny thought that possibly the explanation for the singeing of the hair on his head may have been as a result of a recent haircut at his barber. The other signs of singeing on his hands could possibly have come from having lit some hurricane type lamps or candles during the power failures at the party at his home the evening before; burns may have also resulted from his lighting cigarettes; and further still as a result of his scalding of chickens over the open fires at his chicken farm.

During Captain Barker's cross-examination at the trial by Ernest Callender, he was asked how the fires were set around Sir Harry's room, to which he answered — *"by a match or blow-torch."* *"What kind of torch?"* asked Callender — *"any kind, maybe a piece of paper"* answered Barker.

In an attempt to evaluate the markings on the carpeting on the inside entrance to the bedroom, some black and white photos (only ones available) were shown to a Blood Stain Analyst in the hope of identifying blood pool patterns, blood spill patterns or blood impact spatters.

Following his perusal of the crime scene photos, it was his opinion that some of the stains shown on the carpeting could have been pool patterns of blood, which would have indicated that the body may have lain on the floor immediately inside the door entrance to the bedroom.

A further pool pattern of blood is seen a few feet further in the direction of the Chinese screen past the clothes closet. Splattered between these two pools there appears to be a few droplets of blood.

It would appear from this analysis that possibly Sir Harry's body could have lain face down on the floor and then been dragged or lifted to a second position, thus allowing the blood to run from the ear area, across his left cheek and over the bridge of his nose.

It is interesting to note on closer examination of the photograph of Sir Harry's head that the blood seems to also come down on the right side of the nose, which would possibly indicate that at one point Sir Harry's body may have been lying on its right side after having been dragged along the floor.

According to the testimony at the trial by Captains Barker and Melchen, there were no comments made that any signs of blood spattering were visible anywhere around the crime scene. If there had been, then it would have been obvious that the murder weapon would have been raised at least three times in the air with blood on it, however, this does not appear to be the case and would indicate that the so-called *blunt instrument* did indeed have four possible triangular edges to inflict the wound as described by Dr. Fitzmaurice in one single stroke to the head.

If the crime had been committed while Sir Harry was lying on the bed, there should have been blood stains on the headboard and possibly the ceiling or the remains of the wooden frame of the mosquito net which hung over the bed.

During the trial it was mentioned that mosquito blood was found in Harold Christie's room, which no doubt happened when Christie killed a mosquito during the night when he awoke.

The testimony during the trial also revealed indications of blood stains in the room surrounding the crime scene, as well as in the hallway and stairway and were described as follows:

- *on the north wall of the bedroom, west of the door to Sir Harry's room and about four feet above the floor were several smudged prints of a reddish brown colour, but because of the roughness of the plaster it was impossible to identify the prints;*
- *a telephone book lying on the desk near the south window of Oakes' room had smudge prints and stains of a reddish nature which appeared to be blood;*
- *in the room between Sir Harry's and Christie's, Barker found several small diluted blood spots;*
- *in the far east room (Christie's room) Barker also found a small hand towel which was dirty and had considerable blood stains, which was resting on a small dresser stand.*

One question — is it possible to analyse blood drops as to content i.e., blood and insecticide spray or blood and a blow torch chemical? The answer is yes. However, such facilities were not available at the time. If one could exhume the remains of Sir Harry it is understood that it is still quite possible to find a very minute piece of skin or clothing with possible blood spatters which could be further analysed to determine the chemical content.

The science of fingerprinting is quite an art in itself and one of the challenging aspects of criminal investigation, from fingerprints on little Johnny's stolen bicycle to that on the murder weapon causing the death of a fellow human being.

Fingerprinting encompasses such terms as arches (plain and tented); loops (radial and ulnar); whorls (plain, central pocket, double and accidental); deltas and cores. Some of the terms are quite easy to relate to, but it is only through exposure to fingerprinting tests that one can have an appreciation of its application and identification.

In order to experience this art, I first made a point of having inked fingerprint impressions taken of my fingers on a Personal Identification Card, as used by police enforcement agencies. I then proceeded to have the fingerprint of my left index finger raised from a glass surface and in this regard an empty beer bottle was used for the experiment. Following the normal procedure of lightly dusting the surface of the bottle, the appropriate

137

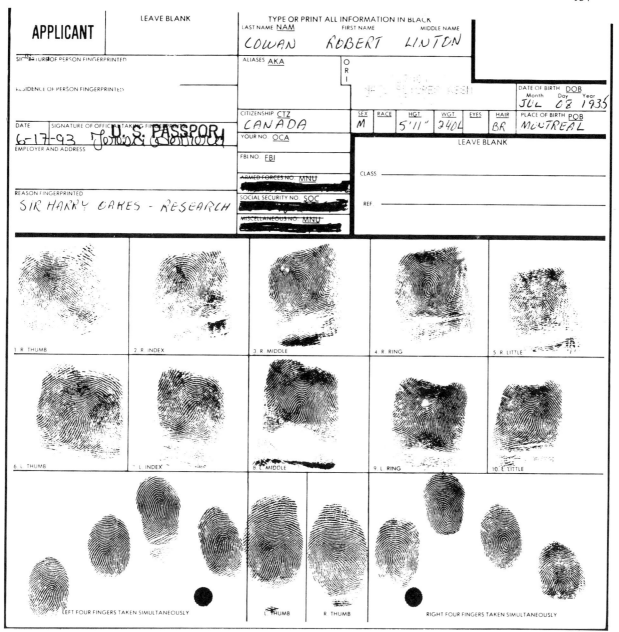

Sample of author's Personal Identification Card showing all fingerprints. *Author's collection*

fingerprint was identified and necessary procedures followed to raise it from the bottle on an adhesive tape.

The Forensic Identification Technician then proceeded to make the proper comparison of identifying marks such as arches, loops and whorls which enabled her to confirm that the fingerprint of my left index finger from the bottle was indeed mine and matched that on my Personal Identification Card.

The next step was to photograph the prints and have them blown up in order to place them on appropriate charts. In the comparison procedure all of the identical characteristics or

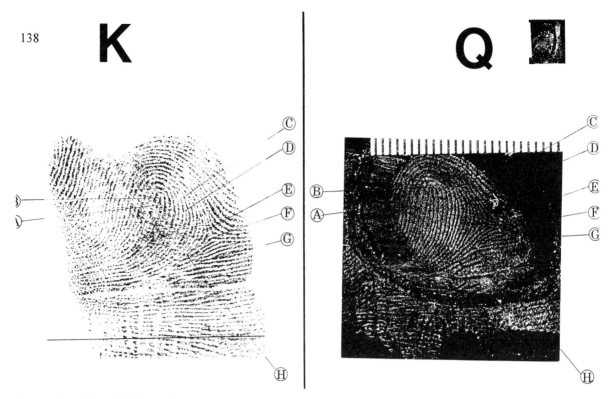

Comparison chart of subject's fingerprints prepared for presentation as an Exhibit during trial. *Author's collection*

points are either numbered or identified in alphabetical order for ease of reference on two charts for presentation in court.

The question of how many characteristics or points are required for proper identification depends on the person preparing the evidence and the quality of the prints. In some cases 6 characteristics could quite possibly identify the individual, but a minimum of 12 characteristics would appear to be normal. In reference to an FBI manual on the science of fingerprinting, it is mentioned that normally twelve characteristics are ample to confirm identification.

According to the testimony given by Capt. James Barker during the trial, when asked about Alfred de Marigny's fingerprint, he confirmed that he had identified 13 identical characteristics between the rolled prints and the latent prints taken from the screen thus confirming that the fingerprint was that of de Marigny. There did not appear to have been any exhibit shown in court to substantiate his comparison statement.

In reverting to the trial of Alfred de Marigny, it would appear that the only presentation made of fingerprinting of the accused was that by Capt. James Barker and recorded as *Exhibit J* (being that of the little finger on his left hand). At no point is there any reference to Barker displaying any inked impression taken during his investigation, when he supposedly took prints from both Harold Christie and Alfred de Marigny.

It was stated by Capt. James Barker, as investigator for the Prosecution, that he had found four or five fingerprints supposedly belonging to the accused in Sir Harry's bedroom and that the one shown in court was confirmed to have been found on the Chinese screen which was beside Sir Harry's bed. Thus in their minds placing Alfred de Marigny at the very scene of the crime.

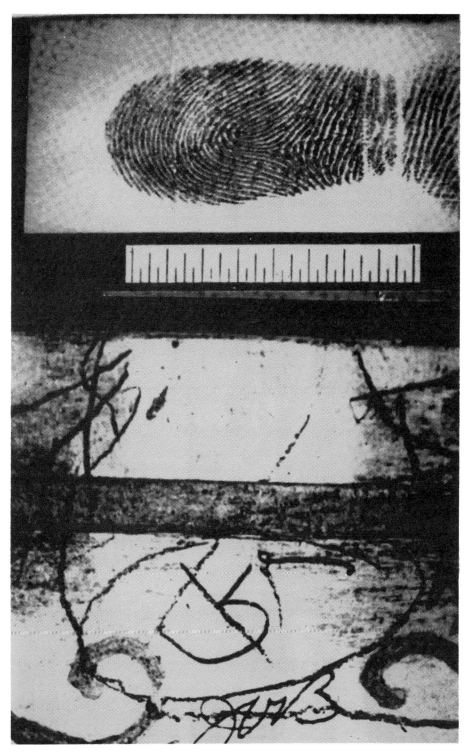

Exhibit J showing fingerprint of Alfred de Marigny's left little finger, together with cross section of the Chinese screen from which it was supposedly taken. Notice initials JOB for Capt. James Otto Barker. *Corbis Images*

The fingerprint was best known as *Exhibit J* during the course of the trial and was allowed as evidence by Judge Sir Oscar Daly, though both Godfrey Higgs and Ernest Callender, de Marigny's lawyers, felt very strongly against it being entered as an exhibit. The main point of contention was the questionable circumstances surrounding the method in which the fingerprint was lifted from the Chinese screen and the lack of any background markings being shown. They had requested Judge Daly to dismiss it as evidence, but after due consideration, he informed the court the following morning, that he would allow the fingerprint to be entered as evidence by the Prosecution and leave it to the Jury to decide on its validity in the case.

Anyone having read any books on the case would notice from the reproduction of the fingerprint, that no material background is shown in the photograph of the print. Therefore it was the Defense's contention that if the fingerprint was lifted from the screen, some of the background design or scroll work should have also appeared on the reproduction of the print.

It is a known fact that because of the high humidity prevalent in the tropics, fingerprints could almost literally melt away from day to day and this certainly applied to the Bahamas.

Under normal circumstances it would have been necessary for Barker to photograph the screen in the room, followed by a close-up photo of the area and eventually one of the immediate area where the print was found, otherwise we have only Capt. Barker's memory to indicate where the print came from. And that appeared to be the case as Barker testified.

Capt. Barker under the circumstances could have easily requested his office in Miami to have his camera sent over on the next flight or, for that matter, to have immediately borrowed the necessary photographic equipment from the Royal Air Force unit stationed in Nassau at the time, who actually were requested to take certain photographs of the murder scene by the Attorney General.

As part of the Defense team, the services of Captain Maurice O'Neil, fingerprint expert with the New Orleans police department was called upon to provide de Marigny's lawyers Godfrey Higgs and Ernest Callender with the necessary fingerprinting expertise, which they needed in analysing the fingerprint. We must remember that Higgs and Callender were not known as criminal lawyers.

This lack of background led many to believe that the fingerprint was taken from another source. The most likely source considered was from the surface of the glasses and the water jug handled by de Marigny, while being interrogated by Capt. Melchen at *Westbourne*. It has also been mentioned that Melchen tossed a package of *Lucky Strike* cigarettes to de Marigny during their conversation, which package had a cellophane wrapper — a very good surface for recording fingerprints.

One question that is never asked seems to be — why would only one fingerprint and at that the one of his little finger on the left hand be the one that was produced in court. There were rumours from Capt. Barker that other prints were found on the screen in other locations, but according to him the quality of the prints was not good enough for them to be identified as those of de Marigny.

If the fingerprint that was claimed by the Prosecution to be that of Alfred de Marigny and was taken from the upper part of the fifth panel from the left of the Chinese screen, why was de Marigny handling the screen in the first place and how come only his little finger was identified? It seems unusual that a person would only touch such a surface with one finger and a little finger at that.

I have tried to touch part of a wall (substituted for the Chinese screen which was six feet in height) that is higher in height than myself with my left hand, however, every time I tried, it seems that at least the two or three extreme left fingers on my left hand appeared to want to touch the wall at the same time. In order to touch the wall with only the little finger, an effort must be made to extend only that particular finger. I also noted that part of the palm of my hand had a tendency to touch the wall.

It was interesting to note that the insecticide spray gun that was found at the end of Sir Harry's bed was dusted for fingerprints, but Capt. Barker claimed that none were found, as supposedly the spray can was covered with fluid from the spray gun itself.

On a number of occasions when showing the fingerprint photo to various members of the police to whom I have referred the print, the immediate reaction is that the fingerprint in *Exhibit J* would appear to be too perfect to be one taken from the crime scene and more likely resembles one that is taken from a suspect on a personal identification card. A crime scene fingerprint is more likely to be partially blurred and cover a smaller surface of the finger itself, as the suspect will handle whatever he touches in a hurry and not allow a finger to record a proper print.

It would also appear in discussion with personnel at the Coroner's Office in Toronto, that one possible medical evaluation that should have been performed at the scene of the murder by a doctor, would have been that of *lividity*, which would have confirmed the fact that the body was indeed moved from one location to another.

An indication of *lividity* usually appears in the parts of the body which touch a surface i.e., a body lying on its side or on its back, could possibly have dark skin colouring on the side of the head, part of the shoulder, thigh and lower part of the leg below the knee.

However, *lividity* can not be used as a specific indicator of the time of death of an individual.

From the description of the murder scene and the testimony given during the trial by Doctors Quackenbush and Fitzmaurice, there is no mention of the existence of any *lividity*. Dr. Quackenbush did admit that there was every possibility that the body had been moved, but did not provide any explanation for his remarks or describe any tell tale signs which would have led him to make that statement. Possibly the blood running across Sir Harry's cheek and nose, may have been Dr. Quackenbush's reason for confirming that the body was moved.

The question of *Rigor Mortis* must also be considered and the following description would seem to be appropriate:

Rigor Mortis is a shortening of both the voluntary and involuntary muscles which stiffen and fix the limbs. This condition is brought about by the coagulation of protein in the muscles, and the earliest signs occur in the eyelids and lower jaw.

Usually about three to four hours after death, the muscles of the body begin to harden. This is called 'rigor mortis'. After twenty four to thirty six hours the condition usually begins to disappear. As with heat loss, however, a number of factors affect the onset and disappearance of rigor mortis. For example, rigor mortis begins sooner in warm weather than in cold; sooner in less muscular people than in those who are well developed; sooner if the victim struggled violently at the time of death than if he or she was passive.

As one can judge *rigor mortis* could possibly in the case of Sir Harry Oakes have set in quite rapidly as the application of warm weather (very appropriate to the Bahamas); less muscular people (Sir Harry was not exactly a physical fitness specimen) and the victim struggled violently at time of death (his violent death would certainly confirm this). In Sir Harry's case all of the foregoing would apply under the circumstances.

The question of the rigor mortis aspect surrounding the death of Sir Harry was further discussed with the Funeral Service Education department at Humber College in Toronto, as it was Harold Christie's statement that following his discovery of Oakes he tried to pour some water down his throat. The question asked of me was "*did Sir Harry have his mouth open at the time?*" and from perusal of the photos taken of Sir Harry, it is obvious that his mouth was found closed, which would have made it rather difficult for anyone to open his mouth under the circumstances. And naturally the photographs were taken some five hours at least after the time of death as estimated by Dr. Quackenbush.

On the question of *rigor mortis* and establishing the time of death the following method is sometimes used by a doctor or medical examiner at the scene of the crime: normal body temperature 37C (99F) — minus the rectal temperature divided by 1.5 will provide the approximate number of hours since death.

Time Since Death:	Changes:
3-5 hours	Lividity is evident as blood drains to lowest parts.
5-7 hours	Rigor mortis begins in the face.
12 hours	Body cooled to about 25C (77F) internally.
12-18 hours	Rigor mortis complete with extension to arms and trunk.
20-24 hours	Body is cold with its temperature down to that of surroundings.
24 hours	Rigor mortis starts to disappear.
24-36 hours	Rigor mortis completely disappeared.
48 hours	Discolouration of abdomen signals beginning of decomposition.

A number of theories have been put forward over the years relative to the possible murderer or murderers by various individuals, who have written on the subject of Sir Harry Oakes, some in a serious vein and others in a novel interpretation. The following is a recap of some of these comments:

One of the more popular theories that has arisen was that Meyer Lansky sent men over to rough-up Sir Harry Oakes, because of his on-again off-again position relative to

Lansky's attempt to obtain a Bahamian gaming permit, but they went too far and killed Sir Harry. (Based on a biography of Robert Vesco)

Another theory which Allan Butler (husband of Shirley Oakes, daughter of Sir Harry) shared, was that the real culprit was the Swedish industrialist Dr. Axel Wenner-Gren, the motive being the millions of dollars that Sir Harry provided him during the Second World War. Wenner-Gren had a Mexican bank operation and persuaded Sir Harry Oakes to help him capitalize it, so the story went. Subsequently, it is said that the Oakes trustees could never locate the money, about $9,000,000. It was thought that Wenner-Gren who seemed broke during the war, suddenly re-emerged as a wealthy man. Who will ever know the truth on this theory?

In his biography on the Duchess of Windsor, the author Charles Higham very clearly states that Harold Christie was the man responsible for the murder of Sir Harry Oakes. He speculated that the killer Christie hired was from a tribe or sect that practised black magic and attributed the peculiar circumstances of the death — the spotty fires around the room and hallway, how the body was burned, the scattering of feathers — to a ritual murder in which Christie himself took part. The murder weapon was described as a fishing spear used at close range.

On the other hand it is Alfred de Marigny's own contention that it was likely that Sir Harry was drugged and then shot — the thick and dark fluid that was found in his stomach, that the doctors did not bother to test according to de Marigny — and that he was killed as he slept. No one but Christie, the only overnight guest was in a position to spike Sir Harry's bedtime drink. There was a subsequent statement made that the dark fluid was in all probability grape juice, which could have been confirmed with the maid Mabel Ellis or for that matter with any of the dinner guests as to whether grapes were served, but this was never done. De Marigny does not believe that Christie participated in the actual murder or was indeed present when it occurred. (based on the book *A Conspiracy of Crowns*)

The author Michael Pye, stopped short of naming Harold Christie as the killer, but he touched on the motive — Christie had a crisis on his hands. For months, even years, the trend of Oakes' thinking was clear — and if he actually decided to leave the Bahamas, then Christie was in deep trouble as he was not in a position to follow Oakes and his finances needed proper attention. (*King Over the Waters*)

Author Montgomery Hyde, special agent for the British government, felt that Sir Harry Oakes was murdered by a syndicate of financial adventurers involved in an intricate plot to get their hands on the Oakes fortune. (based on a book entitled *Crime Has Its Heroes*)

Along that line there has been the theory that as *voodoo* might be part of the murder scene, Sir Harry may have had an affair with a native woman. But as some old time miner once remarked — *the only way that Harry Oakes could get a woman, would be if he found himself on a deserted island with a woman.*

Raymond Schindler, the private investigator hired by Nancy de Marigny in the defense of her husband, claimed that Sir Harry Oakes was murdered because it was his intention to liquidate his large holdings in the Bahamas and move his family to South America and possibly to Mexico. The question is then raised as to who would be most affected by this move — answers: a real estate agent who had benefited from Sir Harry's many property purchases over the years and who would now have a great deal to lose; also a manager of properties for somewhat the very same reasons. Remember that under the circumstances there were only two candidates who were close business associates of Oakes in the Bahamas at the time.

In a newspaper interview in November 1945, Col. Frederick Lancaster, Commissioner of the Bahamas Police Department reported that a mysterious hoard of gold coins was found in a cave near Georgetown on Great Exuma Island. There had always been a theory to the effect that on the night of the murder of Sir Harry, a chest of gold coins had disappeared from his *Westbourne* estate. Col. Lancaster, following a close investigation of the matter on Great Exuma, declared that there was no connection whatsoever with the stories of the gold coins.

All of the above points have been mentioned as possible theories for the murder of Sir Harry Oakes, however, it is up to the reader to surmise which one was a possibility or maybe suggest a further one — at this point in time a new theory may be just as good as the old theories.

Possibly one final scenario would have been plain robbery, as Sir Harry may have withdrawn funds from the bank in anticipation of his trip to Bar Harbor, but on the other hand one would have to remember the story of the night watchmen who were on duty at *Westbourne* and what they saw.

One passing remark, as you may recall the Prosecution's point was that according to the two detectives investigating the murder there was a feeling of hatred by de Marigny for his father-in-law, but not one of the authors has ever brought up this theory as being the motive.

Again, as there have been many theories put forward as to why Sir Harry Oakes was murdered, there are almost as many theories as to what the murder weapon could have been.

During the course of the preliminary hearing in the Magistrate's Court and the trial in the Supreme Court, no weapon was ever identified. The only conclusion that anyone in authority, including Captains James Barker and Edward Melchen on the part of the Prosecution, ever came up with was that the weapon of death was a *blunt instrument*, with no further description of the instrument or for that matter any suggestions as to what the weapon could have been.

The following are some of the theories that have been discussed by various individuals involved with the investigation and also some thoughts expressed by various authors:

A Gun or Revolver

This weapon has been suggested by Alfred de Marigny, but one must remember that Harold Christie was supposedly sleeping two rooms down from Sir Harry Oakes.

The gun theory as you will see later also contradicts in a way what de Marigny himself relates in his book *A Conspiracy of Crowns* regarding the meeting that he had with one of the surviving *Westbourne* night watchmen, who was on duty the night of the murder, as all they heard was the tearing of cloth from their location outside the house.

The description of the wounds as four triangular shaped markings on the side of Sir Harry's head would not be in conformity with the normal markings of a bullet penetration into the skull, which are normally circular in shape. In consultation with the Coroner's Office in Toronto, I was shown photos of actual head wounds, both from a penetration point of view, as well as the exit wound that would be caused by a bullet.

If there had been more than one bullet penetration in the immediate area of the first one, no doubt there would have been quite a shattering of the side of the skull and a great deal more damage, if indeed four shots were fired.

The question of the gun shot not being heard by anyone nearby (Christie supposedly in a room sixteen feet away), would seem unusual. As a result I consulted with the Royal Canadian Mounted Police — R.C.M.P. in Ottawa, who confirmed that silencers on revolvers were indeed available in those days and it is therefore possible that one may have been used if the weapon was a revolver.

A Balustrade

One author who had researched the murder of Sir Harry Oakes came to the conclusion that the murderer had picked up a balustrade from inside Sir Harry's garage before going up to the room.

It is obvious that if one is determined to kill someone or has been hired to do so, it is not at the last moment that one decides to run into a garage and gather up a murder weapon, particularly in complete darkness and on a stormy night. Unless he knew his way around the property or someone was possibly with him and guiding him.

Fishing Spear

Another author claims to have referred the question of a fishing spear to certain authorities, who seem to concur with the theory of the spear as the murder weapon, but no description of the type of spear is given.

However, one should imagine the length of a fishing spear and its maneuverability in inflicting four triangular wounds within inches of each other and no doubt in very quick succession, would seem improbable and next to impossible to handle.

Was the use of a fishing spear a premeditated one? If so, it would have been necessary to have ensured that Sir Harry would not move while the wounds were inflicted within such a small area of the head, as very clearly described in the testimony at the trial. It would seem that if a spear was used four times no doubt the victim would have reacted physically at some point. The depth of the wounds must also be remembered — 1/4 to 1 inch as confirmed by one of the investigating doctors.

In an attempt to further research the question of a fishing spear as a potential murder weapon, I called a friend of mine in Nassau who does a lot of fishing and asked if there was such a spear that would fit in with the description of the wounds to Sir Harry's head.

While the answer was not a resounding yes, there was possibly a four pronged spear somewhat in the shape of an eating fork with a metal handle which extended approximately

146

4 1/2 to 5 1/2 inches in length from tip to tip with a hollow shaft. The entire spear could be handled in one hand. The tips of the prongs were all triangular and would fit the description of the wound as given by Dr. Lawrence Fitzmaurice at the trial, but the only difference is the positioning of the prongs which were all in line rather that in a square shape area. It would appear that the spear was called a *grain*.

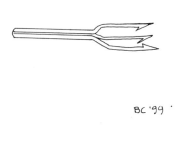

BC '99

Fishing spear. *Author's collection*

A further type of fishing spear noted would be a stainless steel fixed spearpoint called a *trident point* used for small to medium fish and which can be used on a polespear or reef gun. This particular spear has three prongs which are spread out in a triangular pattern with each prong bearing a sharp triangular head. Overall length of the spear is also approximately 4 1/2 to 5 1/2 inches with a hollow shaft.

A wooden rod in the form of a broom stick handle of short length could be inserted into the hollow part of the spears to give them more strength and leverage.

Subsequent reference to a recent fishing equipment catalogue in Canada also described two similar type spears with pretty well the same dimensions, but the main difference was that the spears had five prongs.

Prospector's Pick

A theory put forward by Raymond Schindler was the use of a prospector's pick, which was supposedly removed from Sir Harry's collection in his garage, a point which has never been confirmed. While the tip of a typical pick would seem to indicate a four sided shape one must also realize the weight of such an instrument which is approximately 1 1/2 to 2 pounds and the length of the handle twelve inches, with the steel head in the neighbourhood of nine inches in length, pointed on one end and with a 3/4 inch square head at the other end.

A tracing on paper and actual handling of a prospector's pick was made at the Museum of Northern History in Kirkland Lake and it is obvious that it would not be difficult to handle such an instrument in rapid succession so as to register the four wounds described in close proximity of each other on the side of Sir Harry's head.

A prospector's pick as the murder weapon would add some colour to the murder story, since Sir Harry had been a mining prospector.

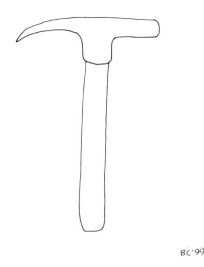

BC'99

Sketch of a prospector's pick as a possible murder weapon as suggested by Raymond Schindler. *Author's collection*

A Boat Winch

In this case the use of a boat winch with a serrated spindle would appear to indicate, based on a number of books, that Sir Harry Oakes had gone down to the waterfront and met with certain individuals on board a boat or yacht and that he was struck down by the use of such a winch.

Now the question is — did Sir Harry indeed leave *Westbourne* on the night in question? — because if you have ever seen pictures of the murder scene, it is quite obvious that spread out on the next bed in the room is a pair of Sir Harry's white sport slacks, which do not appear to bear any stains of any kind or dirt marks and this point was confirmed by Major Herbert Pemberton in his testimony. If Oakes had left *Westbourne* and met his death as many have mentioned it is certain that his clothes would not have been as clean as shown.

It is interesting to note from the book entitled *The King's X* written by Marshall Houts that he makes it very clear that there was involvement in the death of Sir Harry Oakes by one Meyer Lansky, because of Oakes change of mind relative to gambling casinos in the Bahamas.

According to certain informants who were known to Marshall Houts, Sir Harry Oakes and Harold Christie drove down to the dockside area and boarded a cruiser where *three button men* sent over supposedly from Miami by Lansky, met with Oakes and apparently exerted pressure on him in an attempt to obtain his support for the gambling plans.

The *informants* confirmed that one of the *button* men at one point proceeded to strike Sir Harry on the head with a *four pronged winch lever*, who then collapsed to the floor. Each prong was supposedly triangularly shaped.

The story by the *informants* continues to the effect that they then dragged Sir Harry's limp body through the mud in the street and placed it in Christie's stationwagon face down. Christie then sat on the front passenger side and directed the driver back to *Westbourne*.

At this point we should remember the pair of false teeth that were described as being on the night table between the two beds. Alfred de Marigny made a statement during an interview following one of the movies made on the life and death of Sir Harry to the effect *that you do not leave home without them* and this certainly would have been the case.

Therefore, the question of a boat winch as the murder weapon becomes all the more implausible if one were to study the shape and functionality of such an awkward instrument. Its weight of approximately three to five pounds and manoeuverability has been tried and would appear to have been very difficult to handle under the circumstances.

As part of the research on the possibility that a boat winch was used, I spoke to three marina operators, as well as a gentleman whose specialty was the restoration of old boats, all of whom were quite familiar with such winches as were used at that time and in all cases the opinion was that the weapon of death could not have been a winch.

A Machete

As the murder occurred in the islands and may have indeed been committed by a native, the thought has occurred to some that quite possibly a machete may have been used, as it is a very well known tool or weapon as the case may be and easily handled by a native.

However, again we are faced with an object which can best be described as a large heavy knife measuring up to eighteen inches or more in length and would not normally bear any triangular points to correspond to the wounds as outlined by Dr. Fitzmaurice. In addition the machete would be a rather awkward weapon to handle under the circumstances prevalent during the murder and secondly according to de Marigny's interview with one of the night watchman — no weapons were described as being carried by the intruders and a machete is not that easy an item to conceal.

Jack Handle (Lug-nut)

While not in the transcript of the trial it is mentioned that on July 22nd, 1943, Lieutenant Johnny Douglas of the Bahamas Police flew over to Miami to deliver two packages of potential exhibits to Major Herbert Pemberton and Captain Edward Melchen. In one of the packages was an item called a *jack handle*, which had been obtained from Major Pemberton's safe at the police barracks.

JACK HANDLE

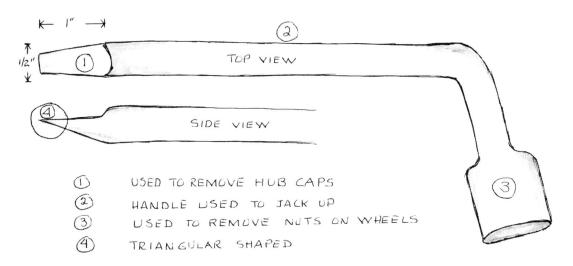

Sketch of a jack handle as a possible murder weapon. *Author's collection*

Following enquiries with various antique dealers, car dealers and auto mechanics, the description of a *jack handle* was narrowed down to a tool which was and still is used for removing hubcaps and unscrewing the nuts from the wheels of a car.

The tool comes in varying lengths (from 12 to 18 inches or more) and is L shaped with the shorter part, which could be used as the handle, terminating at the other end in the form of a screwdriver used for the removal of the hubcaps. The shorter end is basically round and the inside represents six identical sides, used for the removal of the nuts.

The question of the jack handle was only mentioned once and there has never been any further explanation or association of it with the murder of Sir Harry Oakes.

Steel Shaft Golf Club

The following is quoted from an FBI memorandum from their Washington Office under date of October 26th, 1943, relative to a long distance call that they received from someone in Buffalo, New York *"xxxxx stated he desired to submit the following information relative to the Sir Harry Oakes murder case. He offered the opinion that Sir Harry, who was killed by a blunt instrument, was probably hit by a steel shaft golf club which had the driving head broken off, forming a triangular shaped instrument at the point where the head was broken. xxxxx stated that undoubtedly the instrument could be found on a golf course"*.

Ice Pick

One final theory found in my research and which could possibly apply, depending on who did it, is that of an *ice pick murder*, a method once used by organized crime hit men.

As it has often been mentioned the murder of Sir Harry Oakes was quite possibly a *professional job*, the use of an ice pick to make the victim's death seem due to natural causes may very well have been the means. Having seen some ice picks, some of them seem to be three sided — that is in the form of a triangle which would fit into the description given by Dr. Fitzmaurice in his statement at the trial regarding the shape of the wounds to Sir Harry's head.

An ice pick murder is described as — *the murderer would jam the ice pick through the eardrum into the brain. The pick would produce a very small hole in the ear and a very small amount of blood — which could be wiped away.* Additional punctures around the ear, could have caused the larger flow of blood. How deep would the wounds be if an ice pick was used would be hard to determine, however, the first mortal wound would have penetrated right into the skull. An ice pick is also a very easy weapon to conceal.

Ice Pick. *Author's collection*

Blunt Instrument

When Dr. Lawrence Fitzmaurice first described the wound to Sir Harry's head, the term a blunt instrument was used. This theory would in all probability seem plausible to certain people under varying circumstances, but as far as the legal records of the trial are concerned a blunt instrument would appear to be the only conclusion and must remain as such.

Could the blunt instrument have been a plain ordinary hammer? Some hammers have heads which are eight sided with slight triangular edges. Following a discussion with a forensic

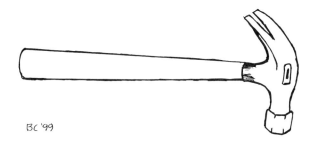

Blunt instrument (carpenters' hammer). *Author's collection*

pathologist and the viewing of certain photographs showing mortal skull wounds inflicted by hammers, it is quite possible that the wound to Sir Harry's head may have been the result of the forceful application of a single blow by a hammer which would shatter the skull causing triangular markings resulting in Dr. Fitzmuarice's theory.

In this regard, it is interesting to note the comments under reference to the murder case investigated by Sir Bernard Spilsbury, mentioned further in this text, where the murder weapon was eventually identified as a hammer.

If the murderer or murderers did not bring any weapons with them — what are the likely blunt weapons that they could have possibly picked up following their arrival at the estate, aside from some of those described above? Would there have been some blunt instruments around Sir Harry's bedroom? Possibly, but none have been suggested and again there is the fact that one does not wait until the last moment to pick one up.

The only likely access to Sir Harry's room, according to the plan drawn by a member of the RAF, was through the main entrance on the ground floor and then up two sets of

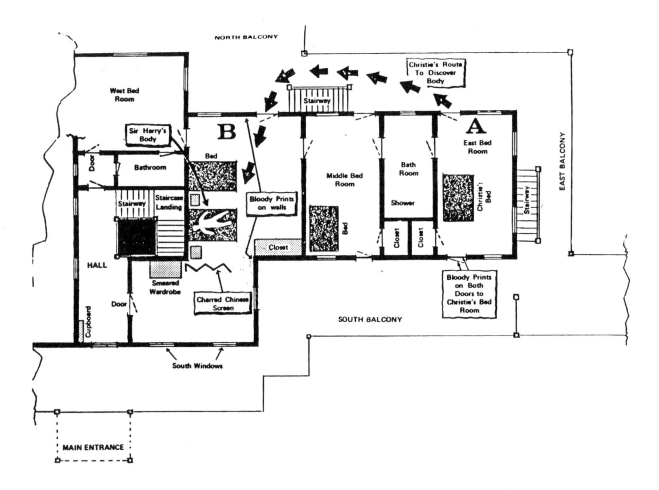

Plan of second floor at Westbourne estate showing Sir Harry's room and that of Harold Christie. (*Based on original plan drawn by LAC John Lord of the RAF in Nassau.*)

'L' shaped stair cases leading to the landing on the second floor, with one door leading into Sir Harry's bedroom. The other choices were through the east side stairway or the north side stairway facing the ocean. In both cases very poor choices unless you really knew your way around the estate or that someone was there to assist you in reaching Sir Harry's room.

In retrospect it should be remembered that no conceivable weapon could drill four neat holes in the head — no weapon, that is, wielded by hand. The strength required to drive a sharp point through the bone would embed the point too deeply to be withdrawn without great exertion. And to repeat this exercise three more times would not be necessary, for Sir Harry would have already been dead.

Another point on this aspect of the crime is that the assailant(s) would have had to know that Sir Harry would be home that night and at that particular residence, as Sir Harry had a tendency to reside also at his other estate the *Caves* when he was on his own in Nassau. During that particular week, Harold Christie had slept at *Westbourne* on two other occasions.

One last note, did anyone ever think of perusing a list of the long distance calls made from Nassau to the mainland possibly during the two weeks leading up to July 7th? In view of the censorship prevailing in the Bahamas at the time, it would have been an easy thing to do, as all calls were supposedly monitored and in some cases details recorded.

It is interesting to note from a biography of Raymond Schindler, that there is reference to a revolver which it is said that Sir Harry had in the drawer of the night table located between the two beds. The investigators supposedly discovered the gun, but as they felt that the gun was not used in the murder, and also as their theory was that a blunt instrument was used, there was no need at that point to retain the gun. The comment was made that it had been given to one of the night watchmen. Interesting that it was given to a night watchman, as there is no reference in the trial proceeding of a night watchman being on duty the night of the murder at *Westbourne*.

In my discussions with Alfred de Marigny, he repeated that it has always been his contention that the murder weapon used to kill Sir Harry Oakes was a small revolver and this is further confirmed in his book *A Conspiracy of Crowns*. This statement would certainly discredit Harold Christie's statement that he spent the night at *Westbourne* and only heard mosquitoes and the odd thunder clap during the course of the night, which no doubt also included the period of time during which the crime was committed.

If de Marigny's claim is correct that a revolver was used, how come there is no mention of it by Rawlins, one of the surviving night watchmen who related to de Marigny what had happened on the night of the murder. We know that silencers were in use at that time, though supposedly Rawlins and his colleague claim that they only heard cloth being torn.

In reading the description of the wounds to the head as described by Dr. Lawrence Fitzmaurice, it would be hard to believe that four identical triangular shaped wounds could have been inflicted to the head in the same immediate area. The wounds were also described as almost identical in shape, surface size and depth. The depth as indicated by Dr. Fitzmaurice, as acting Chief Medical Officer of the Bahamas, in his testimony was confirmed at approximately a quarter of an inch to one full inch, which would seem to certainly discredit any theories that the holes were caused by revolver or gun shots.

This statement must therefore lead to the conclusion that Christie was not in his room or for that matter at *Westbourne* after having said good night to Sir Harry Oakes, but off visiting most likely with his lady friend and this would immediately confirm the statement made by Alfred de Marigny regarding the discussion he had with Rawlins, who claims to have seen Christie leaving *Westbourne*.

I read a biography entitled *Bernard Spilsbury: His Life and Cases* in the hope of increasing my knowledge of forensic investigations. Spilsbury was considered the greatest of forensic scientists in England at the turn of the century and during his medical lifetime he did close to twenty thousand post-mortems, from normal deaths, to suicides and murders.

One case in particular caught my attention, when in 1930 Bernard Spilsbury was called upon to investigate the murder of one Vivian Messiter in Southampton, England, which in a way parallelled the criminal circumstances surrounding the murder of Sir Harry.

In his original testimony at the trial, Spilsbury said that — *in my opinion death was caused by fractures to the skull and injuries to the brain consequent on blows on the head with some heavy blunt object. The head of this hammer might have caused all the injuries.*

Initial evaluation by the investigator at the scene of death was that the cause of the injury was a punctured wound over the victim's left eye, made with the point of a hammer, which was at first mistaken for a bullet hole. Spilsbury performed the post-mortem to which he added the following note:

At least three blows on the head, any one producing immediate unconsciousness. The head of a large hammer, used with great violence, would account for the injuries. Those across the base and on right side produced when the head was on a hard surface. Positions of injuries at the back suggest that the deceased was bending forward.

In retrospect it is interesting to read of Spilsbury's case and compare it to the murder of Sir Harry — the head wounds, the possible bullet hole, a blunt instrument, to the use of a hammer and possibly on a hard surface — the floor at the entrance to his room.

The question of a hired killer has also been mentioned in a number of books with direct reference to voodoo and the Palo Mayombe cult, which was part of the Santeria Sect, consisting of the worship of the saints, the mingling of African tribal religions and Catholicism, established by African slaves brought to the Americas and the Caribbean Islands.

In reference to a book entitled *Cults That Kill: Probing the Underworld of Occult Crime*, there is a section devoted to the Santeria Tattoos, one of which shows three triangular spears on the tip of a handle and could best be compared to the staff held by Neptune, King of the Seas or a type of pitchfork. A further triangular shaped tattoo represents that of stick-ups, loans and other financial related items. In other words the tattoos would appear to be financially oriented.

Examples of the possibility of *voodoo* implications are the references to the actual spreading of feathers in the bedroom, as well as the setting of little fires around the room, a fact that has been documented during the trial.

In Alfred de Marigny's last book, he does mention that in the latter part of the 80's he cruised aboard a yacht with his wife to Freeport, Grand Bahama, together with another couple.

One evening while walking alone around the docks, he was approached by a black native Bahamian who introduced himself as Rawlins. During their conversation, Rawlins further identified himself as being one of the two night watchmen (the other called Cordner) who were supposedly on duty at Sir Harry's *Westbourne* estate on the night of the murder and that they witnessed the arrival and departure of certain individuals to and from the house and apparently at the very time of the murder.

In view of the importance of what these watchmen had seen that fateful night, it is only fair to relate briefly the comments as made by Rawlins to de Marigny of what transpired.

As de Marigny recalled from Rawlins' comments on the evening of the murder, both Rawlins and Cordner were about to leave *Westbourne* to go to their respective homes, but the weather was so bad that in order to protect themselves from the storm they ran into a guard shed located not far from the entrance to the grounds of Sir Harry's estate and within view of the house.

While in the shed, Rawlins claimed that he and Cordner saw Harold Christie come down the stairs from the estate and walk to his car, which was actually parked outside the grounds of *Westbourne* and then drive off in an easterly direction, which would lead him towards downtown Nassau.

Approximately half an hour after Christie's departure, another car drove into the entrance and was driven by none other than Christie's own brother Frank, who was accompanied by two unknown gentlemen. Frank remained in the car, while the two gentlemen got out and went up to Sir Harry's room.

In the ensuing moments, Rawlins claims that he and Cordner saw a reddish glow reflected in the windows of Sir Harry's bedroom and that they heard some cloth being ripped or torn apart. This latter activity was supposedly repeated on three or four occasions while they stood motionless in the guard shed in fear of being detected.

The statement concerning the tearing of cloth is a rather difficult one to believe, due to the fact that the two men who came with Frank Christie were in Sir Harry's room, located on the second floor and some distance away from where Rawlins and Cordner were in the shed. In addition there was a tropical storm underway that night and they were supposedly in the shed trying to protect themselves from the elements. How could they possibly have heard the noise of cloth being torn under such circumstances?

Shortly afterwards, the two gentlemen descended the stairs from the direction of Sir Harry's room, exited through the main entrance and entered the car, driving off with Frank Christie. This time they proceeded in a westerly direction along West Bay Street which would lead them towards Lyford Cay. The glow of fire that Rawlins and Cordner had seen, apparently died off shortly following the departure of Frank Christie and his party. Next, Rawlins and Cordner came out of the shed and headed home as fast they could on their bicycles.

During Rawlins' description of what happened, there is at no point any indication if either of the two gentlemen was carrying any visible weapons, as it must be remembered that the suggestion was made that the murder weapon was a fishing spear which is not a small item to conceal. What about the blow torch?

A rather simple question to be asked is, if they were indeed the night watchmen for Sir Harry's *Westbourne* estate, as well as for the Bahamas Country Club located next door — should not their basic duties have prompted them to investigate the fire in Sir Harry's room or any other potential damage that could have arisen as a result of the activities described, rather than just head home in such a hurry? They were night watchmen after all — were they not?

The fact that the two gentlemen were accompanied by Frank Christie did not raise any suspicion for Rawlins and Cordner and there was probably no reason for them to question their presence at *Westbourne*. The sight of the flames should have prompted them to take some action, i.e., approach those coming out of the house or at least Frank Christie, whom they apparently knew.

There is no comment made concerning the direction from which the car arrived at *Westbourne*. However, as they headed towards Lyford Cay when leaving, it is quite possible that they were the gentlemen who were supposedly seen by the night watchman at Lyford Cay earlier that evening. Or were they?

In a discussion that I had with a certain individual in Nassau in 1992, who wished to remain anonymous, I was informed that his son knew the watchman (expressed very clearly in the singular to me) at Lyford Cay at the time, who claimed to have seen some strangers arrive at the docks that evening.

This gentleman confirmed to me that his son said that the night watchman had died of natural causes in the late nineteen eighties.

While Alfred de Marigny was being held in Nassau prison following the Magistrate Court's decision that there was sufficient cause to hold him for trial in the murder of Sir Harry, a close friend of his, Basil McKinney, sent word to him in prison that he had talked to two caretakers at Lyford Cay, who had seen a motor launch dock there the evening of the murder. As a result McKinney contacted the watchmen two days later and talked to them. He was told that they had managed to obtain the name and registration number of the boat. McKinney then advised de Marigny's lawyer Godfrey Higgs of the incident.

Nothing further was done at that time, to speak to these two potentially important witnesses. On the following morning de Marigny was advised by one of the officers of the jail that the two night watchmen at Lyford Cay had been found dead. And so ended still a further potential follow-up to the case.

It was estimated by Rawlins that the two unknown intruders they saw at Sir Harry's estate with Frank Christie, remained in Sir Harry's room for a period of time ranging anywhere from fifteen to twenty five minutes in total.

As the story continues, Rawlins then informed de Marigny that the following morning Harold's brother Frank went to their respective homes on the south side of the island and asked them where they were the previous night, to which they replied that they had left *Westbourne* around 10.30 p.m. and gone straight home. For some reason, Frank did not seem to believe what they said and told the two of them to be off the island the very next day and proceeded to give each one of them one hundred pounds cash. Rawlins and Cordner departed from Nassau the next morning and headed for Freeport, Grand Bahama where they had relatives and subsequently established themselves. Rawlins said that they both changed their names in order to protect their identities.

This statement by de Marigny in his latest book would seem to have placed at least two authentic witnesses close to the scene of the murder and that they actually saw the perpetrators, which is more than has ever been mentioned in the past fifty seven years or so since the tragedy. Identification of the two gentlemen, aside from Frank Christie, would seem to have been impossible. However, nothing was ever mentioned to the Nassau police about the meeting and even after these statements appeared in de Marigny's book, which was for sale in Nassau book stores in 1990 for everyone on the island to read, no one in authority has ever taken any further interest in the matter. Again as it appears to have been the case on many occasions in this murder scenario, the matter was just left to die.

I am sure that the individual named Rawlins, as it would appear that he was still alive in the late eighties, could have easily been traced and located by the Criminal Investigation Department — CID of the Bahamas Police Force and properly questioned on the matter. Remember that as a start he worked at the casinos in Freeport, which really narrows down the scope of the search if someone is interested in furthering the investigation of the crime, and would only take the trouble to contact the personnel department at the casino and make the necessary enquiries.

Further still, the two night watchmen worked for Sir Harry and the Bahamas Country Club. Under the circumstances would it not be possible for the authorities to investigate their identification? Would there not be some kind of a record of who they worked for as they must have been paid at some time for the job they were performing? The trustees to the Oakes estate would have had access to such information.

One day these two gentlemen were employed and the next day they did not report for work. Surely someone in authority responsible for their employment and the safety of *Westbourne* and the Bahamas Country Club must have missed them and said to themselves — hey, I'm missing two employees, especially since they were involved in a murder investigation.

An interesting note is that Frank Christie knew the two night watchmen and also exactly where they lived in the pine forest area on the southern side of the island when he went to speak to them. Why would Frank Christie have known about these two gentlemen?

This revelation of what seems to have happened that evening also appears to be the only concrete statement ever made by an individual about the murder, since that made by the longshoreman Edward Majava in Oakland, California in September 1950, who subsequently pointed the finger at Harold Christie as being a possible party to the organized plot to murder Sir Harry Oakes. Rawlins' story would seem to substantiate what Edward Majava had said in his statement to Augustus Roberts of the Bahamas Police, who had flown out to Oakland to interrogate him.

However, Rawlins informed de Marigny that his colleague Cordner, with whom he had worked in Nassau, had passed away of natural causes some years prior to this meeting in Freeport.

I should mention that to add to the mystery of what happened during that conversation that evening, in 1992 during the course of a vacation in Nassau I dropped in at an antique shop on West Bay Street in downtown Nassau. I was in search of some old photos of the Oakes family, when a lady approached me to see if I needed any assistance. I mentioned my interest in Sir Harry Oakes and without saying another word, she immediately began talking about that fateful night and said that it was not Harold Christie whom Capt. Edward Sears saw driving through downtown Nassau, but Frank Christie, Harold's brother. These comments fit in exactly with the comments made by Alfred de Marigny when he referred to the conversation that he had with one of the surviving night watchmen at *Westbourne*.

As part of my curiosity in the matter, I wondered if what Rawlins described to de Marigny relative to what had happened on the night of the murder could have been entered into the records of the trial. I therefore spoke to an old friend of mine, who is a retired Chief Justice in the Province of Quebec and the point was confirmed, that the proper authorities in Nassau could have taken a written deposition from Rawlins (under his real name at the time of the murder) and entered it in the court records, even after the passing of some forty odd years.

At least this statement would have been placed on record and further helped clear the name of Alfred de Marigny in a more positive manner. But as usual nothing was done and no one in authority in Nassau seemed to be the least bit interested.

It is regrettable that no action was taken, as it was even Alfred de Marigny's belief at one time that the case should have been reopened, even to the point of exhuming Sir Harry's body from the crypt in the mausoleum at the Dover-Foxcroft cemetery in Maine.

Preliminary investigation into the matter indicated that to proceed with an exhumation requires permission of a surviving member of the family of the deceased and in the absence of such, a court order would be required. In either case there should be an indication as to the legal need of such an exhumation and a valid opinion of what you expect to possibly find that would be beneficial to the case.

As one can see, there have been many stories written about the night watchmen, but the question still remains — which is the true story? De Marigny seems to be the only person who was involved as a suspect in the original tragedy who has committed in writing what he knows.

Sir Harry had planned to leave Nassau on Friday July 9th and the question naturally that would come to mind is — *who knew that Oakes would be leaving the island?*

This point has never been discussed during the investigation of the murder. In my mind it is rather an important question and should have been investigated for the simple reason that whoever murdered Sir Harry or had planned the murder, would have had to make sure that the intended victim would be on the island and in that particular residence. Another important matter is that the person would have also known that Sir Harry was living by himself and that his family was away.

Let us therefore look at the individuals and ponder their knowledge of Sir Harry's plan for his leaving the island:

Harold Christie knew for sure that Sir Harry was leaving the island and had planned to discuss with him some business matters. In addition he stayed with Sir Harry at *Westbourne* on that night of all nights and on two other occasions just prior to the fatal night. He would have also known that Lady Oakes, Nancy de Marigny and the children were away.

Newell Kelly was Sir Harry's manager of his properties on the island. On the morning of the 8th when the murder was discovered, Kelly was apparently out fishing with three friends. He was found the next day and returned immediately to Nassau. Obviously he would have been aware of Sir Harry's departure in view of his responsibilities. Why did he not wait until Sir Harry had left before venturing out on his fishing trip? — possibly Sir Harry could have had some last minute matters to discuss with him.

Walter Foskett, Sir Harry's attorney in the United States, no doubt knew that Harry was going to Bar Harbor to be with his family and would have known where to reach him in case of need. Did he have any interest in Harry's departure date?

Mabel Ellis, the Oakes' housekeeper was also aware of his planned departure, but as hired help she did not have any interest in the matter and was mainly concerned with the upkeep of the house.

Dulcibel Henneage, a close friend of Harold Christie and also of Charles Hubbard, was a dinner guest at Sir Harry's home. She had no interest in Sir Harry's plans.

Charles Hubbard, most likely heard of Oakes' departure during the dinner party. It was obvious that though he was a neighbour of Sir Harry, he was not considered a close friend and his departure from the island was of no interest to him.

Sally Sawyer and *Veronica McMahon*, who played tennis with Sir Harry and Harold Christie the afternoon of the dinner party, possibly may have heard that Oakes was planning on leaving. Their presence was merely a social one and the knowledge that Oakes was departing was inconsequential.

The *Government official* who arranged for Sir Harry's exit visa would have known and probably would not have cared less, provided he did the necessary paper work. It was only part of his job to issue exit visas and other related documents.

Levi Gibson, Harold Christie's chauffeur and so-called man Friday brought Christie's car out to *Westbourne*. Plans for Sir Harry's departure were most likely not known to him or of any relevant importance. Christie's proposed overnight stay with Oakes was probably a normal event as far as Gibson was concerned.

Let us not forget *Meyer Lansky*, to whom the finger of guilt has often been pointed, who would not have necessarily been aware of Sir Harry's planned activities unless he was informed by any one of Sir Harry's close business associates mentioned above. Did Newell Kelly and Walter Foskett know Lansky? Harold Christie did.

Dr. Axel Wenner-Gren; the Duke of Windsor or *Alfred de Marigny* — did any one of these gentlemen have the necessary information about Sir Harry's plans to allow them the time to arrange for someone to do the necessary evil deed or for that matter to participate in it or further still to commit it themselves. I doubt it very much, but the Duke would have known of Harry's planned departure.

It must be remembered that whoever did the actual killing on that particular night had to know that Sir Harry would be in his *Westbourne* estate at a given time, in order that the killer would know where to go, as well as have an idea of the layout of the house in advance. Sir Harry could have just as easily stayed at his other residence, the *Caves*, which he did on a number of occasions when he would be alone.

Almost everyone keeps referring to someone coming over to Nassau from Miami and the knowledge of Sir Harry's whereabouts is all the more important in order to arrange for the proper timing for their trip over.

At the time of the tragedy Dr. Leonard Huggins was the Assistant Medical Officer at His Majesty's Prison in Nassau and Acting Bacteriologist at the Bahamas General Hospital. (now known as the Princess Margaret Hospital)

During the course of the trial, Dr. Huggins informed the court that there was no evidence of alcohol or poison in the stomach of Sir Harry Oakes and indicated that quite possibly the so-called dark fluid discovered was only grape juice.

To confirm this possibility as indeed correct, it would have been quite a simple matter to ask the question of Sir Harry's maid Mabel Ellis if grapes were served at the meal on the evening before the murder. Likewise Harold Christie, Charles Hubbard and Dulcibel Henneage, who were also called as witnesses, could have been asked the very same question and possibly solved one of the minor questions surrounding the medical examination.

Dr. Lawrence Wylie Fitzmaurice was the Acting Chief Medical Officer of the Bahamas at the time of the murder of Sir Harry Oakes. He was born in Amherst, Nova Scotia in March 1900, and graduated in medicine from McGill University in Montreal in the Class of 1925.

At approximately 9.10 a.m. on the morning of July 8th, 1943, he received a telephone call from the Commissioner of Police Reginald Erskine-Lindop and despatched Dr. Leonard Huggins, Assistant Medical Officer with an ambulance to *Westbourne.*

A second telephone call was received by Fitzmaurice at 11.30 a.m. from Eric Hallinan, the Attorney General who requested him to go immediately to *Westbourne.* Fitzmaurice was still there at 4.00 p.m. when the body of Sir Harry Oakes was removed and brought to the Bahamas General Hospital, where later that evening he began a more complete examination of the body. The post mortem was made the following morning July 9th, 1943.

The delay in removing the body of Sir Harry from the crime scene was due to the fact that local authorities were awaiting the arrival of Captains James Barker and Edward Melchen from Miami.

Under the circumstances it is agreed that the best and only details of the head wounds that killed Sir Harry Oakes were those described by Dr. Fitzmaurice during the trial.

Dr. Ulrich 'Ricky' Oberwarth was born in Germany and subsequently moved to England in 1933 and as it was his wish to become a British citizen, he moved to the Bahamas where he would take an assignment as the prison doctor in Nassau.

During his lifetime Dr. Oberwarth was a pilot, a surgeon, a sailor and eventually moved to Cape Breton, Nova Scotia. He passed away in 1978.

At the time of de Marigny's trial, it was indicated that Dr. Oberwarth was attached to the Bahamas General Hospital. He did a physical examination of Alfred de Marigny at the prison following his arrest on the charge of having murdered Sir Harry. Oberwarth subsequently reported that de Marigny was in good health and as far as he could note from his examination that he bore no burn marks, scalds or singed hair on his body. Apparently almost within hours of making his observations known, Dr. Oberwarth was dismissed from his post as prison doctor for reasons unknown.

Following his dismissal, he was asked by a representative of the *Tribune* if this move was due in any way to his involvement in the de Marigny case. At that time he could not say if that was correct or not, as it would appear that he was requested to remain silent on the matter. Dr. Oberwarth was replaced by Dr. Hugh Quackenbush as prison doctor.

After his eventual departure from Nassau in 1943, Alfred de Marigny at one point in time landed in Halifax, Nova Scotia, as a member of a merchant ship which had left Havana, Cuba, and while the ship was held in drydock for repairs de Marigny found his way up to Montreal, where he hoped to be reunited with Nancy.

However, while in Montreal de Marigny attempted, but without success, to enlist in the Canadian Armed Forces. It is interesting to note that following his meeting with the military authorities at the recruiting office, de Marigny was required to undergo a medical examination. The doctor who examined him was none other than Dr. Ulrich Oberwarth, his close friend from the old Nassau days. In retrospect while de Marigny was in Nassau he attempted to join the Free French armed forces of Charles de Gaulle and was turned down by Dr. Oberwarth on the grounds that he had a history of hypoglycemia and chronic stomach pains.

In subsequent conversation between Oberwarth and de Marigny relating back to the murder of Sir Harry, he informed de Marigny that he had not been allowed near the body of Sir Harry Oakes after it arrived at the mortuary, but he managed to view the body. Oberwarth could not speak at the time and told de Marigny that he would come over to his home later, which he did. During their conversation, Oberwarth told de Marigny that he was concerned about the way in which the investigation was proceeding. He said that he was under strict instructions from the Attorney General, not to discuss the case with anyone and that medical reports were not to be put in writing.

It was his conclusion that Sir Harry had been shot in the head with a small calibre gun. Sometime later he urged de Marigny to try and have the body exhumed, following which de Marigny did make some preliminary enquiries relative to the possibility, but the matter was never pursued any further.

At the time of Sir Harry's death, Dr. Hugh Quackenbush who was forty three years of age, was considered by many Nassauvians as a very pleasant gentleman, who had trained for the medical profession at McGill University in Montreal and graduated in medicine in 1927.

Together with Dr. Lawrence Fitzmaurice, they were not exactly considered forensic pathologists as such and regrettably it was the opinion of some that their postmortem observations and evaluations concerning the death of Sir Harry Oakes, were actually more confusing than enlightening, both to the Prosecution and Defense teams.

On the morning that Sir Harry's body was discovered, Dr. Quackenbush received a telephone call from Mrs. Madeleine Kelly at *Westbourne* around 7.30 a.m. requesting his presence as Sir Harry was gravely ill. He proceeded immediately and arrived there at 7.40 a.m.

Dr. Quackenbush went up to Sir Harry's room on the second floor and examined the body from which he noted that a puncture wound in front of his left ear was large enough to allow the penetration of his index finger and also felt that the skull had been cracked. It was obvious at this point that Sir Harry was not ill, but certainly dead.

It was Dr. Quackenbush's estimate that Sir Harry had been dead for approximately 2½ to 5 hours, however, no mention was made of what forensic evaluation brought him to this conclusion.

The description of the head wounds to Sir Harry Oakes by Dr. Fitzmaurice, was the only professional description provided by the Prosecution during the trial. There appeared to be no reasons for the Defense to question the validity of his testimony.

It must also be remembered that both these doctors were the only available physicians on the island with any previous experience. To perform the necessary analysis and await the arrival of more experienced help would have further delayed the immediately required evaluations into the cause of the death of Sir Harry. Assistance from the RAF medical staff stationed in Nassau could have been requested.

All types of conclusions have been drawn as to the weapon used, but none was ever put forth during the trial, with the exception of numerous references to a possible *blunt instrument* which was Dr. Quackenbush's opinion and which has never been challenged.

There is good reason to believe that the wounds to the head were not as a result of gun shots, in view of Harold Christie's so called proximity to the scene of the crime — only sixteen odd feet away in his room that night. It would be difficult to argue this case without pointing the finger at Christie for his possible implication in the matter — his possible false testimony or for that matter that he was not actually in the house and was visiting with a lady friend at the time that the crime was committed.

It should also be noted that when the plane departed from Nassau on its way to the United States with the mortal remains of Sir Harry Oakes, it was suddenly recalled to Nassau and the remains were immediately rushed back to the Bahamas General Hospital, where Attorney General Eric Hallinan, Capt. Edward Melchen, Capt. James Barker and Dr. Quackenbush himself, remained with the body for over an hour.

Various opinions have been expressed as to the reasons for the recall of Sir Harry's remains. One was to allow the authorities time to further clean out the cavities of the skull and to remove any remote trace of the remnants of any bullets, which may still have been lodged in the skull. Another source claims that the original photographs of the body had been lost, possibly stolen or lastly that the original negatives were exposed to light. Regardless of the reason it was necessary to repeat the procedure.

Dr. Quackenbush reported directly to the Duke of Windsor on the morning that the murder was discovered, to inform him of what had happened and that it was his belief at the time that Sir Harry had possibly committed suicide because of the injuries near his left ear. Sir Harry was supposedly left handed. It was only after Dr. Quackenbush saw the x-rays that he changed his opinion and realized that there had been four skull fractures and the cause of death was now murder, but it still remained that the murder weapon was not known nor could any other reasonable suggestion be put forth. According to the trial transcript, the x-rays never made it to court, as there is no mention of them.

Commissioner of Police Reginald Alexander Erskine-Lindop. *Courtesy of Patrick Erskine-Lindop, Nassau*

It was said that Col. Reginald Alexander Erskine-Lindop was a white Bahamian, who also came from the Islands of Mauritius, as did Alfred de Marigny and his cousin Georges de Visdelou.

At the time of the murder of Sir Harry Oakes, Erskine-Lindop was Commissioner of the Bahamas Police and together with his colleagues was more or less forced to wait idly on the sidelines at *Westbourne* under the Duke of Windsor's strict orders not to take part in the immediate investigation being performed by the detectives from Miami.

Following the basic investigation by Captains James Barker and Edward Melchen, they informed Erskine-Lindop's officers that they could scrub the walls of Sir Harry's bedroom and the hallway to remove all hand marks and fingerprints, because as they would say — these prints do not match those of the accused — de Marigny — and would only add confusion to the matter.

Erskine-Lindop held the position of Commissioner of Police from October 1936 to September 1943, at which point he was apparently posted away from Nassau, virtually on the eve of de Marigny's trial, so that he would not be there in person to give evidence in the defense of de Marigny.

In conversation with Judge Daly following the verdict, James Sands as foreman of the Jury, expressed on behalf of the Jury their concern that it was not proper to not have had Erskine-Lindop called back to Nassau to testify during the actual trial, thus allowing the

Defense the opportunity to properly cross-examine him as would normally have been the case.

Some years later, an author reviewing the murder of Sir Harry spoke to Etienne Dupuch, then Editor of the *Tribune*, who felt that Erskine-Lindop's transfer to Trinidad was *presumably the decision of the Duke of Windsor. He claimed that a suspect in the case broke down under his cross-examination, however, Erskine-Lindop refused to name the individual, who, he claimed, continued to move in high circles.*

As was usually the case another opportunity to properly identify a suspect was missed as Erskine-Lindop did not reveal the name of the individual.

Reginald Erskine-Lindop passed away at the age of ninety eight in Nassau.

Another member of the Bahamas Police was Major Herbert Pemberton who was the Acting Deputy Commissioner and Head of the CID (Criminal Investigation Division). It was Major Pemberton who placed Alfred de Marigny under arrest on Friday, July 9th, 1943, at approximately 6.15 p.m. at Sir Harry's *Westbourne* estate on the charges of having murdered his father-in-law.

Pemberton's testimony during the trial regarding the scene of the murder when he first arrived, seems to be the only official description provided. When Captains James Barker and Edward Melchen arrived later that day, the room had been completely overrun by anyone who cared to enter and view the scene of the crime.

Lieutenant Johnny Douglas was a close friend of Alfred de Marigny and at the time of the murder was Assistant Superintendent of the Bahamas Police department. He had been assigned by Capt. Edward Melchen, to guard de Marigny at his home on the evening prior to his arrest.

Douglas escorted de Marigny home and following their arrival expressed his disappointment to de Marigny in having to watch over him that evening, as he had a previous commitment of a more personal nature than to sit and keep an eye on him. As Douglas said — *if the murdered person was just another local Nassau native, there would not have been all this fuss.*

On an hourly basis the Nassau police headquarters would call de Marigny's home to enquire from Douglas if all was well with de Marigny and no doubt to also see if Douglas himself was still awake. Needless to say de Marigny had a rather restless night with all these hourly calls.

While Alfred de Marigny was under the custody of Lt. Douglas prior to his arrest, Douglas confirmed that de Marigny asked him some rather unusual questions — *whether in a British Court, a man could be convicted if the weapon were not found?* to which Douglas answered — *don't worry about it Freddie.*

De Marigny then asked Douglas a further question — *if a man could be convicted on circumstantial evidence?* to which Douglas said — *yes, I think so.*

Two rather significant questions to ask a police officer, even a friendly police officer, especially when you are possibly about to be considered as the prime suspect in an important murder case.

Very little is subsequently known of Johnny Douglas and what happened to him. In a 1959 publication summarising the trial, it was simply mentioned that Douglas had passed away some years earlier.

Mysterious Deaths, Threats and Stories

Elizabeth 'Betty' Renner was a thirty seven year old lady who vacationed in Nassau in 1950 and whose body was found at the bottom of a well. The location of the well was in the Pine Barren area not far from Gladstone Road, which is located almost halfway across the island to the south, but quite some distance from where she was residing with her friend Alison MacDonald at the Loft House down near Bay Street.

It is said that Ms. Renner had dinner one evening following her arrival with one of the trustees of the Oakes estate and the story circulated at the time that she had made it known when she arrived in Nassau, that she was going to investigate the murder of Sir Harry Oakes.

She worked for a law firm in Washington, D.C., who subsequently claimed that it was their understanding that she was only in Nassau on holidays and denied any investigative undertakings by Ms. Renner on their behalf. If she was doing anything, she was doing it on her own.

Prior to working with the law firm, Ms. Renner was a former American Justice Department attorney, who had been involved in the Japanese war crime trials.

It was also Raymond Schindler's contention, that Ms. Renner had gathered some information on the murder that could have been quite damaging to the man involved with the actual murder.

An interesting note on the possible solution of the murder of Ms. Renner was reported in a story which appeared in the *New York Daily News* a short time after the incident, to the effect that the Federal Bureau of Investigation had uncovered a major clue regarding the slaying of Ms. Renner. The information was said to have come from a prominent figure in Nassau. The U.S. State Department was also investigating the murder as Ms. Renner was after all an American citizen.

It was said that Ms. Renner was known to have seen a man who was associated with Oakes and who appeared as a witness in the Alfred de Marigny trial. According to the transcript of the trial proceedings, the only three gentlemen who testified during the trial, who were considered associates of Oakes were Harold Christie (Nassau real estate agent), Newell Kelly (Sir Harry's Nassau manager) and Walter Foskett (Sir Harry's attorney and manager for his U.S. interests).

Following Ms. MacDonald's return to New York after the incident, the *New York Daily News* reported that they had learned that she received several telephone calls from an hysterical woman, who was believed to have said to Ms. MacDonald to keep quiet about anything she might know.

The calls were reported to have come from a maid at the Loft House where Ms. Renner stayed with her, but the *News* subsequently said that it understood that the FBI had checked the calls and found that they did not come from a maid at the resort. The question then is, who did these calls come from? The question was never answered.

Cyril Stevenson was the editor of the Nassau Herald newspaper and co-founder of the Progressive Liberal Party. He was also a prominent figure in the Bahamian Government and the development of their political parties.

In June 1959, some sixteen years after the tragic death of Sir Harry Oakes — possibly motivated by nothing more than the passage of time as they say — Cyril Stevenson stood on the floor of the House of Assembly and called for the Government of the Bahamas to reopen the investigation into the murder of Sir Harry Oakes. It was his feeling that the people of the Bahamas should be entitled to have a solution to the murder and that this was the least they could do in memory of their good friend, benefactor and colleague Sir Harry Oakes.

As a result Stevenson introduced a Resolution in the House of Assembly which read as follows:

Resolved, that it is the opinion of this House that immediate steps should be taken by the Bahamas Government to reopen the Oakes murder case and that Scotland Yard be requested to send investigators to the Colony to conduct an intensive investigation into the murder in Nassau in 1943 of the Canadian gold-mining multi-millionaire Sir Harry Oakes.

Resolved further, that it is the opinion of this House that the Governor of the Bahamas should order the Criminal Investigation Department of the Bahamas Police Force to offer every assistance possible to the officers from Scotland Yard in the investigation of the most brutal crime in the annals of Bahamian criminal history.

Be it further resolved, that a copy of this Resolution be forwarded to His Excellency the Governor for his information, and respectfully requesting him to carry out the wishes of the House as herein contained.

In a moment of high drama, Cyril Stevenson stood in the House and declared that the man responsible for the murder of Sir Harry sat amongst them and must be brought to justice. No leap of the imagination was apparently required to picture the heads turning toward the member of the House in question, who it is said remained motionless in his seat.

In this regard it is interesting to note from a Nassau newspaper report the following comment — *member Harold Christie, who was a house guest of Sir Harry on the night he was bludgeoned to death, voted for the resolution.*

In addition it was Stevenson's feeling *that the Duke of Windsor should come to Nassau to reveal information he had at his disposal concerning the murder. It was the Duke's bungling that was responsible for the investigation not being carried through.*

Stevenson had said that Raymond Schindler, an American detective — *told me without doubt he could put his hand on the murderer.*

Interestingly enough, on June 16th, 1959, some twenty four hours following his speech in the House, there was an attempt made on Stevenson's life. Three shots were fired into the lower floor, housing the newspaper office. Stevenson occupied an apartment upstairs and was in bed at the time of the incident.

Deputy Police Superintendent Stanley Moir confirmed that the police authorities had two of the bullets, which appeared to be from a .38 calibre revolver which was an unusual size in the Bahamas. Did the intruder come from off the island?

Oct. 12, 1950.

Sea Coast Stevedoring
401 Broadway
New York 13 N.Y.

Dear ████████

In my letter to you, I did not go into any details as to the reason for quiting my job as I assumed that you had read the newspapers which stated that I recieved several threats from persons unkown to me as I possessed intimate knowledge of Sir Harry Oaks murderer.

Miss Renner was killed as she had knowledge of the murderer.

It was for this reason that I became irratable and nervous. Being in the 'spot' I was, I felt it best at that time not to reveal the the reason for my leaving.

Yours truly
Edward Majava

62-73177-26

ENCLOSURE

ALL INFORMATION CONTAINED HEREIN IS UNCLASSIFIED
DATE 6/12/80

Copy of letter written by Edward Majava on October 12, 1950, to his former employer.
Freedom of Information & Privacy Act — FOIPA

Nothing ever came of the resolution and without meaning to sound repetitive, another opportunity to take some initiative to properly investigate the murder of Sir Harry was not acted upon.

Sir Oswald Raynor Arthur subsequently announced in the House of Assembly that there would be no further enquiry and the case was closed. Nevertheless, to this day the Oakes case has always remained opened.

What magic powers were there to abort all these efforts over the years will never be known.

On September 16th, 1950, one *Edward Majava*, described as a 31 year old mechanic (or ex-seaman as the case may be) boasted to a number of patrons in a bar in Oakland, California that he knew *the inside story* on the murder of Sir Harry Oakes in Nassau. He was subsequently arrested for drunkenness and brought to a police station.

Majava continued to discuss the matter and claimed that the information had been given to him by a lady named Mrs. Hildegarde Hamilton, who was a society portrait painter from Fort Lauderdale, Florida who in turn had heard the story from the local grapevine and they had been told it by friends of none other than Walter Foskett, Sir Harry Oakes' Palm Beach attorney.

It seemed like a dubious lead to an old murder, however, certain officers of the Oakland police force were aware of the famous murder case in the Bahamas and thought it best to take action.

As a result Patrick O'Reagan, British Vice-Consul in San Fransisco was immediately made aware of the matter concerning Majava and his comments relative to the murder of Sir Harry Oakes, following which O'Reagan cabled the Bahamas Police department with the information.

Augustus Roberts, then Assistant Superintendent of the Bahamas Police force flew to Oakland and questioned Majava on the matter.

Recently declassified Federal Bureau of Investigation files revealed for the first time that what Chief Roberts confirmed about Majava was indeed correct.

At all times during this matter Scotland Yard remained silent, no doubt because royalty had been involved in the person of the Duke of Windsor. Assistant Superintendent Roberts subsequently returned to Nassau from Oakland, but never did pursue the matter though it had received comment in the Nassau press.

Once again what appeared to be a further reliable source was never followed by the authorities in either Nassau or London for that matter, and the murder of Sir Harry Oakes continued in the annals of crime as being an *unsolved murder*.

A subsequent newspaper clipping and a photo of Majava, together with Assistant Superintendent Augustus Roberts, appeared in the Toronto Star on September 18th, 1950, substantiating the story given by Roberts when he returned to Nassau.

An interesting note to the above is that within a week of the Majava incident, one George Boyle, a retired grocery clerk came forward and walked into a newspaper office in Oakland with a claim that he also knew who had killed Sir Harry Oakes. Inspector James Mangini of the Oakland Police questioned him on the matter for a two hour period. Although

Mangini would not reveal what had been discussed and felt there were a few discrepancies, he said flatly that — *I believe his story in some respects*. Boyle at one time lived in the Miami and Palm Beach areas.

Following Augustus Roberts' verbal report of the conversation with Edward Majava, Bahamas Police Commissioner G.H.Ranoe announced that *"there was no new evidence in the case based on the interview, which would justify opening new legal proceedings in the seven year old murder of Sir Harry Oakes."* Commissioner Ranoe when questioned declined to issue any further statement on the matter. And so ended another attempt to investigate the tragic death of Sir Harry Oakes.

On October 12th, 1950, Edward Majava wrote a second letter to his employer in New York explaining his reasons for having resigned his job with the stevedoring company. He did not give his employer any details in his first letter as he thought that they had already read about it in newspaper articles. It had been reported that he had received several threats on his life from persons unknown to him relative to his intimate knowledge of circumstances surrounding the murder of Sir Harry Oakes.

In conversation with a certain individual on a bus trip to Niagara Falls in November 1991, to visit Oak Hall with Max Haines of the *Toronto Sun*, the statement was made to me that a Chief of Police or high ranking officer in the Bahamas Police Department was murdered sometime following the murder of Sir Harry Oakes, but no name was mentioned as he did not recall it. The information seems to have come from one of the doctors who examined the body of Sir Harry Oakes and this doctor was a friend of this individual.

During a visit to Nassau in 1992, the question of the high ranking police officer being murdered was put to Ernest Callender, one of Alfred de Marigny's Defense attorneys, however, he could not recall such an incident. While he did not recall the incident, Callender was quite surprised in a way when asked the question, and tried to extract from me the source of my information. I did not know the name of the officer.

Lord Beaverbrook (Max Aitken), Canadian born newspaper magnate, was one of the founders and original shareholders of the Bahamas General Trust and at one time owned property on which is now established the East Hill Club in Nassau, a very exclusive European styled meeting and dining establishment.

At the Riviera home of Lord Beaverbrook in Cap d'Ail, France during the 1960's, Lord Beaverbrook hosted a party at which Harold Christie was in attendance. Lord Beaverbrook, having lived in Nassau and having read a great deal about the murder of Sir Harry Oakes, asked Christie point blank, *"Harold, now that you are free and clear, why not tell us how you did it?"* in reference to the often mentioned association of Christie with the murder of Sir Harry Oakes.

Christie was said to have only smiled and naturally didn't respond to the question.

One of the main claims to fame of Washington socialite *Evalyn Walsh McLean* is most likely the fact that she was at one time the owner of the world famous Hope Diamond. As history would dictate, anyone who owned the Hope diamond was sure to encounter bad luck at some point during their lifetime.

The following is quoted from the book entitled *RSVP: Elsa Maxwell's Own Story* written by Elsa Maxwell herself, and provides an interesting reference to the Sir Harry Oakes case:

It is a pity that Mrs. McLean was known to the public only as the owner of the Hope diamond — a singularly ugly stone — and as a bit of an eccentric on criminology. Although she was a remarkably perceptive woman in many areas, she was a pushover for any cock-and-bull story relating to crime. She offered $100,000 reward for the return of the kidnapped Lindbergh baby and unhesitatingly gave the money to Gaston Means, a notorious confidence man, on nothing more than his say-so that he had made contact with the culprits. Mrs. McLean also went for a tidy bundle trying to solve the murder of Sir Harry Oakes in Nassau. She did not know the victim or any of the suspects; she simply was fascinated by mysteries. Private investigators convinced Mrs. McLean that a voodoo cult murdered Oakes for seducing a native woman.

Evalyn Walsh McLean, an eccentric on criminology who was interested in the murder of Sir Harry Oakes. Notice the famous *Hope* diamond which she is wearing on a chain. *Copyright Washington Post, reprinted by permission of the D.C. Public Library, Washington*

Mrs. McLean also had a residence in Bar Harbor, Maine and it could be that one day she may have met Sir Harry Oakes, who as you are aware also had an estate there. Would this have been the connection for her interest in his murder?

The Hope Diamond was purchased by Evalyn McLean in January 1911, at a cost of $184,000 and when she died in 1947 she left the stone in trust for her grandchildren. The diamond, however, had to be sold in due course to assist in paying off some of her debts. The appraised value was set at $176,920.

The purchaser of the diamond was one Harry Winston, well known New York jeweller, who eleven years later would donate the stone to the Smithsonian Museum in Washington, D.C., where it can still be seen on display to this day. Interestingly enough, nothing bad ever happened to Winston during his ownership of the diamond. The Hope Diamond weighs 45.52 karats.

An interesting note from an article written by Gary Cohen for *Vanity Fair* on the subject of Evalyn McLean, was concerning James Todd, who was one of the mailmen who delivered the gem to the Smithsonian Museum. Todd had one of his legs crushed by a truck, injured his head in a car crash, lost his wife and dog. Then his house burned down. When asked if he blamed any of his ill fortune on the diamond, he said — *"I don't believe any of that stuff."*

9

The Magistrate's and Supreme Courts

The Magistrate's Court: July 12th to August 31st, 1943 — Determine If There Is Just Cause ..... Supreme Court: October 18th to November 11th, 1943 ..... Sir Oscar Bedford Daly M.B.E., K.C., — The Presiding Judge ..... The Jury — The Twelve Wise Men .....The Ultimate Verdict ..... The Trial of the Century ..... Guilty or Not Guilty ..... Deportation As An Undesirable ..... Certain Arrivals and Departures — Were They Important?

Alfred de Marigny had already been charged on July 9th, 1943, with the murder of Sir Harry Oakes and it was the purpose of the hearing in the Magistrate's Court, to determine if there was just cause, based on the evidence to be presented by the Crown, to bring de Marigny to trial by jury in the Supreme Court of the Bahamas.

The Magistrate's Court under the jurisdiction of Magistrate Frank Eustace Fields was called into session on Monday, July 12th, 1943, at 10.00 a.m., four days following the murder of Sir Harry. Fields' full title was Stipendiary and Circuit Magistrate, as well as Coroner.

It was Magistrate Fields' conclusion on August 31st, 1943, on having heard the case presented by the Prosecution, who called some 28 witnesses, that there was just cause for de Marigny to be brought to trial by jury.

As a result Magistrate Fields made the following announcement to Alfred de Marigny: *From the evidence of the hearing, I am satisfied that a prima facie case has been made out against you and I order you to stand trial at the Court of Sessions in October*, and so ended Alfred de Marigny's hope that he would not have to stand trial for the murder, knowing very well himself that he was not guilty of the charge.

During the preliminary trial Godfrey Higgs and Ernest Callender as the Defense team did not ask many questions, as their main objective during the hearing was to record for themselves the facts that were being presented by the Crown against their client and to prepare themselves for the trial in the Supreme Court, if so was to be the case.

Following his appearance in the Magistrate's Court, Alfred de Marigny was now under the protection of the British judicial system and as such, both Captains James Barker and Edward Melchen were no longer in a position to approach and question de Marigny.

As was the custom under British law, no bail was allowed when the charge was murder.

On the morning of Monday, October 18th, 1943, at 10.30 a.m. in the Supreme Court of the Bahamas, the *trial of the century*, as it was called, was to take place, with Alfred de Marigny to stand trial for the murder of his father-in-law, Sir Harry Oakes during the night of July 7th and 8th.

The following is from the *Tribune's* book published in 1959, for which permission has been granted to reproduce, and which provides a very vivid description of a most historical moment typical of the British legal system, which is very seldom seen in this day and age:

The Chief Justice wore the scarlet robes of his office and his white, meticulously curled wig. The lawyers were clothed in the same academic gowns which identified scholars in the early days of England's revival of learning and they wore wigs which perpetuated a memory of the age when England's snuff-taking gentry, creating another of the transient fashions of human vanity, wore fastidiously curled periwigs with no thought of bequeathing a legacy to posterity. Over the left shoulder of each barrister hung a little black pouch — a nostalgic tradition reminiscent of the days when, allowed to accept an honorarium but forbidden to fix a fee, lawyers sat with money bags across their shoulders and reserved the right to accept or reject a case, contingent on the amount of the honorarium dropped into the pouch by the accused as he passed behind the Bar. And the visitors learned that today the pouch, like the anatomical appendix, serves no practical purpose — except to add polish to the court manner of the barrister who addresses the Jury with greater ease when clutching the draw-cords hanging in front of his gown.

Standing stiffly in the court and pacing back and forth outside the doors and windows were the constables of the Court Guard, wearing the red-striped blue woollen trousers, the immaculate white tunics, the spiked helmets and the sheathed bayonets of the colonial constabulary.

To those witnessing this scene for the first time it was, perhaps, a reminder of a tableau from a Gilbert and Sullivan operetta. But to those reared in the British tradition this scene was a symbol of a vibrant, an ageless, an immortal spirit — a breath from the soul of the world's oldest monarchial democracy.

The *trial of the century* was now underway in the Supreme Court of the Bahamas in Nassau, a two storey building built in 1921 located in what is called Parliament Square. The square and its surrounding area also includes the Senate and the House of Assembly.

In order to obtain proper seating in the Court House during the trial, many of the affluent white residents would send a member of their staff to access the line up outside the Court House, thus assuring themselves of appropriate seating space when the court opened. In viewing some old film footage from the coverage of the trial by Movietone News, there was a large number of RAF personnel in the daily line-up in front of the Court House waiting to enter and witness the administration of British justice.

According to a sketch of the interior of the Court House, the prisoner's dock is clearly shown as a wooden enclosure in which Alfred de Marigny would sit during the entire course of the trial. The dock was self-enclosed with a wooden top and sides, as well as wooden bars that were located in the front through which de Marigny would look around the court room.

Line-up of Bahamians awaiting possible access to the Supreme Court to witness the proceeding of the Trial of the Century. *Corbis/Bettman — UPI*

At the time of the murder of Sir Harry, Sir Oscar Daly was the Chief Justice of the Bahamas and had previously administered the sacred oath of office to the Duke of Windsor on his appointment as Royal Governor General of the Bahamas upon his arrival in Nassau in August 1940. Daly had been appointed Chief Justice some four years earlier and was to be presiding Judge in the Supreme Court during the trial of Alfred de Marigny. Daly had attended Trinity College in Dublin, Ireland, and had been Chief Justice of the Bahamas since 1939 and was knighted in 1942.

Sir Oscar also had an outstanding career in the Intelligence Corp during the First World War and was later at the Bar in Kenya Colony in private practice. He was a member of the exclusive Bahamas Country Club in Nassau, which was situated next door to Sir Harry's *Westbourne* estate.

During the course of the trial, as there were no court stenographers at the time, Sir Oscar was obliged to maintain in his own handwriting a transcript of the trial in a huge

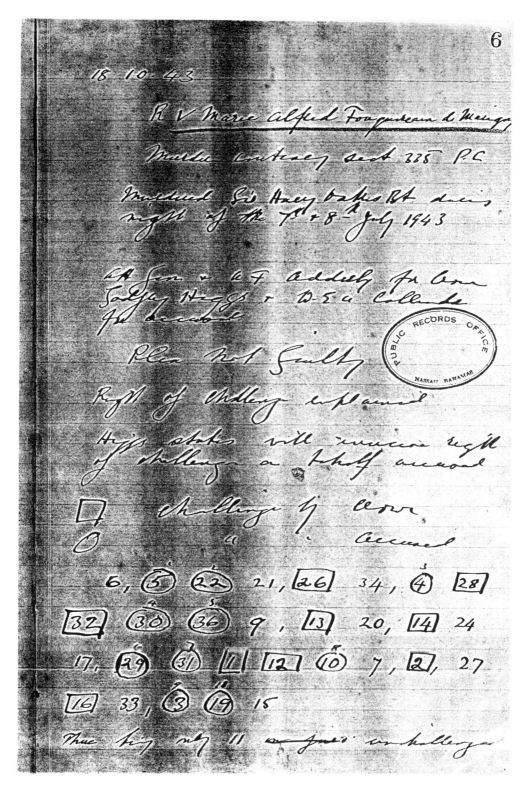

Extract from page six of Sir Oscar's handwritten minutes relative to Alfred de Marigny's plea and the selection of the Jury on October 18, 1943. *Courtesy of the Public Archives of the Bahamas*

Closing page 496 from Sir Oscar's minutes showing the verdict and Jury recommendation for deportation of the accused. *Courtesy of the Public Archives of the Bahamas* five hundred page book. As he wrote the proceedings into the book, he only wrote on the right hand pages, as was the custom. The left side was left blank in case it was necessary to make any changes to the transcript if any one so wished, when the text was read back the following day.

It is estimated that in total some five hundred full size legal pages were hand-written and the author can vouch for this fact, as when I visited the Bahamas in the spring of 1992, I had the opportunity of doing some of my research at the Archives of the Bahamas and viewed the two books which Sir Oscar had maintained. I photocopied the first and last pages of the transcript of the trial, which provided the opening records concerning the not guilty plea entered by Alfred de Marigny, the selection of the Jury and the final page which recorded the verdict, as well as the Jury's recommendation that de Marigny be deported from the Bahamas.

As part of the preparation for the trial, a list of thirty six potential jurors was prepared by the judicial authorities in Nassau and presented in the Supreme Court for the benefit of the Prosecution and Defense.

The selection of the Jury was made by means of thirty six wooden numbered balls enclosed in a wooden box, each numbered ball representing the name of one of the potential jurors. Court Crier Jonah Greenidge extracted one numbered ball at a time, gave the number to the Registrar, who would refer to his list of names and call out the number and the name of the potential juror associated with the ball.

The individual was then subject to the acceptance or rejection by the Prosecution or the Defense teams. If they refused the juror they would simply exclaim *challenge* and the juror would be dismissed. In this selection the Prosecution challenged on nine occasions and the Defense on ten out of a total of thirty six potential jurors. Were these challenges an indication of how well de Marigny was known to some of the potential jurors?

In summary twelve Jury members were finally accepted by both the Prosecution and the Defense, after a certain amount of negotiation. Their names, which would go down in the judicial history of the Bahamas, were as follows:

James Patrick Sands	J.W.F.Grahame
Donald d'Albenas	Howard Hullen Farrington
Louis N. Knowles	Joseph Samuel Johnson
John Psilinakis	Charles Seighbert Russell
Talbot Jerome Bethel	Reginald John Robertson
William Arthur Cole	Joseph Dewitt Albury

The final step was the selection of James Sands as the Jury foreman by the members of the Jury.

The Jury was comprised of three accountants, a bakery owner, a sponge merchant, a liquor dealer, a general insurance agent, a grocery clerk, two general merchants, an ice house manager and the foreman James Sands, owner of one of Nassau's larger grocery stores.

Presiding Judge Sir Oscar Daly (with the cane) accompanied by (left to right) Godfrey Higgs, Alfred de Marigny, Lt. Johnny Douglas and Ernest Callender, as they visited de Marigny's home with members of the Jury. *CP Picture Archive*

One by one the members of the Jury repeated the oath — *"I swear by Almighty God that I shall well and truly try and true deliverance make between our Sovereign Lord the King and the prisoner at the Bar, whom I shall have in charge and true verdict give according to the evidence. So help me God."*

As the trial started, Judge Sir Oscar Daly arranged for the jurors to be transported by taxis to Sir Harry's *Westbourne* estate in order to give them a chance to familiarize themselves with the scene of the crime. The Jury also visited de Marigny's residence on Victoria Avenue.

During the trial, Sir Oscar Daly allowed the members of the Jury on October 20th to attend a movie entitled *Above Suspicion* under police escort. One of the jurors attended the movie under protest, as he was opposed to the viewing of movies on religious convictions, however, the court rules compelled that all Jury members remain together at all times.

Similarly the following Sunday, a beach party was planned for the members of the Jury to which the same juror once again objected on the belief that Sundays were days to be devoted to the Lord. In order not to deprive other members of the Jury of the pleasure of the party he attended and sat under the shade of a palm tree by the beach reading his Bible.

On a few occasions during the trial, the members of the Jury were allowed to meet with their business associates for the express purpose of signing cheques and looking after matters of major importance in the operations of their businesses. At all times police officers were present to ensure that no discussions were held concerning the trial.

All the members of the Jury were sequestered in residence at the Rozelda Hotel (subsequently called the Carlton House), which was within easy walking distance of the Court House and they could be seen every day as they walked back and forth along the street.

A final note on the members of the Jury was the fact that only men served on the Jury at that time, as compared to the present day standards, and all members were white.

Marie Alfred Fouquereau de Marigny, you are charged with murder under Section 335 of the Penal Code, Chapter Two. Particulars of the offence being that during the night of the seventh and eighth of July, 1943, at New Providence you did murder Sir Harry Oakes, Baronet. Are you guilty?

"Not guilty," answered de Marigny.

And so started the trial of Alfred de Marigny, son-in-law of Sir Harry Oakes and husband of Nancy Oakes, a trial for which the motive was never really established, nor the murder weapon properly identified.

It is interesting to note that from de Marigny's point of view all the leading individuals in the trial knew him and likewise he knew them — from the presiding Judge, to the Prosecution team (except Captains Barker and Melchen), the Defense team, the members of the Jury and most of the witnesses. Nassau was a very small place.

Last but not least, the only piece of physical evidence ever presented by the Prosecution against de Marigny, was a fingerprint — the little finger on his left hand or finger number ten, which turned out to have been fabricated. It was admitted as evidence at the trial by the presiding Judge Sir Oscar Daly, though the members of the Defense objected most strongly as they felt that the circumstances surrounding the fingerprint and how it was obtained, left a great deal to be desired as far as authenticity and legal interpretation was concerned.

It was also mentioned at one point that in view of the increased risk to de Marigny, he should be taken to a jail some distance outside of Nassau — the question I raise is where would that have been? I ask this since even when I lived in Nassau in the early 1980's there was mainly the Central Police station and a few minor police stations, which did not have proper holding facilities similar to the Central station and certainly would not have provided de Marigny with the necessary protection.

A number of the individuals involved with the trial, also felt that in view of the strong feeling against de Marigny, possibly the trial itself should have been held somewhere else with a more neutral setting such as Bermuda, Jamaica or even Canada. They were possibly right, but it was felt that the expenses of transferring the entire proceedings would have been prohibitive and de Marigny in particular, would not have had the necessary funds to pay for his defense other than in Nassau.

In Judge Daly's summary to the Jury, he outlined some of the downfalls of Captains James Barker and Edward Melchen in their handling of the evidence that they presented during the trial, and also the fact that there was nothing to show what the weapon was or how the assailant(s) entered the house or for that matter how the crime was committed. It was his opinion that in this case, the evidence was entirely circumstantial and that there were no eye-witnesses to any aspects of the crime.

The members of the Jury returned to the Supreme Court at 7.30 p.m. on the evening of November 11th, 1943, having reached their decision on the fate of Alfred de Marigny on the charges of having murdered his father-in-law Sir Harry Oakes.

Alfred de Marigny was led into the court room under the escort of two members of the Bahamian constabulary and his wife Nancy, having been advised at her home that the Jury had reached their decision, also entered the filled court room. The two of them could not see each other in the court room at that time.

The Jury returned a verdict of *not guilty* nine to three, though the Jury added a rider to the effect that de Marigny be deported from the Bahamas as an *undesirable*. Regretfully, due to the noise and excitement surrounding the announcement of the verdict no one heard the details of the rider as expressed by James Sands, the Jury foreman. Judge Daly informed Sands that it was not within his jurisdiction to act or make any comment on their recommendation.

The question has often been raised as to what authority did the Jury have in recommending deportation of de Marigny as an undesirable, as part of their decision? Was this an admissible statement from a legal point of view or should the question have been raised outside the jurisdiction of the Supreme Court, as the Jury's main concern was to judge de Marigny guilty or not guilty of the specific charge of murder?

In addition to the rider, the comment was made by Sands on behalf of the Jury that Commissioner Reginald Erskine-Lindop should have been called back to Nassau to testify at the trial in the Supreme Court, as he was one of the more senior police officers who assisted in the preliminary investigation into the murder before the arrival of the detectives from Miami.

Judge Daly further informed Sands that these matters would be referred to the Colonial Secretary, in the absence of the Governor General, the Duke of Windsor.

An interesting note in the local Nassau newspapers was that if the Jury had returned a verdict of guilty, the Chief Justice would have put on a black cap, pronounced the findings and would have broken the pen with which he wrote the evidence. In the Bahamas at the time, there was no such charge as second degree murder in the justice system and with a verdict of guilty, the Judge would have had to pronounce the sentence of mandatory death by hanging.

As was the custom under Bahamian court regulations, all members of the Jury would normally be excused from jury duty for the next three to five years, however, in this case they were excused for eight years, with no explanation given for the extended period by the Chief Justice.

Alfred de Marigny met James Sands, the foreman of the Jury, in Nassau one evening following the trial and during their conversation de Marigny was informed that the reason for the nine-three verdict of acquittal was due to the fact that four of the jurors were members of the Plymouth Brethren, an apparently strong religious group who objected to de Marigny's lifestyle and in particular to the fact that he spent his Sundays racing yachts with many members of the younger Nassau male population, whereas, they considered that Sundays were days to be devoted to the Lord.

They originally voted de Marigny guilty eight to four which would have led to a hung jury and they agreed to change one vote thus acquitting him, but a rider would be added recommending de Marigny's deportation. As a result of the verdict, many people then and now still do believe that based on the vote of the Jury at least three of the jurors felt that de Marigny was indeed guilty of the murder of his father-in-law Sir Harry Oakes, which as you can see would not appear to be the case. This was first mentioned in 1990 when de Marigny wrote his second book, though de Marigny knew this for a fact within days of his acquittal back in 1943.

For some unknown reason, no mention was made by de Marigny of this fact in his first book published in 1946, which would have assisted the public in gaining a better understanding of the verdict and the reasons behind his actual acquittal and deportation from the Bahamas.

Following the trial, Jeanne Bellamy, feature writer for the *Miami Herald* reported in her paper — "*thus ended the twenty two day trial that was sequel to the most spectacular murder on record in the islands.*"

As they exited from the Court House, reporters asked the Attorney General Eric Hallinan if any further investigation was contemplated, to which he replied — "*nothing as far as I am concerned. It's completely closed — call it a day.*" And with these comments ended any hope for a foreseeable investigation to find the real murderer and to this day that has remained the case.

Captains James Barker and Edward Melchen were also asked for their comments concerning the verdict and replied to the effect that — "*we did what we were supposed to do and the rest was up to the jury.*"

Based on old copies of the leading Nassau newspapers, the *Tribune* and the *Guardian*, mention was made on a daily basis in both publications of all the arrivals and departures of local residents of Nassau, as well as any visitors.

It is imagined that in those days, before the large influx of tourists, it was a rather easy matter to record and publish all the arrivals and departures in Nassau, which in turn would provide some newsworthy information for those who were socially inclined. It was also a valuable source of information concerning the whereabouts of friends, as well as some indication as to who may be visiting with your neighbours.

The reference to these arrivals and departures was also part of the testimony given at the trial of Alfred de Marigny, by one Phillip Strong Brice, then Acting Immigration Officer for His Majesty's Government, who confirmed for the Prosecution the following arrivals and departures of members of the Oakes family (Sydney) and also de Marigny himself (and his wife Nancy) during the part of 1943 leading up to the date of the death of Sir Harry Oakes:

	Arrivals	Departures
Sir Harry Oakes	January 22	February 5
	March 23	April 1
	May 25	Died July 8
Sydney Oakes (Sir Harry's son)	March 23	April 1
Alfred de Marigny	January 22	January 27
	March 1	April 25
	May 1	December 6
Nancy de Marigny (Sir Harry's daughter)	March 13	April 25
	May 1	May 27
	July 20	December 6

Lady Oakes and the children were off the island at the time of Sir Harry's death and it was Oakes' intention to depart on Friday July 9th for the United States to be with his family in Bar Harbor, Maine.

It was said that prior to the start of the trial of Alfred de Marigny on October 18th, 1943, the Duke of Windsor and his Duchess had left the islands for the United States, as it appeared to be the Duke's wish not to be in Nassau during the trial.

It has always been maintained by some, that the reason the Windsors were away from the islands was due to the possibility that the Duke could have been called upon to testify at the trial and be questioned by the Prosecution or the Defense. It is not known for sure if this would have happened considering the Duke of Windsor's position as Royal Governor General at the time and in particular as a member of the British Royal family. It is a known fact that members of royalty can usually avoid such unpleasant circumstances.

If the Duke had been called to testify it could have caused some potential public exposure to the more questionable financial dealings of the Duke of Windsor with Sir Harry Oakes, Harold Christie and Dr. Axel Wenner-Gren, keeping in mind that the Exchange Control Board regulations were in force in the Bahamas at the time governing the flow of funds.

It is interesting to note that neither the Prosecution, the Defense, the Jury nor the Chief Justice asked any questions concerning the records presented of the arrivals and departures, although this information was entered as an Exhibit at the trial.

10

The Prosecution and the Dynamic Miami Duo

Sir Eric Hallinan — The Attorney General of the Bahamas ..... Alfred de Marigny's Arrest Statement ..... Alfred Francis Adderley — For the Prosecution ..... Captain James Otto Barker — Fingerprinting Was His Specialty ..... Captain Edward Walter Melchen — The Other Member of the Dynamic Duo ..... Detective Frank Conway — A Fingerprinting Consultant ..... Inspector Joseph J.Donovan — We Have An Unknown Witness ..... Finally the Prosecution's Case — Some Fourteen Points to be Proven

---

Eric Hallinan, the Attorney General of the Bahamas, was born in County Cork, Ireland in 1900 and was educated at Downside, one of the finest Catholic schools in England. He subsequently continued his education at Trinity College in Dublin, Ireland.

Attorney General Eric Hallinan accompanied by the Assistant Prosecutor Alfred Adderley as they viewed Alfred de Marigny's home. *CP Picture Archive*

Hallinan was a Barrister-at-Law of the Irish and English Bars and formerly a Crown Counsel in Nigeria before his eventual appointment as Attorney General of the Bahamas.

At the time of the Duke of Windsor's arrival in Nassau, Hallinan had less than a month's experience in the Bahamas. It was nevertheless felt that he likely had the most knowledge in his field and was instrumental in assisting the Duke of Windsor establish himself as the new Royal Governor General of the Islands.

Eric Hallinan as Attorney-General of the Bahamas at the time of the murder of Sir Harry was responsible, together with Alfred Adderley, in preparing the Prosecution's case for the trial of Alfred de Marigny.

As de Marigny recalled it on the day that he was arrested, Hallinan said to him — *"please step this way."* I walked towards him and stopped a few steps short. In a clear flat voice he said,

"Alfred de Marigny, you are accused of the murder of Sir Harry Oakes. Have you anything to say?"

A few moments later Col. Reginald Erskine-Lindop placed his right hand on de Marigny's shoulder and stated, *"Alfred de Marigny, in the name of the Crown, you are under arrest for the murder of Sir Harry Oakes."*

Immediately following his having been charged on the evening of July 9th, 1943, with the murder of his father-in-law Sir Harry Oakes, Alfred de Marigny made the following written statement to Major Herbert Pemberton, then Acting Deputy Commissioner of the Bahamas Police:

Having been charged with the murder of Sir Harry Oakes and duly cautioned make the following voluntary statement: It is a ridiculous charge as I have no reason to do it. I had dinner at my house with my guests and the last ones were Mrs. Ainslie and Mrs. Clarke and I took them home in my car in the morning, car No. 1383, between 1.00 a.m. and 1.30 a.m. I returned home immediately. My servants were still there as it was raining heavily. I entered my car in the garage and went to bed. My servants apparently left they told me around 2.30 a.m. Around 3.15 a.m. my friend Georges de Visdelou-Guimbeau, took Miss Roberts

Major Herbert Pemberton of Nassau's Criminal Investigation Division, together with Captains James Barker (seated) and Edward Melchen from the Miami Police. *Corbis/Bettman — UPI*

home and the noise of the car passing woke me up. He returned about 15 minutes later, entered on the ground floor through the dining room and went into my room to get his cat who was making quite a noise trying to get out. He left in a couple of minutes and I went back to sleep. I woke early having some work to do and went to the farm with some chickens. I returned to town and went to the Post Office to see if there was any mail. I met on the corner of Bank Lane and Bay Street Basil McKinney and Oswald Moseley. We discussed for about a few minutes the races of the previous afternoon. I left and returned to the farm where I stayed until roughly 11.00 a.m. I returned to town to purchase some cheese-cloth to make screens with. I met Mr. J. H. Anderson who told me that Sir Harry had been found dead. We both went home and we announced the news to Mr. Visdelou and Mr. Anderson took me in his car to Westbourne House and I can swear that I have not seen Sir Harry Oakes to talk to since the 29th of March. I have not been to Westbourne before two years ago for a short visit. This is all I have to say.
(signed) M.A.F. de Marigny.

March 29th is actually the anniversary date of Alfred de Marigny's birthday.

It was during the hearing in the Magistrate's Court that Major Pemberton read de Marigny's written statement.

Attorney-General Hallinan recalled seeing evidence of hand prints on the walls around Sir Harry's bedroom on the day the murder was discovered and that Capt. James Barker had taken photographs of them, but they were never referred to again during the entire prosecution of Alfred de Marigny, either in the Magistrate's or Supreme Court.

Hallinan was very critical afterwards of the investigative work performed by the Miami detectives, however, as he said — *"his position during the trial was to lead them through their testimony and let the jury evaluate the validity of their presentation."*

In 1944, the year following the trial of Alfred de Marigny, Hallinan was posted to Trinidad, following in the footsteps of Commissioner Reginald Erskine-Lindop of the Bahamas Police force, who had also been transferred there prior to the start of the trial.

In due course Hallinan was appointed Chief Justice of Cyprus in 1952 and knighted the same year. It is said that he ended his legal career as the Chief Justice of the Windward and Leeward Islands.

Sometime in late 1970, Marshall Houts, author of a book entitled *The King's X*, who investigated in some detail the proceedings of the trial of Alfred de Marigny on the charge of the murder, and had also received certain information from some so called *informants*, decided to write to Hallinan asking him for his comments on the trial. A short time later, Houts received the following reply as quoted from Hallinan's own letter:

On board I. S. Geesthaven   *Good Friday*
Dominica, West Indies   *9th April 1971*

Dear Mr Houts:

I've been preoccupied pulling up my roots in Barbados (after 11 years) preparatory to going to live in Spain. But I now have some spare moments to reply to your letters requesting some information from me concerning the Oakes case.

I fear you will be disappointed in what I have to offer. I am not sufficiently interested in the case to recollect and record all that went on.

I think the attitude of a prosecutor in a British court (such as I was) may be somewhat different to one in an American court. Something you said in your letters (not with me as I write) gave me the impression that I should have been concerned at the failure of the prosecution in this Oakes case ...

In British practice, the prosecutor in an Assize Court (district or superior court) is a barrister whose task is not to conduct the criminal investigation or even supervise it, but to present the evidence which the Crown has in its possession against the accused. A magistrate at the Preliminary Inquiry decides whether the Crown has a prima facie case to go to a judge and jury at the Assize. If the accused is returned for trial, then it is the duty of the prosecutor (myself in the Oakes Case as Attorney General) to present the evidence for the Crown as cogently and at the same time as fairly as possible. It is not the function or duty of the prosecutor to try and obtain a conviction by every means in his power or to make the case appear stronger than it is. On the other hand, he must lead the evidence for the Crown even though he may consider it weak; he must leave it to the jury to assess its value.

The only part of the Oakes case to which you specifically referred in your letter was the fingerprinting evidence. I have no objection in letting you have my recollection of this part of the case which perhaps may be of some interest. You must remember that, once the trial was over, I never pursued the matter further, many things may have transpired since then. I only know what happened before and at the trial.

The Duke of Windsor, then Governor of the Bahamas, thought the investigation into the murder of Sir Harry Oakes was too big for the local police headed by Colonel Erskine-Lindop — in this, the Governor may very well have been right. But his request for aid from the Miami City Police was unfortunate. The Duke had been impressed with the efficiency of their arrangements when he passed through Miami on his journeys to and from the United States. Two officers were sent over from Miami, Melchen and Barker. Melchen was the non-technical CID officer. I do not recollect his making any very material contribution to the investigation, Barker was the fingerprint and photographic expert.

Barker took photographs of Oakes' corpse, and of the bedroom where he was murdered. I remember seeing the imprints of a hand on the wall as if someone had groped his way round the room. Barker took photographs of these which I thought was important. He then announced that he had found the accused's fingerprint on a screen besides Oakes bed. He did not photograph it in situ (the usual practise) but stated that he had taken it on a scotch tape which he later produced in court.

He informed me that proper facilities for developing photographs, making enlargements etc., were not available in Nassau, so he flew over to Miami to do it there. I was then informed by the police that Barker had sent a message to say that light had got into the plates on the way over and had spoilt them.

Sir Harry Oakes' body (which had been embalmed and was being flown to Bar Harbor, Maine for burial) had to be intercepted in mid-air and flown back to Nassau. The cerements were again removed and the ghastly business of photographs gone through again. I inquired what had happened about the hand prints on the wall of Oakes' bedroom but was told they were negative. I regard the way in which the investigation of these hand prints was covered as one of the most sinister and mysterious features of the case.

When Barker's evidence of the fingerprints was brought up to me, I had misgivings as to the method he had used in obtaining it. I wrote to the Federal CID (FBI) of the United States asking them to send an expert as a 'second opinion' to Barker. I was informed that once the police of a U.S. city had been called in, the Federal CID would not join the investigation. I then applied to the New York City police who sent down a most reliable officer, Detective Inspector Conway. Conway confirmed my doubts as to Barker's procedure: the fingerprints should have been photographed in situ and not taken off on a scotch tape.

My position at the trial was perfectly clear. I had to lead Barker's evidence and let the jury decide whether or not they believed him when he said he had taken the fingerprint from the screen beside Oakes' bed. I also put Det. Inspector Conway in the witness box to give his opinion of the fingerprint and the method in which Barker had dealt with it.

It is now over 27 years since the trial, and I have no record, diary or notes of the case. What I have stated is my recollection. However, I am confident that what I have written is correct.

Yours sincerely,
Eric Hallinan

10th April

PS — I have read what I wrote last night. From the point of view of an American about to write a book on a British criminal trial, perhaps the most useful contribution I can make at this distance of time and without notes, is to emphasize the function of a prosecutor in a British Court.

He is not 'out to win' and he is not an investigator. The police conduct the investigation and the prosecutor orders and presents the evidence, which the investigation has adduced (evidenced), to a judge and jury. At the end of a criminal trial where I was the prosecutor, I never felt that the Crown had 'lost' its case, if the accused person was acquitted. If the Crown's case had been cogently and fairly presented, then I was satisfied — whatever the outcome. In the Oakes case, I was satisfied the Crown had done its duty. The judge had summed-up strongly against the Crown as he was entitled to do, and the jury had acquitted.

It would appear from the comments in Hallinan's letter, that even Hallinan himself as Attorney General of the Bahamas and head of the Prosecution team, felt all along that the evidence presented by Capt. James Barker relative to the fingerprint of Alfred de Marigny left a great deal to be desired. He had no choice but to go along with the evidence as introduced by Captains James Barker and Edward Melchen, which formed the main point in the evidence being presented against Alfred de Marigny.

Hallinan's letter is actually about the only comment that has ever been made concerning the murder of Sir Harry, that is by an official or individual involved in the actual legal proceedings of the trial and for that reason alone is most interesting.

Assisting Hallinan was Alfred Francis Adderley, son of Mr. and Mrs. Wilfred Parliament Adderley of Nassau, a very prominent Nassauvian family. Adderley himself was born on November 16th, 1881, and was sixty two years of age when he acted for the Prosecution in the trial of Alfred de Marigny.

The Honourable Adderley was a graduate of Cambridge University and Barrister-at-Law of the Middle Temple.

Adderley was to become a very popular and successful Bahamian criminal attorney over a twenty five year period, who followed in the tradition of his family, his father having served as a Justice of the Peace, as well as being a member of the Bahamian House of Assembly.

In 1938, Alfred Adderley enjoyed international fame when he successfully defended one Forrester Scott, a well known Philadelphia lawyer in the only kidnapping case ever recorded in the history of the Bahamas. Mr. Scott had kidnapped his only son from the Fort Montagu Beach hotel in east end Nassau, while his former wife, a member of the famous Dupont family, was vacationing with her second husband and the child from her first marriage to Scott.

Adderley, while receiving a great deal of opposition, eventually succeeded in becoming the first black Chief Justice of the Bahamas. His most noted case was in assisting the Attorney General, Eric Hallinan in the criminal prosecution of the defendant, Alfred de Marigny.

During the course of his long and distinguished career as a criminal lawyer, Adderley is said to have prosecuted or defended in ten murder cases in the Supreme Court of the Bahamas, nine of which he won. The one loss was the prosecution in the case of Alfred de Marigny.

In June 1953, Adderley went to London as the representative of the Government of the Bahamas, on the occasion of the Coronation of Queen Elizabeth II in London, following the sudden death of her father King George VI. On the return flight on June 17th, Adderley passed away suddenly.

It is interesting to note that following the arrest of Alfred de Marigny on the charge of murdering Sir Harry, it has been mentioned by de Marigny that he had specifically requested the Attorney General, Eric Hallinan, to immediately get in touch with Alfred Adderley and request his services as his defense attorney. Hallinan called Adderley who was out and left a message for him to call back.

During de Marigny's initial appearance in Magistrate's Court, Magistrate Frank Fields informed de Marigny that Alfred Adderley had been retained by the Crown. This was to be the shock of his life for de Marigny when he heard this statement, contrary to his belief that Adderley had been asked to defend him.

It should be remembered that as Nassau was basically a very small community at the time, everyone knew everyone else and your best friend could as easily be your attorney or as in this case your prosecutor. De Marigny and Adderley were indeed good friends.

On the morning of the murder when the Duke of Windsor was informed of the tragedy, a decision was to be made which would shake the whole basis of the eventual prosecution of the accused Alfred de Marigny. At that point in time the question of who would do the investigation was a matter of great importance and concern.

In consultation with Col. Reginald Erskine-Lindop, it was decided in view of the murder of such a wealthy and prominent individual, that the Bahamas Police force was not necessarily in a positive position to investigate such an important case, as they did not have the experience or the necessary equipment to assist with the fingerprinting aspect.

After some lengthy consideration lasting over three hours following his being informed, it was finally decided by the Duke of Windsor that he would request the assistance of the Miami Police Force. The Duke was familiar with Captain Edward Melchen, who had acted as his bodyguard and provided the necessary security during previous visits to Miami and as a result an unforgettable and regrettable telephone call was made requesting his services.

Capt. Edward Walter Melchen was Chief of the Homicide Bureau of the Miami Police Department. Melchen was fifty years of age and had participated in the investigation of approximately five hundred homicides since 1925. His previous experience included the handling of confidence men, pickpockets, cases of burglary, forgery, arson, robbery, counterfeiting and postal violations. Quite a background of criminal investigations.

Following their arrival in Nassau, it was Capt. Melchen who undertook most of the interviews with the individuals closely associated with Sir Harry Oakes. As it would develop, the interview with Alfred de Marigny would prove to be the most important one and best remembered, as de Marigny would eventually be charged with the murder.

Assisting Melchen with the fingerprinting and other technical aspects of the investigation, he suggested that he would need the expertise of Capt. James Otto Barker.

At the time of the murder of Sir Harry, Capt. Barker was Superintendent of Detectives of the Bureau of Criminal Investigation of the Miami Police Force, whose basic responsibilities included fingerprinting records, criminal and technical investigations. Barker was forty years of age at the time.

In preparation for the journey to Nassau, Barker, as the fingerprinting expert, gathered together some of the basic tools of the trade for his part in the investigation. What he brought would prove insufficient, but no attempt was subsequently made by him to immediately obtain some of the missing equipment from his office in Miami. As a result, his performance as an investigator would be questioned by many, including the Chief Justice Sir Oscar Daly, the presiding judge at the trial.

One of the main points of contention raised by the Defense was the validity of the one fingerprint presented by the Prosecution to confirm that de Marigny had been in Sir Harry's bedroom on the night of the murder. The Prosecution claimed that it came from the upper portion of one of the panels of the Chinese screen, the fifth panel from the left to be more precise, which stood on the south side of the bed on which Sir Harry's body had been found.

It was always the Defense's contention that the fingerprint in question had been lifted from another source, completely outside the area of the murder scene.

Barker in his testimony defending the fingerprint had a number of problems explaining how he raised some of his prints around the murder scene; what objects he took them from, not to mention what obvious objects he did not dust for prints.

188

Barker also estimated that he raised anywhere from fifty to seventy prints, including palm prints. A good number of the prints also came from the Chinese screen, however, he could not exactly identify the area that they came from, nor whose fingerprint they actually were.

Godfrey Higgs, as de Marigny's lawyer, asked Capt. Barker why did he not process possible prints from such objects as the headboard of Sir Harry's bed, the thermos on the night table, the lamp, the railing on the stair case and other pertinent objects. In his response, Barker said that he had dusted — *all surfaces that he thought might produce valuable latent (invisible to the naked eye) prints.*

The following cross-examination of Capt. Barker by Ernest Callender, may be of interest relative to the fingerprinting aspect of the Prosecution's investigation:

Q: I suggest, Capt. Barker that there were numerous articles in Sir Harry's room that you never processed.
A: I quite agree with you.
Q: If the accused had left a fingerprint on that screen, wouldn't it be likely that he left fingerprints on other objects?
A: Yes, under ordinary conditions. It is, however, my opinion that the nature of the crime and the extent of emotion or hurry would most likely prevent him from handling a lot of objects. In this case there was no necessity for the assailant to handle many objects.
Q: Well, why did you dust the powder room downstairs?
A: We can't exclude anything in an investigation like this.
Q: But did you exclude a number of articles in the bedroom?
A: Yes.
Q: Did you exclude the possibility of accomplices?
A: I did not exclude the possibility of accomplices.
Q: With all those marks of burning in the hallway, wasn't the railing a likely place to look for fingerprints?
A: There might have been fingerprints on the rail, but it would be difficult to obtain or even locate visible prints.
Q: Why would you say that?
A: It is a natural thing for a person to use the railing in going upstairs. Such a railing is handled to such an extent that in my experience it has been difficult to raise prints from railings because of handling. A number of people went upstairs before me.

Barker said that he had only processed objects which he thought the assailant would have handled. During his original investigation he had obtained rolled impressions of Major Herbert Pemberton, Harold Christie, Dr. Hugh Quackenbush, Alfred de Marigny and the right hand of the deceased Sir Harry Oakes.

There is no indication whatsoever, that Capt. Barker did any examination of Sir Harry's fingernails to see if any foreign material had accumulated under the nails, which could have been related to a possible source.

He did not obtain rolled impressions of Mrs. Babs Henneage; Mrs. Madeleine Kelly; Charles Hubbard; the Attorney General Eric Hallinan; Col. Reginald Erskine-Lindop; Corp. Muir; the coroner; Constables Knowles, Nottage, Kemp and Tynes; Mrs. Gale; Frank Christie; Capt. Melchen or the maid Mabel Ellis.

Q: Why didn't you get any of these rolled impressions?
A: When we arrived, Col. Erskine-Lindop told us specifically that no one had touched anything in the room except Harold Christie and Dr. Quackenbush.
Q: Did you not find a single print of Harold Christie in the room?
A: I did not.
Q: Did you not know that Christie had handled both the glass and the thermos?
A: I knew he handled the glass. But I didn't get a print. It could have been smudged.
Q: You didn't find a single print of Sir Harry's?
A: No.
Q: Although Sir Harry and Christie had lived in the house together for days, you didn't find a single one?
A: No.

During the cross examination of Capt. Barker, Judge Sir Oscar Daly interjected on a number of occasions to ask Barker some pertinent questions relative to the processing of fingerprints as Barker's comments were a little too complicated.

The question of fingerprinting developed into a confrontation of the experts with both the Prosecution and the Defense calling in their own consultants. The Prosecution had Detective Frank Conway of the New York Police Department to assist Capt. Barker and in turn the Defense had Capt. Maurice O'Neil from the New Orleans Police Department as their consultant.

To add to the confusion of Barker's cross examination by the Defense, Barker informed the court that a certain blue line drawn on the Chinese screen outlining the position of the fingerprint that he had raised was not his marking. No sooner said, on further examination of the screen, Barker then wished to correct his statement to the effect that the blue line was indeed his and that his initials JOB were there on the blue line, together with the relative date on which he found it.

Upon further questioning, Capt. Barker continued to express doubts about the area from which de Marigny's fingerprint was really raised.

The more and more he was cross-examined by the Defense, the more doubt was thrown on the entire matter of his fingerprinting examination, as well as his basic expertise.

The following questioning during the trial will also provide the reader with a further example of the cross-examination of Capt. Barker and his responses:

Q: Wasn't the Accused's latent print, Exhibit J, obtained from some object in that northwest bedroom? (the room where de Marigny was interrogated)
A: It was not.

Q: But it was after they had left that room that you claimed to discover his print, was it not?

A: Yes.

Q: I suggest that you and Capt. Melchen deliberately planned to get the Accused alone in order to get his fingerprint?

A: No, sir.

Q: I suggest that Exhibit J never came from that screen.

A: It did come from that screen — No. 5 panel.

Q: You can show none of that scroll work on Exhibit J, can you?

A: I cannot.

Q: (asked by the Chief Justice) When you were working on the screen in the hallway, was it spread out?

A: It was upright and spread out a panel at a time.

Q: (asked by Godfrey Higgs) Would you look at the six prints please — are they prints from the negatives of Exhibit J?

A: Yes.

Q: Do you see those two circles on the right?

A: I do.

Q: How do you account for those two circles?

A: Moisture on the surface where the prints came from — the No. 5 panel of the screen.

Q: Two perfectly spherical objects?

A: I wouldn't say they're perfect but they appear to be circular. The bottom one is not a perfect circle, but the top one is.

Q: In order for these to show in your lift you had to dust those didn't you?

A: Yes.

Q: When you dust, you use a brush and brush over the object, don't you?

A: Yes, I did so in this case.

And the cross examination continued with questions and answers as follows:

Q: Can you find anything on the background of that screen to resemble these circles?

A: No, sir.

Q: Is that another coincidence, Capt. Barker?

A: I have to believe it is.

Q: Did you regard the rubber lift of this print as vital evidence in this case?

A: Definitely.

Q: You never produced the rubber lift in the Magistrate's Court, did you?

A: I had it, but was never asked for it.

Q: You never told Capt. Melchen of the discovery of the print, did you?

A: I told him when I discovered it on July 19th.

Q: This is the most outstanding case in which your expert assistance has been required, is it not?

A: Well, it's developed into that.

Q: And I suggest that in your desire for personal gain and notoriety you have swept away truth and substituted fabricated evidence.

A: I emphatically deny that.

Godfrey Higgs terminated his cross-examination at this point and the Attorney General began his re-examination.

In total Capt. Barker spent almost three complete days in the witness box, defending his findings relative to the fingerprints, against the cross-examination by Ernest Callender and Godfrey Higgs.

After the trial, during which Barker's professional skills were reduced to the lowest possible level due to his bungling of the whole matter, Barker returned to Miami and was placed on sick leave.

Based on an FBI memorandum under date of September 8th, 1944, it would appear that charges were brought against Capt. James Barker by Capt. Maurice O'Neil and Professor Leonard Keeler, relative to Barker's investigation of the murder of Sir Harry Oakes. Both O'Neil and Keeler were members of the Defense team.

The hearing was conducted in a closed session by the Board of Directors of the International Association for Identification. O'Neil and Keeler presented the testimony to the effect that the latent print identified by Capt. Barker as being that of Alfred de Marigny was not lifted from the Chinese screen in Sir Harry's room.

Capt. Barker defended himself against the charge and freely admitted that he had made mistakes in conducting the investigation and indicated in a couple of instances he had become excited and possibly had failed to conduct a good investigation.

The result of the hearing was that Capt. Barker was reprimanded for the faulty investigation which he made. One of the members of the Board felt that Barker was not competent enough to conduct an investigation of this nature and that the case was too big for him. The technique used by Barker for lifting the print from the screen constituted a departure from the best approved orthodox methods of the development, photographing and marking for identification of latent fingerprints and the object on which they were found.

As a result of his experience in this murder investigation, Barker in time became addicted to drugs. During the course of family feuds which culminated on December 26th, 1952, he drew his service revolver in a struggle with his son James Duane, who took possession of the gun. It accidentally discharged, mortally wounding his father. The son was charged with the crime, but he was subsequently acquitted of the charge of murder on the basis of *justifiable homicide*. And so came to a tragic end the life and career of Captain James Otto Barker.

It was a known fact that the RAF station in Nassau at the time possessed the necessary equipment for fingerprinting and that the preliminary investigation could have as easily been done by members of their personnel, pending formal involvement by the proper authorities. Most likely Scotland Yard officers out of the British Embassies in Washington or for that matter Ottawa could have as easily been involved. In reality, the RAF base in Nassau was asked by the Bahamas Police to take some photographs of the crime scene — which they did.

Following his return to Miami after the trial, Capt. Melchen remained with the Miami Police Department, until his death some five years later of a heart attack on July 5th, 1948, at the rather early age of fifty five.

Assisting the Prosecution was Detective Frank Conway, a fingerprinting expert in the New York Police Department who was called upon to give evidence during the trial, concerning the verification of the fingerprinting aspect of the case as presented by Capt. James Barker against the accused, Alfred de Marigny.

In 1939 on the occasion of the New York World's Fair, Conway was part of a group from the N.Y.P.D., who were assigned to educate the public in the art of fingerprint identification. During the fair, he himself processed the fingerprints of some 18,000 visitors.

At the time of the trial, Conway identified the print taken by Capt. James Barker as being that of the defendant Alfred de Marigny. He did not, however, agree with the manner in which it was raised and in fact, was unsure if it was indeed raised from the Chinese screen, as implied by Barker. It was Conway's belief that the print possibly came from another source.

During the cross-examination by Ernest Callender, Conway was asked to place a piece of scotch tape on a portion of the scroll work on the Chinese screen that had not been powdered. Callender then asked him to remove it and confirm if there was an impression of the scroll work on the tape, to which Conway confirmed that there was indeed such an impression. This was the point that the Defense was trying to confirm, in that it was not possible to lift a clear print from the fifth panel of the Chinese screen without some of the background from the area which Capt. Barker had indicated his print came from.

The point had now been made and no doubt the members of the Jury had taken this presentation into due consideration in determining their eventual verdict.

On July 14th, 1943, some six days following the murder of Sir Harry Oakes, Inspector Joseph Donovan of the New York Police Department announced that he had located a witness who could be of assistance to the Nassau police authorities relative to their investigation into the murder of Sir Harry Oakes.

This announcement was duly reported by United Press on July 15th, 1943, and also the fact that Capt. Edward Melchen, one of the Prosecution's investigating detectives in the case, was on his way to New York from Miami to question a man, who was said to be an important witness in the matter of the murder of Sir Harry. It is interesting to note that there was never any subsequent mention of any discussions with the individual in question, who would appear to have been an important witness — nor was his name ever disclosed.

It is believed that Inspector Donovan was at one time a professional associate of Capt. Edward Melchen, who as we know was part of the team from the Miami Police Department brought over by the Duke of Windsor to investigate the murder of Sir Harry.

The following are the fourteen points on which the Prosecution was to base its case against Alfred de Marigny:

1. The compelling motive of hatred, humiliation and gain, which the Crown alleges influenced the Accused to end the life of Sir Harry Oakes;
2. The desperate financial condition of the Accused;
3. His presence alone outside the gates of *Westbourne* on this one night of all nights;
4. His wakefulness on his return home;
5. His curiosity visit, yet significant, to the police station;
6. His anxiety to remove all traces of gasoline from his premises after the discovery of Sir Harry's burnt body;
7. The discovery of burnt hair on his hands, arms, beard, moustache, eyebrows and head;
8. His excuses for burnt hair;
9. His failure to provide the shirt and the tie worn by him on the fatal night;
10. The discovery of his fingerprint, that manual sign of all human beings;
11. His expression of hatred;
12. His callous reference to Sir Harry Oakes after death;
13. His most important enquiry relative to a conviction on the failure of the Prosecution to discover the deadly weapon; and
14. His enquiry into the value of circumstantial evidence in convicting a person.

The Defense: The Other Side of the Case

The Request for Alfred Adderley ..... Godfrey Higgs — The Solution ..... W. Ernest Callender — The Junior Member of the Defense ..... Raymond Campbell Schindler — A Private Detective ..... A Roper — An Unusual Individual ..... Professor Leonard Keeler — A Lie Detector Expert ..... Captain Maurice Bernard O'Neil — The Other Fingerprint Consultant

---

As previously mentioned, Alfred de Marigny had requested the legal services of Alfred Adderley to defend him, however, through a turn of events beyond his control Adderley's services were not to be made available to him. Adderley had in fact been requested by Eric Hallinan, the Attorney General of the Bahamas to assist in the prosecution of de Marigny, quite possibly at the prompting of the Duke of Windsor.

As a result, de Marigny sought the services of Godfrey Higgs, a white Bahamian lawyer, who had previously assisted him in legal matters concerning his day to day needs following his arrival in Nassau. Higgs was not exactly considered a criminal lawyer.

Higgs received his legal training under the guidance of the Honourable Harcourt Malcolm in Nassau and was thirty six years of age at the time of the trial. He was a Barrister-at-Law called to the Bahamian Bar in 1929 and also a close friend of de Marigny as a result of their sailing adventures in and around Nassau.

Initially Higgs had some doubt regarding his role as a defense attorney, but in view of his close relationship with de Marigny, the challenge of being part of a criminal trial was gladly accepted.

Assisting Godfrey Higgs in the defense of de Marigny was Ernest Callender, a native Guinean, who followed in his father's footsteps into the legal profession. He was born in 1909 and was thirty four years of age at the time of the trial of Alfred de Marigny.

His mother was English and had married a gentleman from British Guiana in Georgetown, Guiana (now Guyana) which accounted for Callender's mulatto colouring. The family in due course moved to the Bahamas.

As part of his legal training, he spent twelve years in England, the last four at the Middle Temple where he completed his law training before being called to the Bar in Nassau in 1936 on his twenty seventh birthday.

It was said that he was torn between a career on stage and the legal practice. Callender had sung on the BBC and served as a newscaster in London during the early thirties.

Callender was considered an experienced and witty young criminal lawyer, though he was also known to have a reputation of being utterly indifferent about whose toes he might tread on. This latter characteristic was apparently quite noticeable at times during his cross-

Nancy Oakes de Marigny with attorneys Godfrey Higgs and Ernest Callender for the Defense. *CP Picture Archive*

examination of some of the Prosecution's witnesses and Capt. James Barker in particular — and probably with good reason in view of the latter's attempt to frame de Marigny with questionable fingerprinting evidence.

In April 1992, while visiting friends in Nassau, I had the pleasure of meeting Ernest Callender and the opportunity of discussing with him some of the aspects of Alfred de Marigny's trial.

Callender and de Marigny were very close friends, both before and after the trial and as a matter of fact when de Marigny returned to Nassau at the invitation of the Bahamian Government in 1990 they renewed this friendship after some forty seven years.

Callender wanted to make it very clear to me that he was instrumental in the cross-examination of Capt. James Barker in exposing a great deal of his questionable procedures in the lifting of the prints and in particular the famous fingerprint itself known as *Exhibit J*, which seemed to be the only piece of so-called physical evidence that the Prosecution could present at de Marigny's trial.

During de Marigny's return visit to Nassau on October 7th, 1990, both he and Callender were interviewed on the CTV program W5. One of the comments made by Callender during the interview was that while Harold Christie was on the witness stand he asked him — *Did you kill Sir Harry Oakes?*

According to Callender, Christie turned red in the face, gripped the sides of the witness box and shouted a firm NO. Asked why he put that question to Christie, Callender simply replied that the Defense merely wanted to get Christie's reaction, as they had suspicions about Christie's whereabouts on the night of the murder.

Callender never left the Bahamas and retired with his charming wife into a very beautiful and newly developed residential area of Nassau near Delaporte Village on the northwest side of the island.

Added to the Defense team was one Raymond Schindler, whose services had been retained by Nancy Oakes de Marigny while she was in the United States, before her return to Nassau for the trial. Schindler brought along with him Professor Leonard Keeler, the

Defense attorneys Ernest Callender, Godfrey Higgs and private investigator Raymond Schindler. *Corbis/Bettman — UPI*

reported inventor of the lie-detector, who would assist the Defense team in their attempt to clear Alfred de Marigny's name.

Dr. Paul Zahl, a member of the Haskins Laboratory for Research in New York and a close friend of Alfred and Nancy Oakes de Marigny dropped into the Manhattan offices of Raymond Schindler, recommending that he get into the case on behalf of Alfred de Marigny. Zahl was also known to the Oakes family and had visited with them in Nassau.

Schindler said to Zahl — *First I'd have to get a letter from Nancy de Marigny, saying that if my investigation shows her husband guilty instead of innocent, I have permission to turn the results over to the Nassau authorities.* As a result Raymond Schindler was hired by Nancy de Marigny and arrived in Nassau on July 12th, four days after the murder, for the start of the preliminary hearings in the Magistrate's Court.

Schindler's responsibility was stated to the press during the Magistrate Court hearing as — *I have been asked to confer with the Honourable Godfrey Higgs, Counsel for the Defense, and to study the whole case. My job is to reconstruct the murder of Sir Harry Oakes in the light of conflicting circumstances and to make a private analysis of the case.*

From left to right Baroness Marie af Trolle (close friend of Nancy Oakes de Marigny), Prof. Leonard Keeler, Raymond Schindler and Baron Georg af Trolle. *CP Picture Archive*

His fees were $300 per day plus expenses and as a result both Schindler and his assistant Professor Leonard Keeler who accompanied him, stayed with Nancy's good friends Baron Georg and Baroness Marie af Trolle during their sojourns to Nassau at the time of the trial.

As part of Schindler's attempt to return to Nassau to further investigate the murder of Sir Harry Oakes, he wrote to the Duke of Windsor on January 24th, 1944, some two months following the end of the trial, asking him to reopen the case and that he would be more than pleased to return to Nassau to investigate the matter further and to do so at his own expense.

Schindler's letter to the Duke of Windsor read in part as follows:

It is my considered opinion that the murderer of Sir Harry Oakes can be found, identified, convicted and brought to justice. During the incarceration and trial of Alfred de Marigny no adequate investigation was possible. Statements, which failed to point toward the defendant, were ignored. It goes without saying that I and my associate Leonard Keeler, would welcome an opportunity to work on the case. We would willingly offer our services without compensation.

However, it is said that the Duke of Windsor was not interested in the matter and one of his secretaries sent a brief note to Schindler declining the offer.

Schindler's richest and best known client was one Anna Gould, daughter of Jay Gould who was a U.S. railway tycoon. At the time, he was on a retainer worth $50,000 per year for which he provided amongst other things, security for her mansion on the Hudson River. In addition he lived rent free in a residence provided for him on the property.

Oakes Murdered in Revenge Over Woman, Says Schindler — read the headlines of the first article of a series of twelve which appeared in the *New York Daily Mirror* on November 21st, 1943, a little over a week following the acquittal of Alfred de Marigny, on the charges of having murdered his father-in-law Sir Harry Oakes.

As the articles continued Schindler said that it was his conviction after spending more than two months probing every detail of this macabre case that he was continuing his investigation in the momentary anticipation of a major break in the mystery. As the last article went to press some two weeks later there was no *momentary break* in the case.

It was his feeling that a blow torch was used to inflict the burns on Oakes' body and to try to set fire to the room.

It was a known fact that Schindler kept the Oakes case alive following the trial by periodically making statements in magazine and newspaper articles, as well as on the radio and eventually during television interviews, that he could still solve the murder case and identify the murderer. He maintained that evidence during the trial had been suppressed and implied that the Government and other high ranking Nassau officials were covering up for a prominent individual Bahamian businessman who was well known to Oakes.

In March 1959, Raymond Schindler appeared on the Canadian Broadcasting Corporation (CBC) program entitled *Front Page Challenge* and part of his interview with the panelists produced his familiar claim that there are people still alive at the time in Nassau, who knew who killed Sir Harry Oakes. His one statement to the effect that — *"one man in the Bahamas has full knowledge of how the murder was committed — and by whom"* — has to the best of my knowledge never been followed-up.

In May 1959, Schindler was asked to submit the information that he had concerning the case to the Nassau authorities and to justify his ongoing allegations, however, he was unable to produce any appropriate statements. Schindler died of a heart attack within two months on July 1st, 1959, in New York at the age of sixty one and nothing further had developed in the murder case.

In March 1997, I contacted the CBC in an attempt to obtain a copy of the tape of the show or possibly view the *Front Page Challenge* program in question, but it was with regret that I learned that the 1959 program was missing from their collection of tapes of some of the earlier shows. Could this have just been another one of those Oakes incidents?

An interesting sidelight to Schindler's investigative style was the use of individuals known as *ropers*, a term often used to describe a person that a private eye, an investigator or a detective would hire from time to time to infiltrate certain groups of people, or to associate themselves with suspected criminals and potential suspects, in order to extract or obtain from them some much needed information.

Such individuals were also provided with money to spread around in the hope of obtaining information to help them in their search. I guess another way of describing the whole matter is to say that a *roper* is a person looking for a *stool pigeon* or *squealer*.

It was always Schindler's contention that if the Bahamian Police had allowed him to return to Nassau following de Marigny's acquittal to further investigate the murder of Sir Harry Oakes, he would have been able to use *ropers* to mingle amongst the native Bahamians and obtain the necessary information about the real murderer or murderers. It is interesting to note that even though Schindler never went back to Nassau, he always maintained that he knew who committed the murder, but never seemed willing to provide anyone in authority with the identity of the individual or individuals for further investigation and possible solution to the whole matter.

Professor Leonard Keeler was a colleague of Raymond Schindler and accompanied him to Nassau for the trial. Keeler was apparently responsible for the development of the lie detector testing machine, which at that time was in its infancy and definitely not permitted for use in investigating murders.

At a gathering at Godfrey Higgs' home following the acquittal of Alfred de Marigny, Professor Keeler entertained the guests with the use of his lie detector machine and de Marigny himself in the excitement of the occasion asked that he be tested on the machine, as he felt very confident that he knew he had nothing to hide.

While de Marigny may have felt very confident about himself and still in a state of jubilation, his lawyer Godfrey Higgs questioned the purpose of the test. Higgs had serious concerns that should de Marigny answer just one of the questions in such a way that it would prompt concern to the others and lead them to believe that he could have possibly been implicated in the murder — the results could have been disastrous.

The following, however, were the questions that were asked to de Marigny and his responses are indicated after each one in brackets:

When you took your guests home on July 7th, did you come straight home yourself? (Yes)
Did you enter Westbourne? (No)
Did you kill Sir Harry Oakes? (No)
Were you in the room when someone else killed Sir Harry Oakes? (No)
Do you know who killed Sir Harry Oakes? (No)
Did you put your hand on the Chinese screen between the time of the murder and the discovery of the body? (No)

In all cases de Marigny passed the test with flying colours and not to be outdone Ernest Callender requested he undergo a similar test. Keeler basically questioned him regarding what he had eaten for breakfast and other daily related matters and as Callender said — *I passed the test with flying colours also.*

In addition the Defense brought in Captain Maurice O'Neil, Superintendent of the Bureau of Identification of the New Orleans Police Department to assist in facing one of the major pieces of evidence against de Marigny — the famous *Exhibit J*, relative to the fingerprint of his left little finger. O'Neil was past President of the International Association of Identification.

Capt. O'Neil swore that the circles that appeared on the raised fingerprint produced in court were part of an industrial pattern, such as might be seen on a fancy glass or that the glass had been subject to some form of moisture, as would often be the case in the islands.

We must therefore remember, that during the interrogation of Alfred de Marigny by Capt. Edward Melchen, he asked him to pour two glasses of water, thus handling at least two glass surfaces plus the water jug. The jug would have had condensation on it due to the humidity in the air and the coolness of the water, which would explain the two small circles seen on the print. But why his little finger — if you hold a glass, basically all fingers would touch the surface somewhere. Try it.

12

Witnesses — To Tell The Truth

A Resumé of Some of the Witnesses ..... Geoffrey Jones: Thomas Lavelle: Dr. William Yohannan Sayad — Did They Hear Heated Arguments? ..... Jean Ainslie and Dorothy Clarke — Two Surprised Witnesses ..... Mabel Ellis — A Housemaid at Westbourne ..... Enid Fernandez — Sir Harry's Cook ..... Levi Gibson — Household Assistant to Harold Christie ..... Captain Edward de Witt Sears — Did He See Right? ..... John Gaffney — A Royal Banker ..... Lewis Charles Phillips — Another Banker

---

Close to fifty individuals were called by the Prosecution and the Defense to testify as witnesses at the trial of Alfred de Marigny on the charge of having murdered his father-in-law Sir Harry Oakes. The following is a list of the witnesses in alphabetical order:

Jean Ainslie, wife of an RAF pilot and dinner guest at de Marigny's home on the evening prior to the murder. She was a close friend of Dorothy Clarke;

John Anderson, close friend of de Marigny and General Manager of the Bahamas General Trust, as well as one time employee of Dr. Axel Wenner-Gren;

Captain James Otto Barker, member of the Miami Police Department, brought in by the Duke of Windsor to investigate the murder of Sir Harry Oakes;

Philip Brice, Acting Immigration Officer, Government of the Bahamas;

Alfred Victor Cerreta, former employee of Pleasantville Constructors Ltd., Nassau, and close friend of de Marigny;

Harold Christie, prominent Bahamian real estate businessman and close friend of Sir Harry Oakes, the Duke of Windsor and Dr. Axel Wenner-Gren, was also a dinner guest at Oakes' estate;

Dorothy Clarke, wife of an RAF pilot and dinner guest at de Marigny's home on the evening prior to the murder. She was a close friend of Jean Ainslie;

Detective Frank Conway, member of the New York Police Department, who had been called in by the Prosecution as a fingerprint consultant;

John Vincent Cox, Crown Lands Officer, Bahamian Government;

Alfred de Marigny, the accused, husband of Nancy Oakes and son-in-law of Sir Harry;

Nancy Oakes de Marigny, wife of the accused and daughter of Sir Harry Oakes;

Georges de Visdelou, cousin of Alfred de Marigny, who lived at his residence;

Lieutenant John Campbell Douglas, member of the Bahamas Police Department;

Mabel Ellis, housemaid at the Oakes' estate;

Col. Reginald Alexander Erskine-Lindop, Commissioner of Bahamas Police Department, transferred from Nassau to Trinidad just prior to the start of the trial;

Frank Eustice Field, Stipendiary and Circuit Magistrate, as well as Coroner;

Dr. Lawrence Fitzmaurice, Acting Chief Medical Officer of the Bahamas;

Walter Foskett, Sir Harry's attorney for his holdings in the United States;

John Gaffney, staff member of the Royal Bank of Canada in Nassau;

Flight Lieutenant Reginald Arthur Gates, stationed at the RAF base in Nassau;

Corporal John Gay, member of the Bahamas Police Department;

Edward Henry Godet, employed by Alfred de Marigny;

Mrs. Dulcibel Effie Henneage, close acquaintance of Harold Christie;

Charles Hubbard, retired Woolworth executive and neighbour of Sir Harry Oakes;

Dr. Leonard Huggins, Assistant Medical Officer at His Majesty's prison;

Geoffrey Jones, plumber who had done work at Tom Lavelle's home on Victoria Avenue;

Professor Leonard Keeler, Chicago criminologist and associate of Raymond Schindler;

Newell Kelly, Sir Harry's manager for his properties and interests in Nassau;

Madeleine Kelly, wife of Newell Kelly and neighbour of Sir Harry Oakes;

Corporal Cleophas Knowles, member of the Bahamas Criminal Investigation Dept.;

Thomas Lavelle, neighbour of Alfred de Marigny on Victoria Avenue;

Howard Lightbourn, neighbour of Alfred de Marigny on Victoria Avenue;

L.A.C. John Lord, stationed at the RAF base in Nassau;

Basil McKinney, sailing friend of Alfred de Marigny;

Donald McKinney, sailing friend of Alfred de Marigny;

Captain Edward Melchen, member of the Miami Police Department, brought in with Capt. James Barker, by the Duke of Windsor to investigate the murder of Sir Harry Oakes;

Oswald Moseley, insurance agent and sailing friend of Alfred de Marigny;

Captain Michael Muir, stationed at the RAF base in Nassau;

Constable Bernard Nottage, member of Bahamas Criminal Investigation Dept.;

Dr. Ulrich Oberwarth, attached to the Bahamas General Hospital;

Charles O'Malley, handwriting expert of the New York Police;

Captain Maurice O'Neil, Superintendent of the Bureau of Identification of the New Orleans Police Department called in by the Defense;

Lady Eunice Oakes, wife of the late Sir Harry Oakes;

Constable Wendel Lamond Parker, member of the Bahamas Police Department;

Major Herbert Pemberton, Acting Deputy Commissioner of the Bahamas Police Dept.;

Lewis Charles Phillips, officer of the Royal Bank of Canada in Nassau;

Dr. Hugh Quackenbush, Nassau physician;

Elizabeth 'Betty' Roberts, girl friend of Georges de Visdelou;

Charles Rolle, Alfred de Marigny's butler;

Dr. William Yohannan Sayad, eye, ear and throat specialist in Palm Beach, Florida who treated Nancy Oakes;

Captain Edward de Witt Sears, Superintendent of the Bahamas Police Dept.;

Edith Smith, cook employed by Alfred de Marigny;

Sgt. Jeremiah Storr, officer in Charge Room, Bahamas Police;

Curtis Thompson, chauffeur and right-hand man to Alfred de Marigny;

Edith Thompson, housemaid employed by Alfred de Marigny;

Constable Eric Tynes, member of Bahamas Police.

An interesting comment was made by Godfrey Higgs after the trial to the effect that *it was a strange case in more ways than one. The characters were unusual and the nature of the crime strange. It was extremely difficult to reconstruct the crime. What he regarded as the most extraordinary feature of the whole case was that although the Prosecution had called 35 witnesses not one of them with the exception of Captains Barker and Melchen had given evidence to support the contention of the Crown that Alfred de Marigny killed Sir Harry Oakes.*

The following is a brief resume of some of the witnesses not previously mentioned in the text:

Geoffrey Jones was a plumber by trade living in Nassau and had done some work for Thomas Lavelle, who lived opposite Alfred de Marigny's home on Victoria Avenue and ran the Victoria Guest House.

Jones was called as a witness by the Prosecution, as he was present one evening near de Marigny's home and had overheard one of the so-called arguments between de Marigny and Sir Harry. It was the Prosecution's contention that de Marigny hated Sir Harry to the point that he would have killed him and these witnesses were called in the hope of proving that there was sufficient hatred by de Marigny towards Sir Harry.

However, in his testimony Jones described the so-called argument as merely a question of hearing Sir Harry in his usual loud voice, which was normal and not an indication that he was having an argument with de Marigny.

Thomas Lavelle, a neighbour of de Marigny on Victoria Avenue was another witness called by the Prosecution and his main contribution to the trial was a statement to the effect that he had also overheard arguments on a number of occasions between Sir Harry Oakes and Alfred de Marigny, outside the latter's home.

Dr. William Yohannan Sayad was an ear, nose and throat specialist, who had practised medicine in Palm Beach, Florida since 1926. He operated on Nancy Oakes in February 1943.

It was Sayad who suggested to Nancy that she get away from the warm and humid weather prevalent in the Bahamas during the summer and seek a cooler climate — which resulted in Nancy heading for Bennington, Vermont and the Martha Graham School of Dance in May 1943.

Sayad was also brought to the trial by the Prosecution to provide character reference relative to possible detrimental remarks that de Marigny may have made at some point about Sir Harry Oakes in his presence.

This was a further attempt by the Prosecution to show that de Marigny and Oakes argued on many occasions, however, again it boiled down to the fact that Oakes and de Marigny did have a tendency at times to raise their voices to each other and in particular Sir Harry who did not hesitate to express his opinion.

Following his testimony, Dr. Sayad was leaving the witness box and at the same moment de Marigny had been released from the prisoner's dock and the two of them bumped into each other. De Marigny turned around, patted Sayad on the back, shook his hand and the two went about their own way. Again de Marigny knew Sayad very well.

Jean Ainslie and Dorothy Clarke were the wives of two RAF Ferry Command Pilots stationed in Nassau, who were introduced to Alfred de Marigny by Freddie Ceretta at the Prince George Hotel two days prior to the murder of Sir Harry.

As a result of the introduction, de Marigny, who was planning a dinner party the following evening at his home on Victoria Avenue, seized the occasion to invite Jean Ainslie and Dorothy Clarke, together with their husbands who had to decline as they were on duty that evening. The Ainslies and Clarkes shared one of the Hubbard Cottages on West Bay Street, next door to Sir Harry's *Westbourne* estate and more specifically cottage Number Two as it came to be known.

Following his dinner party, de Marigny drove both Jean Ainslie and Dorothy Clarke to their home and would have occasion to pass Sir Harry's *Westbourne* estate, where Oakes was found murdered the next morning.

Both ladies appeared at the trial, originally as witnesses for the Prosecution in helping to establish that de Marigny was indeed near *Westbourne* estate at around the time that the murder occurred and that he had every opportunity to go into *Westbourne* after driving the

Three of the Defense witnesses at Alfred de Marigny's trial — Dorothy Clarke, Freddie Cerreta and Jean Ainslie. *CP Picture Archive*

ladies home next door. The detectives supposedly already had a so-called fingerprint establishing de Marigny's whereabouts that evening within the premises of *Westbourne.*

During the cross examination, both Godfrey Higgs and Ernest Callender were successful in using Jean Ainslie and Dorothy Clarke to their own advantage as alibi witnesses. Their recollections of the time at which they were driven home by de Marigny, as well as the incident of de Marigny lighting the hurricane lamps during his party proved beneficial to the Defense. In their testimonies the ladies very clearly referred to the fact that they had checked the time shortly after they left de Marigny's home and also as they were passing Christ Church Cathedral on their way to West Bay Street.

Dorothy Clarke estimated that they arrived home around 1.15 a.m. and de Marigny left immediately. It was 1.30 a.m. when they went to bed, not knowing what was awaiting them the next morning following the discovery of the murder of Sir Harry Oakes.

Mabel Ellis was a housemaid employed by the Oakes family and was one of the three staff members who would normally be on duty. She did not reside at the estate and went home every evening to her residence on Brougham Street in east end Nassau, when her housekeeping chores were complete.

She was called as a witness at the trial of Alfred de Marigny and confirmed that on the evening of the dinner party at *Westbourne*, she served dinner to Sir Harry and his guests, and provided them with certain liquid refreshments before and after dinner.

During her testimony Ms. Ellis also confirmed that before leaving for her home that evening she had prepared Sir Harry's bed for the night and placed a flit gun on the floor near the bureau in close proximity of the eastern door. The flit gun contained some insecticide spray (Fly-ded), which was used for spraying mosquitoes. This was a normal routine for her every evening. In addition she mentioned that no windows or doors were locked at *Westbourne*, as was usually the case.

She further explained the various accesses to Sir Harry's room, which included a stairway from the main entrance in the downstairs hallway which led to the upstairs landing. From there a doorway then led in to the southern portion of the bedroom. She also mentioned that from the north side (or ocean side), there was an entrance to the room. The third means of entry was from Christie's room through the adjoining smaller room and into Sir Harry's room.

During cross-examination by Ernest Callender for the Defense, it was established that on a number of occasions Harold Christie would spend the night with Sir Harry whenever he was alone at *Westbourne*. On this particular night Ms. Ellis was not aware that Christie would be staying overnight, but she confirmed that whenever he did he would use the east room, which is the room he supposedly slept in on that particular night.

She did not know the names of the guests who stayed for dinner in the persons of Charles Hubbard and Dulcibel Henneage, but she did know Harold Christie.

Ms. Ellis remembered serving Sir Harry and his guests drinks before supper on the northern upstairs veranda, which faced the ocean and around 8.45 p.m. she served them dinner. The meal as she recalled was completed around 9.30 p.m. and the entire party then proceeded to the card room for drinks and a game of Chinese checkers.

She left *Westbourne* for home with Enid Fernandez, the cook, around 10.15 p.m. after finishing her chores and returned the next morning around 7.45 a.m., July 8th, when she met Mrs. Madeleine Kelly at the entrance, who informed her as to what had happened.

In November 1930, Levi Gibson, then only sixteen years of age, was given a temporary job in the Christie household where he was to serve as butler and eventually become an aide and confidant to Harold Christie. Gibson also acted as chauffeur and general handyman in subsequent years.

In the cross examination of Harold Christie during the trial, there seemed to be a great deal of concern relative to Gibson's parking of Christie's car outside of the *Westbourne* property on the evening before the murder. Christie's argument was that he wanted to save fuel and by parking outside the property, he would not be asked to use his car the next morning to visit Sir Harry Oakes' sheep farm.

Others have subscribed to the more logical fact that by leaving his automobile outside the property and out of sight, no one would see him leave or for that matter hear his car as he departed from *Westbourne*.

According to Alfred de Marigny's interpretation of what actually happened that night, this statement would appear to have been correct, as Christie was seen leaving *Westbourne* in his car by two of the so-called night watchmen.

In the years following the death of Harold Christie, Gibson had developed a very good knowledge of the real estate business and in due course set up his own real estate agency in Nassau to be known as Levi Gibson & Associates. As he once said during an interview, he owed all his knowledge to having worked for the king of real estate in the Bahamas.

Captain Edward de Witt Sears was a white Bahamian, who had been a sponge merchant for many years until 1939 when the *red rust* plague destroyed his livelihood and as a result he took to police work.

Sears was the Superintendent of the Bahamas Police at the time of the murder and testified for the Defense at the trial, to the effect that during the night of the murder, he was driving along West Bay Street near George Street in downtown Nassau and saw Harold Christie in a stationwagon going in the opposite direction. Christie always claimed that Sears must have been mistaken in his identification and should have been more careful in making such a statement.

According to Sears it appeared that Christie was on the passenger side, which would have placed him very close to Sears, who would have been in the driver's seat of the other car. One must remember that in Nassau one drives on the left side of the road and the vehicle in which Christie was a passenger was a north American stationwagon, whereas Sears was in a right hand drive or British style automobile, where the driver is on the right hand side. This would explain the fact that they were within a few feet of each other as they passed.

During the cross-examination of Capt. Sears, the Prosecution was a little concerned that Sears was unable to identify the owner of the stationwagon or for that matter the driver, as apparently there were only twenty six stationwagons on the island at the time and Sears was responsible for the Traffic Department of the Nassau Police. Sears did not note the license number, which was only comprised of four digits.

For all intents and purposes the testimony as given by Capt. Sears remained and was to be part of the official court records of the trial.

In due course Sears became Commissioner of Police and in 1959 he retired and was appointed Acting Comptroller of the new Transport Authority.

We must now remember that Alfred de Marigny subsequently spoke with one of the surviving night watchmen, who identified the driver of the stationwagon as Frank Christie, which would appear to discredit Sears statement at the trial.

Likewise when I visited Nassau in 1992, I was approached by a lady in an antique shop on West Bay street, who informed me that it was not Harold Christie who was driving the stationwagon but his brother Frank, which would further confirm de Marigny's statement.

The lady to whom I spoke, while identifying the driver as Frank Christie, did confirm that there was indeed a close facial resemblance between Harold Christie and his brother Frank.

John Gaffney, Manager of the Royal Bank of Canada, Nassau. *Courtesy of Gordon Gaffney, Toronto*

John Gaffney was a Canadian employee of the Royal Bank of Canada in Nassau and during the Second World War, was seconded to head up the Exchange Control Board in the Bahamas, to supervise the Bank of England's monetary restrictions which were in effect and governed the movement of currencies in the British Colonies.

Gaffney arrived in the Bahamas in the late thirties as an Accountant with the Royal Bank. He was single, eccentric, kept to himself and was known as a very caring person and did a great deal of travelling. He died in 1981.

During the trial of Alfred de Marigny, he was called upon to testify as to the financial responsibilities of de Marigny and the movement of funds from his account and at one point there was mention that de Marigny had a 20,000 pound line of credit with the Royal Bank.

As a result of this remark, Chief Justice Daly turned towards Gaffney in the witness box and asked, *"And how much would you loan me?"* To which Gaffney replied, *"Possibly a thousand pounds, My Lord — no offense intended." "None taken"* replied a smiling Sir Oscar.

Lewis Charles Phillips was the Manager of the Current Account and Savings Departments at the Royal Bank of Canada in Nassau. During the course of the trial he was also called upon to testify regarding the financial status of Alfred de Marigny. Phillips confirmed during the hearing in the Magistrate's Court that on July 7th, 1943, the account in de Marigny's name showed an overdraft of only *twenty eight pounds, one shilling and six pence* (approximately $300 based on the exchange rate prevalent at the time).

Naturally, it was the intention of the Prosecution to try and establish that de Marigny was in dire need of money and every effort was made to question all large entries to his account going back to June 5th, 1942, almost one year earlier and actually almost to the date of his marriage to Nancy Oakes on May 19th.

The Prosecution even went so far as to question the account balance of de Marigny's cousin Georges de Visdelou for a purpose that did not seem to be clear to anyone, including Alfred de Marigny himself.

As was noted in the Prosecution's opening remarks at the hearing in the Magistrate's Court, *the desperate financial condition of the accused* was another one of the reasons that they felt prompted de Marigny to murder Sir Harry Oakes. Surely an overdraft for the equivalent of $300 is not an indication that the person is broke and in dire need of funds and much less willing to go to the trouble of murdering someone as close as his wife's father.

Let us now review some of the true assets that de Marigny did have at the time according to his testimony — a piece of property at the corner of Malborough and West Street in Nassau valued at 400/500 pounds, property on Blue Hill Road at 1,000 pounds, two houses and 100 acres of land at Governor's Harbour on the Island of Eleuthera valued at 3,000/4,000 pounds, a profitable chicken farm, a sail boat, a car and most important of all, a twenty thousand pound line of credit as previously mentioned by John Gaffney — the exchange rate was approximately $5 to the pound. Again a poor excuse on the part of the Prosecution to show that de Marigny was in need of money.

In addition to the above assets, Alfred de Marigny also had a good sum of money with a New York brokerage house, however, he did not wish to disclose this additional source of funds as he would have been forced to transfer the money by order of the Exchange Control Board. This transfer would have been at the prevailing exchange rate which in de Marigny's mind would have caused him quite a substantial loss.

13

Sir Harry Oakes — Some Other Notes

Some of Sir Harry Oakes' Estates — Bar Harbor, Maine: British Colonial Hotel, Nassau: The Caves Estate, Nassau: Westbourne Estate, Nassau ..... Some Memorial Services for Sir Harry Oakes ..... Sir Harry Oakes — Some Legends ..... Sir Harry Oakes — Some of His Philanthropies ..... Trees — Sir Harry's Pet Peeve ..... Sir Harry Oakes — His Will ..... The Canadian Mining Hall of Fame — At Last Some Recognition ..... Exhumation — A Possible Last Resort ..... The Federal Bureau of Investigation — Some Interesting Memos

---

Over the years following the discovery of his gold mine and as a result of his new found wealth, Harry Oakes began to purchase estates and properties in various parts of the world and the following is a list of the main ones that have been mentioned:

Oakes Chateau in Kirkland Lake, Ontario, which was built by Harry Oakes.
Oak Hall in Niagara Falls, Ontario.
The Willows in Bar Harbor, Maine.
Property on Barton Avenue in Palm Beach, Florida.
Property at Kensington Gardens in London, England.
Land at Tottingworth Park in Sussex, England.
The *Caves* and *Westbourne* estates in Nassau, Bahamas and the British Colonial Hotel.

In addition to the two above-mentioned residences in Nassau, other members of the Oakes family owned a number of other private residences located throughout the fashionable areas of Nassau.

Bar Harbor, Maine is a quaint resort town on the eastern coast of the Atlantic ocean, that for a century was the exclusive summer domain and playground of many of the rich and famous, including the likes of J. P. Morgan, Joseph Pulitzer, John D. Rockefeller, Evalyn Walsh McLean (at one time owner of the Hope diamond) and others, including Sir Harry Oakes.

As part of Sir Harry Oakes' estates, he purchased a residence in 1935 in Bar Harbor which was called the *Willows* and renamed it the *Seven Oakes*, no doubt in recognition of the Oakes family of seven. The estate was originally constructed in 1913. Lady Oakes and the children spent a great deal of time in the summer months in Bar Harbor and Sir Harry would join them there on a number of occasions. The main reason for their spending time in Bar Harbor was to get away from the heat and high humidity prevalent in Nassau at that time of the year.

Sir Harry Oakes' estate *The Willows* at Bar Harbor, Maine. *Author's collection*

In 1958, some years following the death of Sir Harry, Lady Eunice Oakes donated the estate to Bowdoin College, Sir Harry's alma mater, with the purpose of using it as a summer educational center. The plan was not a success and the residence was sold in the early 1970s. It is presently used as a bed and breakfast complex as part of a hotel resort known as the *Atlantic Oakes By The Sea*, which provides full resort amenities with tennis courts, indoor and outdoor swimming pools. If you are daring, you can always go for a swim in the Atlantic Ocean at the edge of the property.

On July 9th, 1943, it was Sir Harry Oakes' intention to leave Nassau for the remainder of the summer and join his family in Bar Harbor. Necessary exit visa papers had been obtained from the authorities in Nassau. But fate played its part and during the night of the 7th and 8th he was murdered by parties unknown in his *Westbourne* estate in Nassau.

A funeral service for Sir Harry was held in Bar Harbor and it is there that Captains James Barker and Edward Melchen visited with Lady Oakes at her request. She then heard from them first hand the gruesome details surrounding the murder of her husband. It was also at this point that they informed Lady Oakes and Nancy de Marigny, that Alfred de Marigny had been charged with the crime and that they had sufficient evidence to bring him to trial in the Supreme Court in October.

The *Willows* portion itself is closed during the winter months, but during a visit there in April 1996, I was given a grand tour of the establishment which was not open to the public. Most of the interior and exterior remains as it was back in the days when the Oakes lived there. The building incorporates eleven rooms, many with fireplaces, and has a great deal of charm and architectural beauty.

The *Willows* is located within a stone's throw of the beautiful and sometimes rough Atlantic Ocean. The ferry terminal between Bar Harbor, Maine and Yarmouth, Nova Scotia is also situated on the adjoining property.

In 1947 a disastrous fire ravaged most of the elegant estates in Bar Harbor with losses estimated at the time at $23 million. The area where Sir Harry resided was not affected.

According to an article in the April 22nd, 1931, issue of the *Palm Beach Post-Times*, it was reported that Harry Oakes purchased two parcels of property in the central part of Palm Beach adjoining the Palm Beach Golf Club. The purchase price was reported at $250,000.

A view of Sir Harry Oakes' property in Palm Beach. *Historical Society of Palm Beach County*

Oakes also bought houses on Barton Avenue which fronted on the ocean and on Flagler Road, with extensive alterations planned for later that summer to include a swimming pool and tennis courts. It was expected that following completion of the remodelling, the property would be one of the outstanding beauty spots in Palm Beach.

Interesting to note that Walter Foskett of the law firm of Winters, Foskett and Wilcox in Palm Beach represented Harry Oakes in the transactions.

The British Colonial Hotel was originally the site of Fort Nassau, located in downtown Nassau at the entrance to the harbour area. The Fort was erected in 1697, as one

Sir Harry Oakes' British Colonial Hotel in downtown Nassau. *Author's collection*

of the main defence locations against possible attack from the pirates roaming around the Island of New Providence and the Caribbeans at the time.

The railway tycoon Henry M. Flagler decided to invest in the Bahamas and was one of the first foreign investors to do so on a large scale, in the interests of Bahamian tourism, and no doubt also from a personal and financial point of view, as many of his ventures in Florida were most profitable.

Flagler at the time entered into an agreement with the Bahamian Government and constructed the Colonial Hotel, which opened for business in 1890, the very same year that a winter steamship schedule was inaugurated between Miami and Nassau.

The original hotel building was destroyed by fire on March 31st, 1922, and a new hotel was subsequently constructed with surplus Government funds, supposedly from the duty collected during the rum-running days of Prohibition. The hotel was completed within eight months and was opened for the second time on February 19th, 1923, under the name of the New Colonial Hotel.

In 1939 Sir Harry Oakes purchased the British Colonial Hotel from one Henry L. Doherty and began to operate it as an all year round resort, making it possible for Nassau to then enter the winter tourist trade.

Part of the interior ruins of Sir Harry's *The Caves* estate in Nassau. *Author's collection*

The hotel is now known as the British Colonial Hilton and still remains one of the great landmarks in the downtown waterfront area of Nassau with its stucco facade.

The *Caves* was the name of Sir Harry Oakes' largest residence in Nassau and was located on a hilltop on the west end of the island overlooking Lake Killarney to the south and the blue Atlantic ocean to the north, with easy access from West Bay Street. It was considered Sir Harry's favourite residence on the island and was quite an elaborate domain.

In 1959 the property was reported as worthless in view of the dilapidated state of the buildings, which had for the most part crumbled to the ground, though some of the stone walls and certain roofs had survived.

The land appeared to be waiting for someone to come along and plan a development of this choice piece of real estate. In a 1987 issue of the journal of the Bahamas Historical Society, it is interesting to note an ad for the sale of some 300 acres at Westridge Estates of the hilltop and lakefront property referred to as *that which the late Sir Harry Oakes loved so dearly.*

Sir Harry Oakes' main residence in Nassau was *Westbourne* estate, located on the ocean front on West Bay Street near the Cable Beach area and which was eventually to become the site of the Ambassador Beach Hotel and home of the Playboy Club and Casino.

It seems ironic that one of the gambling establishments in the Bahamas was built on the very site where Sir Harry once resided, as it was often said that he deplored the thought of gambling casinos becoming part of the lifestyle of his beloved Nassau. It is this point that

The Ambassador Beach Hotel and Playboy Club and Casino on the fomer site of Sir Harry's Westbourne estate. *Author's collection*

has led many an author to conclude that the murder of Sir Harry Oakes was due in part to his objections to the idea of having gambling casinos in *his* islands.

On one occasion I drove over to the Ambassador Beach Hotel and had a conversation with an elderly taxi driver who recalled Sir Harry Oakes. As we discussed the hotel and Oakes' former estate, the driver mentioned that not all was lost, as some of the original foundation of *Westbourne* was still visible down by the beach front.

At his suggestion I strolled down the west side of the hotel towards the ocean and sure enough, within a few hundred feet or so of that beautiful blue Atlantic Ocean, I discovered a small section of the remains of the foundation. Lying there within a few feet were a number of tourists sunning themselves, no doubt not even aware of the history behind the site where they were.

Westbourne was purchased in 1934 by Sir Harry, through his new found real estate friend Harold Christie, for an estimated $250,000 from the American film actress Maxime Elliott, though another reliable source indicates that Oakes purchased the home for $100,000 from a Mrs. B.F. Johnson of Rye, New York.

The twenty five room estate was situated next door to the Bahamas Country Club. Also on the west side of the estate were the *Hubbard Cottages* where Jean Ainslie and Dorothy Clarke resided at the time of the tragedy, as well as Charles Hubbard who was the owner of the cottages and a dinner guest at Sir Harry's on that fateful evening.

Upon the arrival of the Duke and Duchess of Windsor in August 1940, following his appointment as Royal Governor General, the conditions at Government House were not exactly to their liking and required a great deal of refurbishing, in order to make the residence live up to the standards of the Duchess of Windsor.

At this point, the Duke and Duchess required a temporary residence and Sir Harry came forward with the offer of the use of his *Westbourne* estate.

It is said that the Duke and Duchess slept in the very same room in which Sir Harry was subsequently found murdered.

In August 1961, a press report confirmed that Sir Harry's estate, which comprised 3,200 acres and the Bahamas Country Club, including the golf course, had been sold to a British developer by the name of Roland Lawrence.

Although no dollar value was officially announced, it was estimated that local sources in Nassau had placed the price at approximately ten million pounds ($28.8 million).

Lawrence announced that he felt that the property would be the hub of a development which would include hotels, apartments, public buildings, as well as residential and shopping areas. However, that would not be the case as the Ambassador Beach Hotel would be the only commercial establishment to be built on the former site of Sir Harry's *Westbourne* estate. Nancy Oakes was in Nassau at the time that the announcement of the sale was made and commented to the effect that — *I must admit that I am very sad. I had hoped that we would do the developing of the estate ourselves.*

In tribute to a great man and benefactor, a number of memorial services were held for Sir Harry Oakes following his death. The following are brief summaries of the services held in Nassau at Gambier Village, Christ Church Cathedral and at the Southern Recreational Grounds, as well as one at Dover-Foxcroft, Maine. It is interesting to note that there did not appear to be any memorial services held for Sir Harry in Kirkland Lake or Niagara Falls.

Dover-Foxcroft, Maine

On Friday July 16th, 1943, an official memorial service was held in the small town of Dover-Foxcroft at twelve o'clock noon, officiated by Rev. Gordon Reardon, a 69 year old friend of Harry Oakes. Amongst those in attendance were Dr. George Cameron, physician and Frederick Blomfield, Managing Director of Lake Shore Mines from Kirkland Lake.

Sir Harry's older brother Louis Oakes from Greenville, Maine, and his sisters Myrtice of Dover-Foxcroft and Jessie of Leesburg, Virginia, were also in attendance as were members of his immediate family.

Also present from Nassau were Capt. George Woods, OBE., representing the Duke of Windsor and the Government of the Bahamas; the Hon. and Mrs. A.K. Solomon and Mr. and Mrs. Newell Kelly, who had accompanied the body of Sir Harry Oakes from Nassau.

Christ Church Cathedral, Nassau

On the same day as the memorial service in Dover-Foxcroft on July 16th, a further service was being held at Christ Church Cathedral in Nassau which started at 5.30 p.m. in the afternoon and was officiated by the Very Reverend, the Dean of Nassau. In attendance at this elaborate memorial were the following prominent citizens of Nassau:

The Duke and Duchess of Windsor
Commander James Dugdale, ADC to the Duke of Windsor
Chief Justice Sir Oscar and Lady Daly
The Hon.W.L.Heape, Colonial Secretary and Mrs. Heape
Sir Walter K.Moore C.B.E., President of the Legislative Assembly, and Lady Moore
Asa Pritchard, Deputy Speaker of the Nassau House of Assembly
Members of the Nassau Executive Council, the Legislative Council (of which Sir Harry was
    a member)
Members of the Nassau House of Assembly
Commander R.Langton Jones, R.N., of the Ministry of Transport
Major Frederick G.Lancaster, M.C., Security Department
Col. A.W. deWolfe D.C.M., representing the Canadian Armed Forces
Col. Reginald Erskine-Lindop, representing the Bahamas Police Force
Major d'Arcy Rutherford and Capt. George Lightbourn, representing the Bahamas Defense
    Force Company.

A detachment from the Bahamas Red Cross was also present, together with the children of the Belmont School and one of Sir Harry Oakes' close friends, Reverend Robert Hall, of Gambier Village.

The very simple service at the Cathedral lasted approximately twenty-five minutes.

Gambier Village, Nassau

Reverend Robert Hall, teacher at the school in Gambier Village and friend of Sir Harry and Lady Eunice Oakes led the memorial service for Sir Harry at the Community Hall at Gambier held on Monday, August 2nd.

A number of residents from Gambier Village, Delaporte, Adelaide, Carmichael and Old Fort, which were neighbouring villages also attended. The Honourable Harold Christie, Sir Harry's best friend and business associate, delivered a tribute to Oakes during the service.

Southern Recreational Grounds, Nassau

At the request of the people of the Southern District of Nassau, arrangements were made by the Representatives of the Districts to organize a memorial service in honour of Sir Harry at the Southern Recreational Grounds, in order to accommodate the large number of people who wished to attend.

The gathering was held on Monday August 9th and was said to be the largest ever seen on the Grounds, which included several lodges and other organizations dressed in their full ceremonial regalia.

This service was by the people of Nassau, whom Sir Harry assisted the most and who in turn had a great deal of respect and affection for one of the greatest philanthropists that the Bahamas has ever known, and wanted to show their respect for him. During the service a collection was held to raise funds to establish a memorial in the Southern District in honour of Sir Harry. An account was opened with the Royal Bank of Canada to receive all future donations.

Over the years since Harry Oakes arrived in Canada and his subsequent move to the Bahamas, many stories and legends have followed him wherever he has gone — some have been true and others just plain fabrication.

Foremost amongst the legends and most often referred to is the one whereby Oakes arrived in the Kirkland Lake area in 1911 hungry and penniless, and was *grubstaked* by some individual who started him on his way.

Along the same vein is the story that Oakes was thrown off a train near the town of Swastika because he could not pay his fare. It is often said that all Oakes had in his pockets was $2.65.

As regards this story concerning his train trip, a further story goes on to point out that some time later, when Harry became wealthy he sought out the conductor of the train, built him a home, retired him from the Canadian Pacific Railway and established a trust fund that would pay him an income of $500 a month for life. If I am correct the CPR was not even in that area at the time?

In December 1946, Lady Eunice Oakes during an interview in Nassau refuted the above stories and clarified Harry's arrival in Kirkland Lake saying that, *"Actually, what happened was that Harry got off the train at Swastika. This was at the time the nearest station to Kirkland Lake, four miles away — a very hard, rugged and wild country in those days. He prospected at Swastika for a while and then gradually wended his way towards Kirkland Lake where he struck his pick and that was it. And that's all there is to the tale."*

In 1925 when Harry Oakes was searching for financial investors for his newly discovered gold mines, he met some American executives in a commodious private railroad car on a siding near Kirkland Lake. Arnold Hoffman, author of *Free Gold*, was in the rail car at the time and had an opportunity to interview Harry Oakes, and amongst the questions asked was, "And is it true that the conductor put you off the train when you weren't able to pay for a ticket?" Oakes replied that there was no truth to this story but felt that there was nothing he could do to suppress it. Under the circumstances Harry Oakes figured that these stories were now all part of the lore of the north and part of his legacy.

Another legend that is often related is that concerning Sir Harry in Nassau and his visit to the British Colonial Hotel. On this particular day Oakes asked to be seated in a certain area of the hotel dining room. Since the maitre d'hotel noted that Sir Harry was attired in his usual prospector's rig which comprised his plaid shirt, mining pants, boots and his hat — in other words his mining outfit that he basically wore around Kirkland Lake in harder times — he refused to allow the seating requested and Harry turned around and walked away. It is said that he then purchased the hotel for $1,000,000 and returned the following day and fired the maitre d'.

How true is this story is often questioned, but like his being thrown off the train — the story lives on and on. Until someone can claim otherwise these legends will always remain with Sir Harry Oakes, but he did eventually buy the British Colonial Hotel.

Following ownership of the hotel he decided that only black Bahamians would be hired and he established a hotel training school for the development of the employees.

Following an interview on CBC North in Kirkland Lake in March 1996, broadcast from the Sir Harry Oakes Chateau on the occasion of the inauguration of the new radio transmission facilities for the north from Kirkland Lake, I was approached by Tom O'Hare, an old time resident of Kirkland Lake. Tom asked me why I did not talk about some of Oakes' philanthropies while he lived there. I explained to him that as the timing for the interview was limited, certain points of his life had to be regrettably omitted, though they were part of my notes.

As I returned home and continued to write my notes on Sir Harry, I remembered Tom's comments. It became rather interesting that indeed Harry Oakes had shown a number of philanthropic gestures in almost all the places he touched and as a result I researched the matter and came up with the following interesting notes:

Sangerville, Maine

Although he had been born and raised in Sangerville, it was only following his death in 1943 that Harry Oakes' name was brought forward as a philanthropist, with land donations by his surviving wife Lady Eunice Oakes. These included the property on which his family home was built and which was donated to the Grace Bible Church & Christian School, for which ground was broken in the spring of 1981. Across the road a further piece of land was donated and became Oakes Manor, an equal housing opportunity residence for seniors, dedicated to the memory of Sir Harry and Lady Eunice Oakes.

Dover-Foxcroft, Maine

Harry Oakes attended Foxcroft Academy and as a result, some years following his gold strikes, Oakes returned to Dover-Foxcroft and made some sizeable donations to the Academy for the development of playing fields and additional space for the library.

Not to be outdone, his brother Louis also made numerous contributions to the school during his lifetime.

Brunswick, Maine

While attending Bowdoin College, Harry became a member of the Zeta Psi fraternity house and a number of years later he returned to the college for a class reunion. While renewing acquaintances Harry was approached for a financial contribution towards the funds being raised to build a new fraternity house. At this point Harry had already discovered his gold mine and was well unto financial independence.

As a result, he gave them a cheque for $40,000, for which he received a rather startling look of surprise. Harry immediately asked the gentleman if it was because the amount was too small, to which he received a negative response and a rather hearty handshake. Harry told them that if they needed additional funds to contact him and he would be more than pleased to make a further contribution. It is understood that Harry's original donation alone, covered more than half the cost of building the new fraternity house.

The old Zeta Psi fraternity house at Sir Harry's alma mater Bowdoin College in Brunswick, Maine. *Bowdoin College Archives, Bowdoin College Library*

In addition to his financial donations to his alma mater, Harry Oakes had become a collector of fine art and as a result purchased five masterpieces and lent them to the Bowdoin College Museum of Fine Art for an indefinite period.

Kirkland Lake, Ontario

Following his departure from Sangerville and Dover-Foxcroft, Maine, Harry Oakes' next residence was to be Kirkland Lake, where in due course he would spread more of his philanthropic benefits.

Oakes donated land for a school, which later became the Central Public School which opened in 1917, and also provided them with books.

As plain Harry Oakes, he built a skating rink for the younger people of Kirkland Lake apparently at an estimated cost of $75,000 and also made available to them the necessary skates. The arena was completed in June 1927.

220

Niagara Falls, Ontario

When Oakes left Kirkland Lake for Niagara Falls, his philanthropic gestures continued to follow him, such as the Oakes Garden Theatre which was developed by the Niagara Parks Commission and the modern Oakes Athletic field operated by the City of Niagara Falls on a site donated by Oakes. Most of these sites are presently tourist attractions.

In March 1945, it was reported in one of the Niagara Falls papers that Lady Eunice Oakes, formerly of Oak Hall had donated the sum of $10,000 for the purchase of new x-ray equipment for the Niagara Peninsula Sanatorium. The new equipment was to replace the original equipment generously donated by the then Harry Oakes in 1929 when the sanatorium was first established.

Following the death of Lady Eunice Oakes in 1981, the following comment was made in a local Niagara Falls newspaper — *no greater philanthropists lived in Niagara Falls in the 1920s and early 1930s than Harry Oakes and his wife Eunice. Their names are perpetuated in many ways here as reminders of their generosity.*

At the Niagara Falls public library one of the rooms was named the Sir Harry Oakes room and was furnished through a gift from Lady Oakes in 1973. The room was used to house a special collection of books on the early settlement and pioneer life on the banks of the Niagara River.

As he did in many other places where he resided, Harry donated land and amongst the more important gestures was the fact that he also provided much needed employment to hundreds and hundreds of individuals in times of hardship. Niagara Falls was no exception and it is said that each man was paid $2 for a half day's work and was paid in $2 bills.

Aside from having Oakes Field in Nassau, Sir Harry also had in the mid to late thirties a 400 acre property near Chippawa, Ontario on the Niagara River Parkway, of which a part was licensed privately to be used as an airfield and which was also called Oakes Field. Sightseeing flights were available to the public at the field at a cost of $5 per passenger.

Nassau, Bahamas

Immediately following his arrival in Nassau in 1937, Harry Oakes donated one thousand pounds to Sir Bede Clifford, then Governor General of the Bahamas, to assist the government in developing employment and training in Nassau for local Bahamians.

During his residency in the Bahamas, Oakes established a bus service for the natives of Nassau, as well as an inter-island medical emergency air service.

In addition to the transportation services that Oakes initiated, he developed land that he owned and established Oakes Field, an air field in the eastern section of the island. The airfield was also used as a training centre for the RAF personnel who were stationed in Nassau during the war.

During a visit to Nassau in 1994, I searched for and located Oakes Field. All that is left are the runways which have been overgrown by vegetation. One of its main uses at present is as a short cut by some of the local residents when driving home.

Again, possibly not considered an out-of-pocket donation to charity or to the people of the Bahamas, Sir Harry did provide over the years steady employment to close to one thousand labourers who would have been otherwise unemployed and as a result he was very popular amongst the native Bahamians.

In January 1948, some five years following the tragic death of Sir Harry Oakes, the real citizens of the Bahamas as we would call them, helped erect a memorial obelisk in his memory.

The obelisk itself is situated on an open piece of land measuring approximately one hundred square feet in area and bordered by a two foot high cement wall.

There is an inscription on the base of the obelisk which reads as follows:

In Memory of Sir Harry Oakes, Bt. 1874-1943
A Great Friend and Benefactor of the Bahamas

It has been estimated that Sir Harry Oakes' contributions to the well being of the people of the Bahamas approached $500,000 during his lifetime in Nassau.

Inscription on the obelisk erected in Nassau in memory of Sir Harry Oakes. *Author's collection*

St. George's Hospital at Hyde Park in London, to which Sir Harry made substantial financial contributions for the restructuring fund. *Courtesy of the London Metropolitan Archives*

London, England

Following his purchase of a residence in London, Harry Oakes began to make financial donations to the fund-raising efforts at St. George's Hospital in Hyde Park. The amount donated has varied from source to source, however, a close estimate would be in the neighbourhood of $500,000.

In 1937 it is said that Oakes had startled an official of the hospital by handing him a cheque for the equivalent of $100,000 telling him that a further contribution would follow for the hospital's rebuilding fund.

In June 1940, it was reported in the press that the Ministry of Aircraft Production in London announced a gift of $22,000 received from Sir Harry and Lady Oakes, then residents of the Bahamas and again in July it was also reported in the Nassau press that Lady Oakes had cabled $27,812 to England to be used toward the purchase of a fighter plane.

During the course of the early years of the Second World War, it was estimated that Sir Harry and Lady Eunice Oakes had donated sufficient funds to the war effort alone to cover the cost of apparently five fighter planes.

On June 6th, 1939, on the occasion of the birthday Honour List of King George VI, Harry Oakes was created a Baronet of the British Empire in recognition of his many generous contributions to the various charities in London and in particular to St. George's Hospital.

Up in Kirkland Lake, there is a story that has circulated over the years, which I am told is true, that Sir Harry had an oil painting made of himself in the full regalia of his new title as a Baronet of the British Empire. Apparently the painting was shipped to Kirkland Lake, so that all his mining friends and foes alike could see the recognition that he had finally received. To this day no one has ever located this oil painting of Sir Harry Oakes, however, should anyone ever find it, please contact the Museum of Northern History in Kirkland Lake.

Palm Beach, Florida and Bar Harbor, Maine

It is interesting to note that of all the places where Sir Harry Oakes established residences, the only two that did not seem to benefit from his philanthropies were Palm Beach, Florida and Bar Harbor, Maine, often referred to as the homes of the rich and famous.

Lady Eunice Oakes

While Sir Harry made numerous donations to various causes during his lifetime, it should also be noted that Lady Eunice Oakes continued his tradition following his death and made many donations of her own.

A Lover of Trees

Some years ago I had the pleasure of speaking with the late Val Clery, who had written a story for the Toronto Star relative to his interview with Alfred de Marigny, when he was in Toronto promoting his book in 1990.

We discussed Sir Harry Oakes at some length and Clery asked me if I knew the answer to Sir Harry's pet peeve concerning the destruction of trees, to which I could not really give an intelligent answer. The comments quoted below no doubt support my ignorance of the subject and hopefully will act as a souvenir of my conversation with Val Clery:

Fortunes in the Ground — Michael Barnes

Harry Oakes had a different encounter over trees. When fire rangers approached Lake Shore Mines to cut down some standing timber for a firebreak, he chased the rangers off with an axe. Harry loved trees and the rangers felt that their $2.50 a day pay less room and board was not worth the argument.

Sir Harry and Lady Eunice Oakes in London following his investiture. *Museum of Northern History*

Who Killed Sir Harry Oakes? — James Leasor

He planted thousands of citrus plants, coconut palms and acres of strawberries. "I have been planting trees all morning," Oakes told them. "I thought you'd rather cut them down" said Hubbard, Sir Harry's neighbour. "Every time I see you on a tractor or a bull dozer — and that's nearly every day — always tearing trees down all over the place." "I like trees" replied Oakes defensively, "I cut them down only because I need to make way for a road or an airfield."

The Life and Death of Sir Harry Oakes — Geoffrey Bocca

Visitors who knew Oakes only in his last years talked about his phobia without realizing the significance of what they were saying. The Duchess of Windsor's innocent recollection of Oakes is of — *a man levelling acres of Palmetto trees in a series of furious rushes.* Every day he was out on the job. The great bulldozer whirred and ground. The trees leaned, creaked and crashed. In the country and sporting clubs the soda water in the highballs of the rich residents shuddered and foamed and the ice tinkled as the bulldozer echoed for miles through the still, sticky air of the Nassau summer. In one area Oakes levelled so many trees that he was able to build an airport on the spot. On one occasion Sir Harry tied a chain around a tree and hooked it on to the bulldozer and pulled away to the astonishment of golfers on the course, however, as he had built and owned the golf course, he could do as he pleased.

Article from MacLean's Magazine

Around the staff quarters in Kirkland Lake at the gold mine, Sir Harry even landscaped the camp leaving natural stands of birch and pine on the point. He loved trees. Some provincial forestry men arrived to cut a fire ring and he met them at the property line threatening to sink an axe into the first man to touch one of his trees.

History of the Bahamas — Michael Craton

A lover of trees in his youth, Oakes became known as a savage destroyer of unwanted timber on New Providence. Near *Westbourne* estate, he cleared a magnificent new golf course. Two miles south-west of Nassau, no doubt persuaded by Christie, his closest confident, he levelled and paved Oakes Field, the first land airfield in the Bahamas.

A Conspiracy of Crowns — Alfred de Marigny

Something about his house puzzled me. The lawns were lush and manicured, but there were no trees or bushes within a hundred feet of the house. Harry had cleared the land, having decided that trees attracted mosquitoes and bugs.

The Kirkland Lake Story — Andre Wetjen & Lorrie Irvine

One year Oakes came up to find one of his five management homes nestled neatly in the trees behind the other four. The assistant manager had ordered his house built in this quiet secluded spot, but Oakes decided no one should receive special treatment and ordered it put alongside the other four homes, where it still is today. Up on the blocks the house went, but a birch impeded progress and an axeman prepared to chop it down. Oakes happened along just then, fired the man on the spot and ordered the house cut in half to negotiate it around the tree. The Lake Shore is gone. Oakes is dead. But that birch tree still stands.

Famous Last Words — Timothy Findley

Some years before when he first arrived and began to buy up all the land that Harold Christie had for sale, the first thing that Oakes had done was plant a thousand trees. Evergreens mostly — spruce and pine and other trees that like a sandy, shallow soil. They had been his pride and joy, these trees — and everyone had said: *a man who plants so many trees where no trees were before can't be all that bad.* It had been the first good sign that Harry Oakes was civilized. Now he went down to the Public Works and came back out along the road with an army truck and trailer. When the trailer was unloaded, what came down the ramp was a dirty yellow bulldozer.

For days, what he did was go out early in the morning, while the sun was still at a tolerable angle in the sky, and knock down trees — all the thousand trees and more he'd planted and nourished and cultivated over the past ten years. He destroyed them — every one.

Passion and Paradise — The Movie

While this was just a movie, there still was a scene when Sir Harry arrived back at his home, walked away from his tractor and had a few words with his butler, who asked him what kind of a day he had. Oakes replied that he had planted another five trees.

Solved and Unsolved Classic True Murder Cases

In this particular book there is an extract from a book written by Julian Symons, which reads as follows: *There was nothing unusual about the last day in the life of the Canadian millionaire, Sir Harry Oakes. He planted trees at Westbourne, his home near the Bahamian Country Club in Nassau.*

There is also a notation to the effect that two small spruce trees guard the approach to the mausoleum at the cemetery in Dover-Foxcroft, Maine, where members of the Oakes family are buried.

This latter statement is indeed true as I had the opportunity in July 1992, of visiting the site of Sir Harry's mausoleum. The two trees are now rather tall and it is interesting to note that on the land immediately adjoining the cemetery behind the Oakes section is a tree farm. Rather ironical when one reads about Sir Harry's relationship with trees.

Crime: An Encyclopedia

Oakes was happy with his bulldozer and he went on buying land from the local real estate promoter, Harold Christie, so that he could knock down trees. As the editor of the *Nassau Times* (more likely either the *Tribune* or the *Nassau Guardian*) commented — *as long as Christie could find something for Sir Harry to destroy, he knew he had a sale.*

Afterwards

In September 1943, some two months following the untimely death of Sir Harry Oakes, his will was still a secret. The only people knowing the contents of it were his widow Lady Eunice Oakes as executrix, and the two trustees, U.S. attorney Walter Foskett and Nassau business manager Newell Kelly.

Rumours persisted that the worth of the Oakes estate was estimated as high as $200,000,000, a great deal of it in land holdings in the Bahamas.

At the time it was foreseen that the will would not be made public until after the trial of his son-in-law, Alfred de Marigny. It was understood that this was normal British Court procedure in order not to prejudice the proceedings of the trial.

However, on October 3rd, 1943, contrary to the previous statement that the contents of the will would not be released until after the trial, it was confirmed that the Last Will and Testament of the late Sir Harry Oakes had now been made public.

The release of Sir Harry's will appeared to have no bearing whatsoever on the process of the trial and the eventual outcome.

The will itself was only five pages long and involved an estate valued at three million six hundred and seventy one thousand, seven hundred and twenty four pounds, thirteen shillings and five pence, with the bequests confined to Lady Eunice Oakes and family, with Lady Oakes receiving a cash settlement of 50,000 pounds and one-third of the entire estate. The remainder was divided equally amongst the five children, who would receive an annual income of US$12,000 each.

It was further stipulated that only when the children would reach the age of 30 would they come into full possession of their respective shares with Nancy Oakes de Marigny to receive her share on May 17th, 1954; Sydney Oakes on June 9th, 1957; Shirley Oakes on April 10th, 1959; William Pitt Oakes to have received his share on September 10th, 1960, (William Pitt died on April 26th, 1958) and finally Harry Phillip Oakes on August 30th, 1962.

The Bahamian Government was to collect a 2% succession tax which amounted to approximately $320,000. However, according to lawyers in Niagara Falls, Ontario at the time they estimated that if Sir Harry had died there, the estate would have been required to pay a provincial estate tax in the neighbourhood of $4,800,000 plus a surtax of 31% and a further federal tax of 17%.

It should be noted that some ten months following the marriage of Nancy Oakes to Alfred de Marigny, due no doubt in part to Sir Harry and Lady Eunice Oakes' feeling — that nothing good would come from the marriage, Sir Harry changed his will on February 15th, 1943, to ensure that Alfred de Marigny would not in any way benefit financially from his marriage to their daughter Nancy.

Canadian Mining Hall of Fame

On January 6th, 1995, some fifty two years following his tragic death and some eighty four years following his discovery of gold in Kirkland Lake, Sir Harry Oakes was at last inducted into the Canadian Mining Hall of Fame — one of the last honours to be conveyed to this great pioneer of the Northern Ontario mining scene.

The criteria for selection of candidates to be inducted into the Canadian Mining Hall of Fame is that the candidates must have first demonstrated an outstanding lifetime of achievements in Canadian mining in one or more of the following categories: exploration; building the corporation; technical contribution; supporting contribution and mining in society.

A lifetime of service to the industry will normally be evaluated after the individual has retired and reached the age of 70.

In the brochure produced on this occasion, the following is the excerpt of the testimonial given in reference to Sir Harry:

Adventure, fame and fortune all came the way of Sir Harry Oakes, the self-made prospector and mine-finder who transformed Ontario's Kirkland Lake district into one of the world's most famous gold camps. His outstanding achievement was the discovery and development of the Lake Shore Mines, the first significant find in that area.

Sponsors for the Canadian Mining Hall of Fame comprise the following organizations:

Canadian Institute of Mining, Metallurgy and Petroleum
Prospectors and Developers Association of Canada
The Mining Association of Canada, and
The *Northern Miner* newspaper

In a 1943 announcement of the death of Sir Harry Oakes, there is mention that he was President of the Ontario Mining Association in the years 1927-28 and was actively connected with the Canadian Institute of Mining, as well as the American Institute of Mining.

Since the death of Sir Harry Oakes, there have been references to the possibility of having the remains of Sir Harry exhumed for further forensic evaluation. Even at this late stage, there are some people who are still convinced that such an investigation could lead to new clues and bearing in mind the new DNA technology available there is no doubt some truth to it.

The first incident was raised by Marshall Houts in 1973, some thirty years after the death of Sir Harry, when Houts wrote directly to Lady Oakes who responded in a negative manner.

A few years later Alfred de Marigny brought up the point himself and it was strongly suggested to him that he pursue the matter, but it appears from having spoken to him that he never did follow through with the suggestion.

On two occasions I had the opportunity of visiting the Office of the Chief Coroner in Toronto (better known to some as Club Med) and had discussions on the subject of Sir Harry Oakes, the circumstances surrounding his death, the possible identification of the weapon used, as well as the benefits of having such an exhumation of his remains after all these years.

It would appear that Sir Harry's skull could be well preserved and such an exhumation would allow the forensic authorities to most likely identify from the wounds to the head, the type of weapon that would have been used. The investigative authorities would then be in a position to quite possibly identify the origin of the murderer or murderers based on the type of weapon identified.

When asked questions concerning the state of any remains of flesh or clothing the answer was that it would most likely be completely disintegrated. The reason for this particular question was to try to identify the flammable chemical used in setting fire to the room, to Sir Harry's body and the bed clothing. There has always been some doubt as to whether a blow torch was used, or whether the contents in the insecticide spray container were sufficient to cause all the burns inflicted, and as well as to set the fire to the mosquito netting, the bed and the other small fires which were seen around the bedroom including the carpeting, walls and outside wood finish on various pieces of furniture.

Apparently in order to request an exhumation it would be necessary to provide the legal and judicial authorities in the State of Maine the primary importance of the evidence you are seeking and why you wish to obtain it.

In addition proper permission must also be granted from a surviving member of the family of the deceased or if such is not available, an appropriate court order must be requested.

The Prosecution party would normally request the exhumation, however, in the case of Sir Harry Oakes, all members of the Prosecution and Defense have since passed away. In addition there would be further legal complications as the deceased died in the Bahamas and his remains are in the State of Maine in the United States.

During the war years in Nassau, there was a vested interest by the Federal Bureau of Investigation and in particular by its head J.Edgar Hoover, to monitor the activities of certain well known suspected residents, as well as various incoming visitors to Nassau who were known Nazi sympathisers, and other individuals of questionable background.

The following is the text of a letter written on September 30th, 1943, by the New York Office of the FBI. There are a few names and lines of text which have been obliterated by the FBI which appear as continuous marks as follows *xxxxx* and the *x*'s show the approximate length of the words, however, there is sufficient text to shed some light on the cast of characters mentioned:

JLQ:PAR   *September 30, 1943*
62-7430

Director, FBI

Re: Harry Oakes Murder Case

Dear Sir:

On September 17, 1943, xxxxxxxxxxxxxxxx telephonically advised xxxxxxxxxxxxx in the New York Field Division that he wished to furnish the following information:
"On Sir Harry Oakes case, at one time there was supposed to be a big investment group in Mexico, this about a year ago, consisting of Sir Harry Oakes, Alexander Wennergren, Harold Christie and the Duke of Windsor. xxxxxxxxxxxxxxxxxxx points out this is the first link between Oakes and Wennergren, which indicates something mysterious about the Nassau murder if Wennergren was mixed-up with Oakes.
xxxxxxxxxxxxxxxxxxxxxxxxxxxxxxxxxxxxxxxxxxxxxxxxxxxxxxxxxxxxxxxxxxxxxxxx
xxxxxxxxxxxxxxxxxxxxxxxxxxxxxxxxxxxxxxxxxxxxxxxxxxxxxxxxxxxxxxxxxxxxxxxxxx

xxxxxxxxxxxxxxxxxxxxxxxxxxxxxxxxxxxxxxxxxxxxxxxxxxxxxxxxxxxxxxxxxxxxxxxxxxxxxx
(*a paragraph of three complete lines of obliterated text*)
"Wennergren is going around saying he is the one who settled the war between Finland and Russia, before Germany invaded Russia several years ago; also, that Wennergren is supposed to be on the black list but through dummy (corporations) operates one of the largest silver places in Mexico City, known as La Conquistadore. Oakes made it known he planned to move with his family to Mexico, but concealed fact that he was Wennergren's silent partner (one of them). If we knew the reason for the secrecy, would we know why Oakes was killed?"
Very truly yours

E.E.Conroy
Special Agent in Charge

The following is the text of a second letter written on October 23rd, 1943, subsequent to the start of the trial of Alfred de Marigny on October 18th, 1943, on the charge of having murdered Sir Harry Oakes. This letter was written by the Washington Office of the FBI and addressed to the Director (presumably J. Edgar Hoover — though his name is not mentioned):

DHL:OSH   *October 23, 1943*

MEMORANDUM FOR THE DIRECTOR
RE: HAROLD G. CHRISTIE

You will recall that former Attorney General Homer Cummings telephoned your office and was referred to me, at which time he stated he desired to make an appointment for xxxxxxxxxxxxxxxx to see someone with the Bureau.

On October 22, 1943, xxxxxxxxxxxxx called at my office at least partly in connection with the murder of Sir Harry Oakes, in Nassau. He said that he understood that the FBI had ascertained that Harold Christie, one of the principal witnesses for the Crown, had a criminal record in the United States. He was also aware that Christie had paid one or more visits to the Bureau to intercede for Axel Wenner-Gren, who has been black listed by Naval Intelligence and is presently believed to be in Mexico.

xxxxxxxxxxxxx said he was calling on behalf of Mr John H. Anderson, general manager of Bahamas Trust Company and an employee of Axel Wenner-Gren. Anderson is described as being concerned that he might be left "holding the bag" in the wake of Wenner-Gren's troubles. He would like to put his role on the record and is available for an interview. Anderson says that Christie and Wenner-Gren brought the Duke of Windsor into a plot to divert millions of dollars to Mexico, to be exploited there after the war. Anderson claims he warned them of the risks and was rebuffed in his effort to alert the British Foreign Office or the Currency Exchange Board.

I was told that Anderson does not know where the records were kept or how, but Wenner-Gren let be known that he was holding $2,500,000 (US currency) for Windsor — some of it the Duke's money, all of it available to him. According to Treasury, currency from

occupied European capitals pouring into the Bahamas. Unthinkable that former King of England might have a hand in it. Recommend we examine Anderson soon as possible, after the trial has ended. He is for now a material witness.
COPIES DESTROYED

Respectfully
D.H.Ladd

It is interesting to note from these two memos that indeed all the names mentioned are those of the main characters noted throughout this text and are considered to be well known businessmen in high place in Nassau. The name of Alfred de Marigny can be eliminated from both memos, as he was awaiting trial in jail on the date of the first memo and secondly he was being tried in the Supreme Court on the latter date.

It has always been mentioned by reliable sources, both publicly and to the author, that indeed the person who organized the death of Sir Harry was part of that special circle of individuals. The list of names is limited and the identity of the person(s) should once again be easy to conclude.

However, who was the party who *telephonically advised* the FBI's New York Field Division — any possibility that it could have been either Walter Foskett or Newell Kelly?

14

Some Authors; Some Books and a Few Movies

Geoffrey Bocca ..... Erle Stanley Gardner ..... Max Haines — A Crime Columnist ..... Marshall Wilson Houts — A Letter to Lady Oakes ..... Cholly Knickerbocker — A Social Columnist ..... James Leasor — From a Book to a Movie ..... Sydney Albert Pain — The North Was His Dream ..... Julian Symons — A Crime Writer ..... The Miami Herald, the Nassau Guardian and The Tribune — The News As Reported ..... Newspaper Correspondents — Who Was There From the Press? ..... Newsweek and Time Magazine — Further Reports on the Murder and Trial ..... The Sunday Times Magazine — An Eye Opener ..... Eureka — The First Movie ..... Passion and Paradise — The Second Movie ..... Scales of Justice — The Last Screen Effort ..... The King's X — Some Informants

---

The following is a summary of some of the authors who have written about Sir Harry Oakes, as well as movie productions which have been made in an attempt to cover the life and death of Sir Harry Oakes and the trial of Alfred de Marigny.

A fair number of books, newspaper and magazine articles have made for good reading, though in some cases authenticity has been lost and in other cases they have gone to extremes in making their material more attractive to the reader or viewer.

Geoffrey Bocca

Geoffrey Bocca, educator, journalist and author, was born in 1923 and passed away in London at the age of sixty. During the Second World War, Bocca was a newspaper correspondent for the London Daily Express and eventually moved to the United States on a so-called temporary basis.

He wrote in excess of thirty books during his lifetime, including one entitled *The Woman Who Would Be Queen* in 1953, which related to the Duchess of Windsor and led up to the possibility that had she married the Prince of Wales when he was expected to be King of England, quite possibly she could have become Queen of England. At the time that the book was to be released, the Duke of Windsor apparently made every effort to have its publication suppressed in England, but without success.

In 1959, Bocca wrote a further book entitled *The Life and Death of Sir Harry Oakes*.

Erle Stanley Gardner

Erle Stanley Gardner was born in July 1889, in the town of Malden, Massachusetts and is best remembered as the creator of the fictional detective *Perry Mason*, both in writing, radio and eventually on television with Raymond Burr playing the lead role.

In the early part of his career, Gardner devoted at least twenty years as a practising attorney before he began writing his numerous mystery novels.

His first novel was entitled *The Case of the Velvet Claws*, which was published on March 1st, 1933, and during the course of his lifetime, he was to write in excess of 80 full length novels which sold over 300 million copies. It was from these novels that numerous radio episodes were produced.

Gardner wrote articles for a number of detective magazines and other periodicals, some of which you may remember, including — *All Detective, American Weekly, Argosy, the Atlantic Monthly, Black Mask, Collier's, Detective Fiction Weekly, Dime Detective, Look, Saturday Evening Post, True Police Cases* and many more.

He was to be one of the founding members of *The Court of Last Resort*, a group of forensic and legal experts established to review cases where potential miscarriages of justice were prevalent. Amongst some of the other founders of this elite group were Marshall Houts, Raymond Schindler, Alex Gregory, Dr. Lemoyne Snyder, Harry Steeger and Park Street. It is interesting to note that Gardner himself, together with Raymond Schindler and Marshall Houts would be involved in the events surrounding the murder of Sir Harry Oakes as writer, investigator and reporter.

In 1943 Gardner was sent to cover the trial of Alfred de Marigny. The newspaper articles appeared from October 14th, 1943, until November 12th, 1943. Gardner was said to have been assisted by two stenographers to take down his dictations and ongoing comments about the trial.

It was during this trial that Gardner became good friends with Raymond Schindler, the private investigator who had been hired by Nancy Oakes de Marigny to assist in the defense of her husband.

Gardner kept notes and at one point during the cross-examination of Harold Christie, Gardner noted the time Christie took in answering some of the questions put to him by Godfrey Higgs. In some cases the pauses were in excess of ten to fifteen seconds before Christie would utter a word and when everything is quiet in the court room, it seemed like an eternity before the answers would come forth.

Gardner died in March 1970, and the eulogy at the funeral was given by his very good friend and associate Marshall Houts.

Max Haines

Max Haines is the crime columnist for the *Toronto Sun*, the other leading daily and weekend newspaper in Toronto. The title of his column is *Crime Flashback* and reviews murders from around the world.

I first had the pleasure of meeting Max on the occasion of one of his famous *Weekender* trips, which he organized from time to time, to visit various famous Canadian crime scenes or landmarks within the Toronto area.

What brought this trip to my attention was the fact that Max was going to cover Sir Harry Oakes. We departed from Toronto and headed for Hamilton, Ontario on a very dreary Sunday morning to first pass by the home of one Evelyn Dick, who had been accused of killing her husband and dismembering his body. The weather was very appropriate for the occasion of our visit.

From Hamilton we continued on our trip to the second destination, which was to be Oak Hall in Niagara Falls, Ontario, which at one time was one of the Canadian residences of Harry Oakes, prior to his final move with his family to Nassau in the Bahamas in the mid thirties.

As we travelled by luxurious coach on the way out to Hamilton and then on to Niagara Falls, Max provided us with some background information on the individuals being honoured with the trip. During the return journey later that afternoon, Max organized a kind of trivia session, whereby he would ask questions concerning the subjects of our trip and gave out prizes accordingly. Before we knew it, we were safely back at our starting point in Toronto.

Max Haines is also known as the author of a number of books concerning criminals and their crimes, amongst which are such titles as *Bothersome Bodies*, *Murder and Mayhem, Canadian Crimes* and other criminally oriented titles, which are recaps of some of the more than one thousand cases of crime, which he has researched over the years. Readers of the Sunday editions of the *Toronto Sun* can always count on a weekly outline of some well known murder for their reading enjoyment.

Max Haines, Crime Columnist for the Toronto Sun, the other newspaper in Toronto. *Courtesy of Max Haines*

Marshall Houts

Marshall Houts was born on June 28th, 1919, in Chattanooga, Tennessee. He was the author of a book entitled *The King's X* which when first published was banned from the Bahamas at the insistence of Harold Christie, as it appeared to make some disparaging remarks about him. In 1989 the book was re-published under the title of *Who Killed Sir Harry Oakes?* as part of a series on crime for a book club.

During a visit to Nassau in 1988, I had a similar experience when a copy of the book was lent to me. I was asked to keep it to myself and not let anyone know how I came into possession of the book if asked.

In the book entitled *The King's X*, the author makes reference on a number of occasions to information that he obtained through so-called *informants*, in his very concise description of the scene surrounding Sir Harry's room, as well as the activities leading up to the brutal murder.

It is said that the title of the book itself is short for the expression *the King's excuse*, which was a cry used in children's games to claim exemption from being tagged or caught or to call time out (the source was said to be Webster's Third New International Dictionary).

The book in question was originally written in 1972, however, all the information that Houts appears to have gathered from his so-called *informants* was never released to the proper authorities, which could have solved the mystery once and for all. It should also be noted that in reading the text describing what went on in the room, he clearly mentions informants in the plural indicating more than one eye witness to the crime.

Who were these so-called *informants* and how did Houts contact them for their story of what happened at Sir Harry's estate that evening? Where were they from — the islands or the mainland? In addition, it should be noted that it is a well known fact, in view of the size of Nassau, that very little can happen without someone else on the island knowing what transpired.

Houts was an American crime expert and a graduate of the University of Minnesota School of Law. During his career he was a U.S. Coroner and Judge as well as a professor of Criminal Law and Evidence at the Michigan State University School of Police Administration.

A number of years following the murder, Marshall Houts, having attended the annual meeting of the American Academy of Forensic Sciences, wrote Lady Oakes requesting her concurrence to have the body of Sir Harry exhumed, in the hope of answering some of the remaining questions on the murder of her husband. However, a response was received within two weeks from one of the trustees of the estate, to the effect that — *no useful purpose could be served and would he please spare Lady Oakes any unnecessary pain and suffering.*

The following is the text of the letter that Marshall Houts wrote to Lady Oakes and would appear to have been written in early 1973, some thirty years following the death of Sir Harry Oakes:

I have just returned from the annual meeting of the American Academy of Forensic (Courtroom) Sciences in Las Vegas where the subject of Sir Harry's death was discussed in considerable detail by many of the world's leading forensic pathologists and criminalists. It was the general consensus that the real facts of the cause and manner of Sir Harry's death were never adequately established. Drs. Quackenbush and Fitzmaurice were not forensic pathologists; and regrettably their postmortem observations actually were more confusing than enlightening. There can be little doubt that valuable physical evidence was either overlooked or destroyed by Captains Melchen and Barker.

There is still possibility that definitive information can be developed as to the cause and manner of Sir Harry's death by an exhumation of the body. In the event that you are interested in seeing whether these answers are still available, I can offer you the services of the most outstanding men in forensic pathology and science to preside over the disinterment and subsequent investigation.

In my opinion, Sir Harry is entitled to far better treatment in death than he received at the hands of the blundering Miami detectives; and while the results of exhumation can never be predicted in advance, it is possible that the findings will make an invaluable contribution to the forensic sciences that will benefit mankind in the future.

The exhumation will be performed in private, and in the same respectful, professional manner employed by surgeons as they approach a live patient in the operating room.

Sincerely yours
Marshall Houts

Cholly Knickerbocker

Cholly Knickerbocker was a well known society columnist, to whom Alfred de Marigny wrote following certain statements that had been made about him in the press following the arrest in September 1950, of Edward Majava in Oakland, California and the latter's comments concerning the murder of Sir Harry Oakes.

In the book from which this letter is quoted (*Gone with the Windsors* by Iles Brody), no date is given, but it must be assumed that it was in late 1950 and the text read as follows:

Dear Cholly:

A few days ago a man was arrested after having made a statement in a bar that he knew the name of the murderer of Sir Harry Oakes. I was interviewed by the Press about the incident. Unfortunately, as usual, comments were passed on my accent, my clothes and my being broke. But nothing about my statement was printed.

I stated that neither the Government of the Bahamas nor the Oakes family have the slightest desire to have the party involved in the murder of Sir Harry Oakes made public.

Had they so desired, it would have been an easy matter at the time. Mr. Raymond Schindler, to whom I owe my life, endeavoured to clear me by showing to the Nassau Police who was the party. An Aide-de-Camp of His Royal Highness, Edward Duke of Windsor, then Governor of the Bahamas, informed Schindler in the name of the Government that his action was an insult to the Crown.

He, Schindler, could not prove my obvious innocence by accusing the guilty party. The Crown had arrested me and my innocence had to be proven first before some one else could be accused.

Schindler returned to Nassau after my acquittal and subsequent deportation. He offered his services free of charge to the local authorities.

He wrote a letter to the Duke of Windsor stating that he felt certain he could bring the guilty party to justice if he were allowed to do so. HE RECEIVED A CURT NEGATIVE ANSWER. Undaunted, Schindler returned to Nassau again. The Bahamian Immigration informed him that he would be deported immediately if he were to make the slightest attempt to investigate and re-open the Oakes case.

Therefore, I doubt that seven years later, the same people should make a sudden about-face. I would rather state that every effort will be made to choke the issue and continue the venomous campaign against me, and use me as a smokescreen to protect the large and influential interests who carry on their hands the blood of Sir Harry Oakes.

The murder of Sir Harry Oakes appears to have followed de Marigny wherever he went and whenever the subject came up, someone would find him and ask for his comments on the matter.

It would appear from de Marigny's letter that Raymond Schindler believed that he had the solution as to who the murderer was, but once again Schindler did not divulge any name and never would.

James Leasor

James Leasor was the author of a book entitled *Who Killed Sir Harry Oakes?* published in 1983, on the occasion of the fortieth anniversary of the murder of Sir Harry Oakes. The book was used as the basis for the movie produced for TV entitled *Passion and Paradise* which aired on the CTV and ABC networks in February 1989.

In discussing the movie with people who are familiar with the Oakes tragedy and his life style, everyone seems to confirm that the movie in many aspects does not relate the facts as they happened. It is a case of a movie made for television and a great deal of authenticity has been lost in the hope of making the movie more attractive to the TV viewing audience.

A Los Angeles newspaper columnist once asked the question — *what is Rod Steiger doing in this thing?* in reference to his leading part as Sir Harry Oakes and I feel that the same can be said for Armand Assante who played Alfred de Marigny in the movie.

In a June 1990 interview with the *Montreal Gazette*, de Marigny was asked about his comments on the made for TV movie, to which he replied that he was quite upset with the movie, his own portrayal and also the fact that it was made without his knowledge. He felt that as one of the main players in the whole event, he could have at least been consulted by the producers.

There are a number of individuals or characters appearing in the movie who bear no resemblance whatsoever to the real life individuals and a number of important events described in the book are not covered in the movie.

One interesting aspect is that there is no mention of any of the other Oakes children aside from Nancy and in the movie, the burial of Sir Harry Oakes appears to be in the Oakes' property in Nassau, which naturally is not the case.

The book was placed on sale at the Island Shop on Bay Street in Nassau, without any fanfare and it was there that I bought it and was led into the research that I have undertaken over the years relative to Harry Oakes, Alfred de Marigny and others.

I feel quite convinced in reading the text of the book that certain portions of it are indeed quasi-fictional, as a number of the characters are just that — characters. They do not in most cases relate to any of the real life people or for that matter to the events which occurred.

Sydney Albert Pain

Another author was Sydney Albert Pain who was born in June 1896, educated in England and gained his first interest in mining at the historic tin mines of Wales and subsequently through his attendance at the well known Camborne School of Mines.

Pain could have been considered in a way, a small scale version of Harry Oakes, as in his early days he travelled through South America in search of mineral deposits. In 1924 he moved to Kirkland Lake and established himself there. He was the author of at least two great books entitled *The Way North* and *Three Miles of Gold: The Story of Kirkland Lake*.

Both of these books cover the history of the North and the latter book is in particular a detailed account of the complete exploration and founding of Kirkland Lake, together with its development of the mining industry. It also includes a close account of Harry Oakes and his Lake Shore Mines, which was to become the second largest gold producing mine in North America.

Julian Symons

Julian Symons was born in London, England. As part of his early career he worked as a shorthand typist, copywriter and reviewer for local newspapers following which he wrote a number of novels, as well as some poetry.

Symons was also the author of many books on crime and criminal investigation and in particular one book entitled *A Reasonable Doubt* which he wrote in 1960 covering 13 famous criminal cases, some of which had been solved and others that remained unsolved. Needless to say the story of the murder of Sir Harry Oakes was amongst the unsolved murders.

During an interview on May 25th, 1987, with Elwy Yost for the TV Ontario show *Saturday Night at the Movies*, Symons mentioned that there was a well known individual and businessman in Nassau who should have been questioned concerning the murder of Sir Harry, however, you guessed it — Symons did not reveal the name of the individual whom he suspected. But once again we must remember that the number of prominent Nassau businessmen at the time was limited.

The Miami Herald

In the initial stages following the murder of Sir Harry Oakes, the Duke of Windsor exercised his right of government censorship concerning the release of news relative to the murder to the media and as a result the only news available to the world was based on interviews in Miami by the *Miami Herald* with returning tourists from Nassau.

As a result of the lack of proper information due to the censorship imposed, the *Miami Herald* sent over their feature writer Jeanne Bellamy to Nassau. Other news agencies sent their own reporters and finally a meeting was held with the Attorney General, Eric Hallinan in Nassau, who cooperated in arranging for the release of more factual information on the murder case.

During the actual trial of Alfred de Marigny, the *Miami Herald* was one of the main sources of news and provided a very broad distribution of the stories concerning the day to day activities from Nassau.

The Tribune

At the time of the death of Sir Harry Oakes, the *Tribune* was known as one of the leading Nassau newspapers and was owned and managed by the Dupuch family.

In 1959, some sixteen years after the murder of Sir Harry Oakes and the trial of his son-in-law Alfred de Marigny, the *Tribune* published a book entitled *The Murder of Sir Harry Oakes*, which basically gave a full account of the proceedings of the trial on a day to day basis.

It should be remembered that in those days there were no court stenographers and it was the responsibility of Judge Sir Oscar Daly, to write down in his own handwriting the text of the testimony as it happened during the trial. The text would be read back the following day for possible corrections, additions or deletions to the notes as requested by the Prosecution, the Defense, the Jury or the witnesses themselves.

The *Tribune* book is an immense source of information on the trial and has been used as a basis of reference by many an author who has written about the murder of Sir Harry Oakes.

The original price of the book was 25 shillings (the amount would be one fourth of a pound and at the exchange rate in force at time of publication in 1959 of approximately $5 to the pound, the book would have cost in the neighbourhood of $1.50).

Other Papers

The murder of Sir Harry Oakes, one of the most prominent murder trials ever to take place within the British Colonies, brought in a large representation of foreign newspaper reporters, who gathered in Nassau for the trial of Sir Harry's son-in-law Alfred de Marigny in October 1943.

In order to accommodate all of the newspaper representatives, Sir Oscar Daly, the presiding Judge at the trial, had a table constructed for his court room, in order to seat the ever increasing number of foreign press people who were attending.

The correspondents were to be divided between the local newspaper personnel and foreign representatives. As a matter of interest the following is a list of those who attended the trial and the various newspapers or wire services which they represented:

Local Newspaper Representatives:

Mary Moseley M.B.E.	Nassau Guardian
	London Daily Mail
Etienne Dupuch and	The Tribune
Eugene Dupuch	The New York Times
	Associated Press
	Reuters
	Canadian Press
	London Daily Telegraph and
	Morning Post
	Toronto Star
	London Daily Express
Mrs. Valerie Moss	Nassau Guardian

Raymond Moss	Nassau Guardian & United Press
Stanley Lowe	Nassau Herald &
	INS — International News Service

Foreign News Representatives:

Jeanne Bellamy	Miami Herald
Edward Jones	Associated Press
John McDermott	United Press
James Kilgallen (*)	INS — International News Service
Erle Stanley Gardner (**)	New York Journal American
Mrs. Elizabeth Townsend	New York Post
Miss Ruth Reynolds	New York Daily News

(*)   His daughter was Dorothy Kilgallen, who would one day become one of the star panelists on a TV show entitled *What's My Line?* which appeared weekly with such co-stars as Arlene Francis, Bennett Cerf and others. The moderator was John Daly. Do the names sound familiar to you?

(**)   Author and writer of the famous TV detective stories — Perry Mason.

Foreign Newspaper Photographers:

Earl Shugars	Associated Press
Raymond Mills	INS — International News Service
David McLane	Acme News

These photographers were often seen standing outside the Magistrate's and Supreme Court, photographing the leading players in the trial of the century.

Newsweek and Time Magazines:

Similar in style to the weekly *Time* magazine, *Newsweek* magazine made its own effort to provide news coverage on the murder of Sir Harry Oakes and the subsequent trial of Alfred de Marigny.

It must be said that the *Newsweek* reports were a great deal more attentive to the tragedy that occurred and as a result, articles, together with excellent photos appeared almost every week. The details of the murder and the proceedings of the trial were reported in eleven issues of the magazine.

The dates and titles of the articles are noted as follows and are a good source of information, though as mentioned with regard to the same press provided in *Time* magazine, if one is a serious researcher into the murder one will immediately notice a few flaws in some of the material reported during the trial period:

Date:	Titles of the Articles:
July 19, 1943	Death in the Bahamas
August 9, 1943	Bad News for Nancy
August 16, 1943	Who Moved the Body
August 23, 1943	Fleeting Fingers
September 6, 1943	Sir Harry's Will
September 13, 1943	Count of Mauritius: de Marigny is Bound for Trial in Oakes Murder
October 18, 1943	Sir Harry's Will
November 1, 1943	De Marigny's Trial
November 8, 1943	Little Finger
November 15, 1943	Lady's Story
November 22, 1943	De Marigny's Final Triumphant Playboy Celebrates Acquittal in Oakes Murder Case

Time magazine also reported on an ongoing basis the events surrounding the murder of Sir Harry Oakes, as well as the subsequent trial of Alfred de Marigny.

The following are the four titles of the articles which appeared in *Time* magazine as their contribution to the story:

Date:	Titles of the Articles:
July 19, 1943	The Great Oakes
September 6, 1943	Faith and Circumstances
November 1, 1943	The Bahamas: The Ruffled Sheet
November 22, 1943	The Bahamas: Killer at Large

As part of Alfred de Marigny's promotion of his book *A Conspiracy of Crowns: The True Story of the Duke of Windsor and the Murder of Sir Harry Oakes*, he managed to get a full review in the June 17th, 1990, weekend edition of the *Sunday Times Magazine* in London.

The cover story was entitled *Did the Duke of Windsor Help Frame This Innocent Man for Murder?* and included a full front page photo of the Duke and a very good insert photo of de Marigny himself.

The story contained a two page spread of photos, including the leading individuals involved in the murder scenario, together with very appropriate headings and descriptions of the parties concerned. The captions read as follows under each of the photos and are reprinted with permission from the *Sunday Times*, London:

THE VICTIM: Sir Harry Oakes: slept with a gun but was killed in his bed and set on fire.

THE REAL CULPRIT:	Harold Christie: Sir Harry Oakes' agent. He was heading for a big showdown with Oakes.
THE ACCUSED:	Alfred de Marigny: called the Duke *'nothing more than a pimple on the ass of the British Empire'*.
THE NAZI AGENT:	Axel Wenner-Gren helped the Duke to invest $2 million in a bank to launder looted cash for the Nazis.
THE GOVERNOR:	The Duke of Windsor: worried that de Marigny knew all about his secret deals. He took action.

Some pretty strong words followed by basically an elaborate review of the book and quotations from the text.

It is interesting to read the review of the book in the *Sunday Times Magazine*, as it is the first time that there is reference to Federal Bureau of Investigation file memos relating to their investigation and surveillance of the Duke of Windsor, Sir Harry Oakes, Dr Axel Wenner-Gren, Harold Christie and John Anderson, but never any mention of Alfred de Marigny.

Films

Eureka was the title of a film produced in 1983 starring, amongst others, Gene Hackman in the leading role of a self-made millionaire, who discovered gold in the Klondike in the early 1920's and who later moved to the Caribbeans where he was murdered.

According to the credits at the end of the movie, the film was based on a book written by Marshall Houts and is no doubt the one entitled *The King's X*. The original book was principally based on the proceedings of the trial of Oakes' son-in-law Alfred de Marigny who had been charged with the murder.

Mention is made that the movie was inspired by the Oakes murder case and presented the millionaire as one Jack McGann. The other characters are Helen McGann (Eunice Oakes); Tracy McGann (Nancy Oakes) and Claude Maillot Van Horn (Alfred de Marigny).

If the movie was indeed inspired by the life and death of the real Harry Oakes, it is in my mind the worst interpretation of Harry Oakes that I have yet seen.

During the scenes of the trial of the son-in-law, the latter decides midway through the proceedings to discharge his lawyers and to act as his own defense council. The first witness that he calls is none other than his wife.

There is a great deal of shouting during the subsequent cross-examination and then all of a sudden, out of nowhere, in bursts a large group of natives into the Court House carrying banners proclaiming the end of the war and that the allies have won. And basically that is how the movie ends.

In other words the movie is a little on the ridiculous side and offers quite a few scenes of nudity and a great deal of violence in executing the murder which I feel goes beyond what would be called the norm.

Even the rental of the movie at $1.99 was not worth the trouble, but research is research and you must take the good with the bad — and this was certainly bad.

In 1993, a third movie starring Scott Hyland as Sir Harry Oakes and Eric Murphy as Alfred de Marigny was developed under the CBC's *Scales of Justice* program, hosted by noted Toronto attorney Edward Greenspan.

The movie was a little more realistic in content than the previous movie *Passion and Paradise* and it would appear that they did their homework in researching the main players in the persons of Sir Harry, Lady Eunice Oakes, Nancy Oakes de Marigny and Alfred de Marigny himself, as well as the events that took place.

The conclusion at the end of the movie is that Sir Harry met his tragic death at the hands of certain individuals in a yacht down in the harbour or waterfront which is indeed incorrect, as it has been proven that Sir Harry did not leave his estate on the night of the murder. This is the second movie that has come to the same conclusion in the matter.

15

Some Closing Remarks or The Last Chapter

So — How was Sir Harry Oakes Killed? ..... Harold Christie and the FBI files ..... Remembering Sir Harry ..... Thanks For The Memories ..... To The Experts for their Comments and Guidance

---

So — *How was Sir Harry Oakes Killed?* — A challenging question to answer, but based on the evidence produced at the trial; the testimony given by the witnesses; interviews with some of those involved, as well as researched material, the following could be a possible interpretation of what happened on that fateful night:

Following the departure of two of Sir Harry's dinner guests Charles Hubbard and Dulcibel Henneage that evening, Oakes and Christie then retired to Sir Harry's bedroom on the second floor around 11.30 p.m. when the two of them had a brief discussion. Shortly afterwards Harold Christie borrowed a pair of pyjamas from Sir Harry and went to the bedroom located approximately sixteen feet away.

Sir Harry had already changed into his pyjamas while Christie was in the room and proceeded to get into the bed under the mosquito netting which was hanging from the ceiling. A copy of the July 6th *Miami Herald* was in his hands.

Christie claimed during his testimony that he spent the night of July 7th and 8th at *Westbourne*, although there appears to be some contradiction to this fact. The bed in which Christie slept *had not been ruffled* and the pillow had *a slight indentation in it*. In other words it would appear that no one really slept there the whole night.

No photos were ever taken of Christie's room though blood stains were found in the room as a result of Christie's use of a towel with which to wipe some blood from Sir Harry's face. Blood stains were also seen on the handles of the doors leading to his room.

We only have the testimony of Major Herbert Pemberton of the Bahamas Police in the matter, as one of the first officers on the scene who went through all of the adjoining rooms.

Based on these circumstances there is every possibility that Harold Christie left *Westbourne* following his having gone to his room and this point is further substantiated by Alfred de Marigny in his book *A Conspiracy of Crowns*, whereby he relates the story given him by Rawlins, one of the surviving night watchmen, who was on the grounds with his colleague the evening of the murder and saw Christie leave the estate.

So now we have Sir Harry by himself in his bedroom and suddenly he is disturbed by some noise coming from the stairway and the landing outside his bedroom. Harry gets out of bed, throwing the newspaper he was reading onto the bed. At this point he proceeds to the doorway, pauses and looks for the cause of the disturbance.

As Sir Harry steps out and glances around, he is confronted by two men and in the ensuing struggle, is struck on the side of the head and knocked to the floor. How and with what weapon he was struck was not known and may never be, unless someone is willing to authorize an exhumation of his remains from the mausoleum in Dover-Foxcroft, Maine, which could possibly assist in identifying the markings of the wound and possibly lead to the eventual identification of the weapon.

Returning to the scene of Sir Harry lying on the floor there are apparently blood stains on the carpeting in addition to some burn marks which would indicate that he lay on his side immediately inside the doorway. At all times Sir Harry would have been in a face down position on the carpeting thus allowing the blood to trickle down from the wound beside his left ear, along his cheek and over the bridge of his nose. Under the circumstances the blood is allowed to coagulate along the side of his face.

The result is the photograph shown as an exhibit during the trial of Oakes lying on his back on the bed, which would appear to indicate that the flow of blood was defying the law of gravity. The explanation of how the blood coagulated is also proof that the body had been moved from its original position near the doorway.

During the course of the murder, the body of Sir Harry lay on the floor and was then lifted by the two men and placed on the bed following which the bed was set ablaze and most likely by the use of a blow torch as evidenced by the photos of the room showing the burn marks, all of which appear to be as a result of a back and forth sweeping motion. The murderers then proceeded to further burn the body.

Attempts at this point were made to set fire to the bed itself, the door to the clothes closet near the entrance to the bedroom, the door leading out of the room, as well as parts of the carpeting. The Chinese screen was not overlooked as photographs indicate that flames were applied to the screen in a further attempt to set fire to the room.

Was it the intention of those behind the scheme to murder Sir Harry Oakes, to have the estate burnt down and Harold Christie would return the following morning to find the place completely destroyed?

There is a certain photograph taken from the main floor downstairs looking up the staircase, which shows burn marks on the outside part of two of the top steps, which would indicate that the individual involved would have leaned over the railing or reached it by stepping on a chair shown below on the ground floor. How the attempt to set the fire was made in such an awkward position is difficult to establish and the reason still more difficult to understand. Likewise burn marks on the door and the wall immediately outside Sir Harry's room leading to the top of the staircase are shown in a further photograph which would lead to the aforementioned burns at the top of the staircase.

We are also faced with the question of the feathers from the pillow, spread over Sir Harry's body and blown around the room by the electric fan located on the floor at the end of the beds. These feathers adhered to Sir Harry's head and body. It is also noted from one of the close-up photographs that the feathers do not appear to have been burned by fire and were more or less spread over the body after the attempts at setting the fires. The news of the feathers immediately set off rumours in Nassau that voodoo was involved. On the other hand quite possibly the pillow was used to further suffocate Sir Harry as he lay on the bed.

Some unusual burn marks on the staircase leading to the second floor. *Source Unknown*

The question of the weapon of death was a mystery then and will most likely always remain a mystery, as well as the person(s) responsible for the murder of Sir Harry Oakes, though a number of names have been mentioned and it would be up to the reader to draw his or her own conclusion based on what has been read or what may have been read between the lines.

According to a memorandum dated May 31st, 1944, prepared by a Special Agent in Charge of the FBI office in New York, it would appear that Harold Christie had lunch with a certain individual in New York on May 22nd, 1944, whose name has not been declassified as yet. The individual thought that the FBI would be interested in the details of the meeting which took place.

Christie said that he was in New York at the request of certain influential persons in Nassau to employ an investigator or investigators to re-open the Oakes murder case and determine the identity of the true culprit. Christie advised the individual that he personally believed de Marigny was the murderer although acquitted on trial in Nassau.

Christie asked if it would be possible to employ the FBI on such a project, but he was informed that it would not appear that an official Federal Agency would be interested in a crime committed in Nassau.

Christie further informed the individual that the expenses for such an investigation would be raised by contributions of a few influential people in Nassau and it was expected to raise a fund of from ten to fifteen thousand pounds. The interest of these people in clearing up this murder was that they felt that Nassau had an extremely bad name in the eyes of the American public because of the murder and for public relations reasons, the murder should be solved.

A further note of interest in this matter, is that the following appeared in the *New York Daily News* edition of May 27th, 1944, in Ed Sullivan's column: *Understand the principals in the Sir Harry Oakes unsolved murder conferred in this city a few days back.*

Some questions raised in this regard would be who were the influential people in Nassau? Would some of them have been members of the Bay Street Boys? Would Walter Foskett or Newell Kelly have had an interest in the matter surrounding the murder of Sir Harry Oakes and, finally, who was the individual with whom Harold Christie was speaking?

The perusal of numerous Freedom of Information and Privacy Acts — FOIPA files released through the Federal Bureau of Investigation in Washington relative to the Duke of Windsor; Sir Harry Oakes; Harold Christie; Dr. Axel Wenner-Gren; Walter Foskett and others has made for most interesting reading into the backgrounds of these individuals and their possible involvement in the crime and other illegal activities in the Bahamas at the time.

It would now appear that we have the possibility of a different interpretation of Harold Christie's involvement in the events surrounding the murder of Sir Harry Oakes based on the above. Over the years the finger of suspicion and accusation seems to have been pointed at Harold Christie for a number of reasons. Could we have possibly been wrong?

As you have no doubt surmised a great deal has been said about Sir Harry Oakes and the cast of individuals associated with him from his early days in Kirkland Lake and down to his last days in Nassau.

We are now fifty seven years following his tragic death in 1943 and a number, if not all, of the basic investigative questions remain unanswered: What was the motive? What was the weapon of death? What was the manner of death? And last — Who would have killed him or wanted to have him killed?

None of the above questions have ever been properly addressed and answered and probably will never be.

A possible final thought is that if the actual murderer or murderers were in their mid twenties to mid thirties at the time of the crime, it is quite possible that even today one or both of them may still be alive and well somewhere.

It is doubtful that they would have been residents of the Bahamas, as information on who they were would not have been kept a secret over all these years. In addition there is no comment by the surviving night watchman that the two gentlemen were indeed natives, therefore it could be assumed that they came from the mainland. But where or through whom would they have obtained a blow torch? as such an item is not something one carries around at leisure. Could it have been stolen from the RAF base?

How will Sir Harry Oakes best be remembered? Will it be for finding his gold mine in Kirkland Lake leading to his becoming a millionaire and one of the world's great philanthropists or for having been murdered in his palatial home in the Bahamas? So far when the name of Sir Harry Oakes has been mentioned the answer seems to point to his tragic death.

If Sir Harry had continued with his apparent plans to move his family and wealth to Mexico what would have become of him? What kind of a life would he and his family have led? Would he have adjusted to the more hectic life in Mexico as compared to the peace and quiet of the Bahamas? One thing for sure would be that he would not have had Harold Christie trying to sell him real estate at every opportunity.

As is the case in researching any material, there are a number of individuals, professionals and friends alike, with whom one must at some point sit down and discuss facts, review data and more importantly request their opinions and personal experiences, as well as share in their recollections of times gone by.

One of the first persons that I approached was the late Alfred de Marigny, former son-in-law of Sir Harry Oakes and former husband of Nancy Oakes, who had been charged with the murder and subsequently acquitted. My meeting with de Marigny and his charming wife in Houston, Texas in 1993 was indeed the highlight of my research efforts. While I only shared a few hours of his lifetime, we covered a lot of ground relative to his experiences in Nassau.

A few years earlier while on a return holiday to Nassau, I had the opportunity of spending some time with Ernest Callender, one of the members of de Marigny's Defense team and also with Reverend Robert Hall, an old friend of Sir Harry and former school teacher at Gambier Village, both of whom shared some memories of those memorable years in Nassau.

Needless to say my research has brought me to many places including Kirkland Lake, Ontario, which I have visited on a number of occasions and where I would meet Lydia Alexander, curator and director (since retired) and Lynda Sinclair of the staff at the Museum of Northern History (Sir Harry Oakes Chateau) and a most valuable source of assistance in researching material on Harry Oakes and providing some memorable photographs; Tom O'Hare, Kirkland Lake old timer; Lorrie Irvine, Canadian author; Mark Monette, Mark Monette and Associates; Michael Barnes, Canadian author; Sgt. Claus Fey and Cst. Gene Larocque, Kirkland Lake OPP detachment; and Olga Neely Cassel, Kirkland Lake old timer with many fond memories of Rosie Brown.

A meeting with retired photographer Eddie Duke in Kirkland Lake was most interesting, as was a discussion with Lynda Enouy, a member of the Celebrity Hall of Fame Committee who provided me with some background on the past members of the National Hockey League who had passed through Kirkland Lake.

Also assisting me were members of the staff at the Cobourg Public Library including Valerie Scott in the Information Services section; Paula Jones at the CAA in Cobourg relative to my various research trips; and Jan Carr at Mail Boxes Etc., Cobourg for her assistance in my faxing requirements and quick photocopying needs.

A side trip to Boston Creek, Ontario, would lead me to Beatrice Lavictoire, who would provide me with some interesting background into that little hamlet and to what life was like in the early mining days.

In Sangerville and Dover-Foxcroft, Maine I had the pleasure of meeting Debra Davis at Foxcroft Academy, who very kindly allowed me access to their files on Harry Oakes; Eric Annis and Carol Blanchard at the Lary Funeral Home, who guided me to Sir Harry's mausoleum and assisted in developing background research on funeral arrangements for Sir Harry; and finally to Bowdoin College in Brunswick, Maine where I met Susan Ravdin and Lorena Coffin, who assisted me with some very old files on Sir Harry and more recently Susan Burroughs who assisted me with some old photos. A trip to Bennington, Vermont also provided me some background on Nancy Oakes' attendance at the *Martha Graham School of Dance*.

In order to research some of the material concerning the criminal aspect of the tragic death of Sir Harry, it was necessary to have many discussions with individuals involved in criminal investigation including the following: Karen Anderson, Forensic Identification Technician (fingerprinting), Cobourg, Ontario police; Mike Illes, Blood Stain Analyst, OPP detachment in Peterborough; Sgt. Ross Nelson, OPP Northumberland Detachment, Cobourg; Glen Wright, RCMP, Ottawa; Dr. Martin Queen and Jack Press, Coroner's Office, Toronto; Don Foster, Funeral Service Education, Humber College, Toronto; Marcel Lalonde, Office of the Fire Marshall, Kingston, Ontario and Louis Lang from Montreal, former officer with Ferry Command RAF in Nassau.

A meeting with Canadian author Peter Fancy in Barrie, Ontario a number of years ago, pointed me in the right direction in so far as translating my research material into a potential manuscript.

Dr. Gail Saunders, Archives of the Bahamas allowed me to access many of the old files concerning life in Nassau during the late thirties and early forties, as well as some of the trial evidence including Judge Sir Oscar Daly's handwritten transcript of the trial.

Conversations were possible with Joan Albury at the Bahamas Historical Society; and with Sir Durward Knowles, close sailing friend and competitor with Alfred de Marigny who provided additional background information not only on Oakes and de Marigny, but on Nassau itself.

Naturally visits to second hand bookstores were a necessity and thanks must go to Lois Pollard at Highway Book Shop in Cobalt, Ontario; Ken Saunders of Old Favourites Book Shop at Green River, Ontario and Geoffrey Cates in Oshawa, Ontario who specializes in true crime books.

Barry Mercer and Eric Moore of CBC North radio during an interview in Kirkland Lake in 1996 which provided me with the opportunity of talking to some senior residents who had come to the Sir Harry Oakes Chateau for the broadcast.

Discussions with Muriel Cole and Dean McCaughey of Dean Marine, in Cobourg, Ontario and Ron Cox, boat restorer, at Gore's Landing, Ontario were helpful in an attempt to establish the use of a boat winch as a possible murder weapon. Bev Chrisomalis at Ready

Print in Cobourg, Ontario assisted me with my early printing requirements. Georges Carter, former working colleague who would rescue me from my PC problems.

On the subject of fishing spears, consultation with Roman Mizanski at Innerspace Dive and Marine in Pickering, Ontario, together with Miles McGinn at Gone Fishing in Cobourg, Ontario proved most interesting.

Also Frank Medoro and Jeff Schneider, in Toronto and Mexico City, assisted in accessing the libraries at Banco de Mexico and Instituto Bancario de Mexico relative to Banco Continental; and also Howard Morgan helped me locate Alfred de Marigny in Houston, Texas a number of years ago.

Special thanks to Angela Quinn at Fourteen Island Lake, in the Laurentians north of Montreal for having volunteered to spend a number of evenings one winter proof reading my first draft of the manuscript. Also to her daughter Janet who helped in obtaining background information on some of the medical officers involved with the investigation of the murder.

Others who have shared information and memories were Paul Kavanagh, whose efforts to promote Sir Harry Oakes to the Canadian Mining Hall of Fame were indeed rewarded; Gwen Conmee, who attended Harry Phillip Oakes' wedding and provided some background information on Sir Harry. Discussions with John Cooke, former longtime Executive Publisher of the *Northern Miner* newspaper were indeed informative on the history of the mining areas of Northern Ontario and on Harry Oakes himself.

Peter Smith at the E.B.Eddy Match Company in Pembroke, Ontario made helpful comments regarding the use of match flaps and wooden match boxes around the murder scene and how the fires may have been set at Oakes' estate. Likewise I spoke with Brian Pierce, Technical Director at Wilson Labs in Dundas, Ontario concerning the possible use of an insecticide spray gun for the spreading of flammable liquids around the murder scene.

Dawn Jollymore at the Department of Natural Resources in Toronto was very helpful in tracing back some of the initial records concerning Harry Oakes' mining career in Northern Ontario. Also of assistance was George Gaffney, Royal Bank of Canada, Toronto and nephew of the late John Gaffney, who worked for the Royal Bank in Nassau; Rita Carinci and Anita Fernandes also at the Royal Bank of Canada in Toronto and Lois Wadden at their office in Kirkland Lake, who confirmed some stories about Charlie Chow.

Thanks also to Craig Currie at the Kirkland Lake Cemetery for pointing me in the right direction to the final resting place of Charlie Chow and to Jim Hurd at the Hillcrest Cemetery in Smiths Falls covering some research information.

Mickey Herskowitz of the *Houston Chronicle* newspaper, shared some thoughts on his part in co-writing *A Conspiracy of Crowns* with the late Alfred de Marigny.

To Bill Martin, restorer of antique cars in Cold Springs, Ontario and John Hammond Sr., and Jr., of Hammond's Motor Auto Repairs of Cobourg, thanks for their thoughts and evaluation of a certain potential murder weapon.

Thanks to Larry Schwartz and Eric Young at Archive Photos in New York; John Beaton and Andrea Gordon at The Canadian Press, Toronto; Kevin Rettig and Seshu Badrinath at Corbis Images in New York and Michael Toogood of Toogood's Photography in Nassau, Bahamas, all of whom assisted in researching and providing some of the old photos used with the manuscript; and to Mike Williams at MotoPhoto in Cobourg for handling my early photo requirements. Also to Christine Bourolias at the Special Collections of the Archives of Ontario in Toronto.

Patrick Erskine-Lindop and Peter Higgs in Nassau and George Oberwarth in Trenton, Ontario all of whom shared some thoughts on their fathers who were in Nassau at the time of the tragedy. A meeting and discussions with Alex Phelps from Hartland, Vermont were indeed interesting.

In February 1999, I met with Fred Sampson of Port Hope, Ontario who at one time was personal secretary in Nassau to Lady Eunice Oakes and who provided some interesting background into the Oakes family.

A special thanks to Dr. Douglas Pollard and his wife Lois at Highway Book Shop, Cobalt, Ontario, for their interest and assistance in publishing this manuscript and to Paul Bogart for his guidance through the publication, as well as to John French for his review and critique of the manuscript.

And not to be forgotten, my wife Norah for her enduring patience in listening to my numerous discussions on Sir Harry Oakes and the cast of characters, as well as acting as my sounding board on the whole matter.

And so, in parting — to those who very kindly shared some memories and provided background information, but who wished to remain anonymous and whose wishes I indeed respect — Many thanks.

Bob Cowan
June 24, 2000

BIBLIOGRAPHY

Albury, Dr. Paul: *Paradise Island Story*, Macmillan Caribbean, London, 1984

Albury, Dr. Paul: *The Story of the Bahamas*, Macmillan Caribbean, London, 1976

Bahamas Government Publications: *Preliminary Hearing Testimony of de Marigny Case*, 1943

Bahamas Historical Society: *The Journal of the Bahamas Historical Society*, 1979-1990

Barnes, Michael: *The Town That Stands on Gold*, Highway Book Shop, Cobalt, Ontario, 1978

Barnes, Michael: *Fortunes in the Ground*, The Boston Mills Press, Erin, Ontario, 1986

Barnes, Michael: *Gold Camp Pioneer: Roza Brown of Kirkland Lake*, Shaft Publishing, Kirkland Lake, Ontario, 1984

Barnes, Michael: *Kirkland Lake: On the Mile of Gold*, The Boston Mills Press, Erin, Ontario, 1994

Bloch, Michael: *The Duke of Windsor's War: From Europe to the Bahamas*, Coward McCann Inc., New York, 1983

Blundell, Nigel: *Fact or Fiction: Unsolved Crimes*, Promotional Reprint Co. Ltd., London, 1995

Boar, Roger and Blundell, Nigel: *The World's Greatest Unsolved Crimes*, Hamlyn Publishing Group, London, 1981

Bocca, Geoffrey: *The Life and Death of Sir Harry Oakes*, Weidenfied & Nicholson, London, 1959

Brody, Iles: *Gone with the Windsors*, Winston Publishers, Philadelphia, 1953

Brown, Douglas and Tulette, E. V.: *Bernard Spilsbury: His Life and Cases*, Geo. G. Harrap & Co. Ltd., London, 1951

Canadians All 8: *Portraits of People*, Gage Educational Publishing, Toronto, 1989

Chodos, Robert: *The Caribbean Connection*, James Lorimor and Co., Toronto, 1977

Cohen, Gary: *The Lady and The Curse: Evalyn Walsh McLean and the Hope Diamond*, Vanity Fair Magazine, August 1997

Coleman OSB, J. Barry: *Upon These Rocks*, St. John's Abbey Press, Collegeville, Minnesota, 1973

Craton, Michael: *A History of the Bahamas*, San Salvador Press, Waterloo, Ontario, 1962

de Marigny, Alfred: *Ai-Je Tué?: Le Monde Est Ma Prison*, Editions Serge Brosseau, Montreal, 1946

de Marigny, Alfred: *More Devil Than Saint*, Beechurst Press, New York, 1946

de Marigny, Alfred: *A Conspiracy of Crowns: The True Story of the Duke of Windsor and the Murder of Sir Harry Oakes*, Crown Publishing Co., New York, 1990

Dupuch Publications, Etienne: *Bahamas Handbook*, Nassau, 1983/84/87/88

Fancy, Peter: *Temiskaming Treasure Trails, Volumes 1-8*, Highway Book Shop, Cobalt, Ontario, 1992-1995

Federal Bureau of Investigation: *Freedom of Information & Privacy Acts* — FOIPA, United States Department of Justice, Washington.

Federal Bureau of Investigation: *The Science of Fingerprinting*, United States Department of Justice, Washington, 1984

Fethering, Douglas: *The Gold Crusade: A Social History of Gold Rushes*, Macmillan of Canada, Toronto, 1988

Forbes, Rosita: *Appointment With Destiny*, E.P.Dutton & Co., New York, 1946

Gaute, J. H. H. and Odell, Robin: *Murder 'Whatdunit'*, Harrap Ltd., London, 1982

Gaute, J. H. H. and Odell, Robin: *The Murderers 'Who's Who'*, Optimum Publishing Co. Ltd., Montreal, 1979

Haines, Max: *The Collected Works of Max Haines*, The Toronto Sun Publishing Corp. Ltd., Toronto, 1985

Hammer, Richard: *Playboy's Illustrated History of Organized Crime*, Playboy Press Book, Chicago, 1975

Herzog, Arthur: *Robert Vesco*, Doubleday, New York, 1987

Higham, Charles: *The Duchess of Windsor: The Secret Life*, McGraw-Hill Book Co., New York 1988

Hoffman, Arnold: *Free Gold*, Rinehart and Co., New York, 1947

Houts, Marshall: *The King's X*, William Morrow & Co. Inc., New York, 1972

Kahaner, Larry: *Cults That Kill: Probing the Underworld of Occult Crime*, Warner Books Inc., New York, 1988

Kobler, John: *The Myths About the Oakes Murder*, Saturday Evening Post, October 24, 1959

Lambourne, Gerald: *The Fingerprint Story*, Harrap, London, 1984

Leasor, James: *Who Killed Sir Harry Oakes?*, William Heinemann Ltd., London, 1983

Le Bourdais, D. L.: *Metals and Men*, McLelland and Stewart Ltd., Toronto, 1957

Liston, Robert: *Great Detectives: Famous Real Life Sleuths and Their Most Baffling Cases,* Platt & Munk Publishers, New York, 1966

Messick, Hans: *Lansky*, G. P. Putman's Sons, New York, 1971

The Murder of Sir Harry Oakes, The Nassau Daily Tribune, Nassau, 1959

Pain, S. A.: *Three Miles of Gold*, Ryerson Press, Toronto, 1960

Pain, S. A.: *The Way North*, Ryerson Press, Toronto, 1964

Pratt, Insp. Gabrielle and Simmons, Sgt. Morris: *A History of the Royal Bahamas Police Force,* A Flair for Hollywood Creative Services, U.S.A, 1990

Preston, Anthony: *U-Boats*, Excalibur Books, London, 1987

Pye, Michael: *The King Over the Water*, Holt, Rinehart and Winston, New York, 1981

Rouleau, Leonard: *The Rugged Life of Sir Harry Oakes*, Laval, Quebec, 1971

Russell, C. Seighbert: *Nassau's Historic Buildings*, Historic Society of the Bahamas National Trust

Saunders, Dr. Gail and Cartwright, Donald: *Historic Nassau*, Macmillan Caribbean, London, 1979

Schindler, Raymond: *I Could Crack the Oakes Case Open*, Inside Detective, November 1944

Sifakis, Carl: *The MAFIA Encyclopedia*, Facts on File Publications Inc., New York, 1987

Smyth, Frank and Ludwig, Myles: *The Detective: Crime and Detection in Fact and Fiction*, J.B. Lippincott Co., New York, 1978

Stacey, C. P.: *Six Years of War*, Ottawa, 1957

Stevens, Louis E.: *Dover-Foxcroft: A History*, New Hampshire Printers, Somersworth, New Hampshire, 1995

Stockdale, R. E.: *Science Against Crime*, Exeter Books, New York, 1982

Symons, Julian: *A Pictorial History of Crime*, Bonanza Books, New York, 1966

Taylor, Sir Henry: *My Political Memoirs*, Nassau, Bahamas

Unsolved Crimes, Time-Life Books, Alexandria, Virginia, 1993

Wardell, John Michael: *Oakes Murder Mystery: New Developments*, Atlantic Advocate, July 1959

Wetjen, Andre and Irvine, Lorrie: *The Kirkland Lake Story: A Pictorial History*, reprint, Highway Book Shop, Cobalt, Ontario, 1988

What Metals and Minerals Mean to Canadians, The Northern Miner [pamphlet, undated]

Wilson, Kirk: *Investigating Murders: The Top Ten Unsolved Murders*, Robinson Publishing Ltd., London, 1990

MOVIES AND VIDEOS:

Edward on Edward, 1996
Eureka, 1987
Great Crimes & Trials, 1998
Passion and Paradise, 1989
Scales of Justice, 1990

INDEX